Emotion in Animated Films

Ranging from blockbuster movies to experimental shorts, documentaries or health campaign videos to scientific research, computer animation shapes a great part of media communication processes today. Be it the portrayal of emotional characters in moving films or the creation of controllable emotional stimuli in scientific contexts, computer animation's characteristic artificiality makes it ideal for various areas connected to the emotional. This book looks at international film productions using animation techniques to display and/or to elicit emotions, with a special attention to the aesthetics, characters, stories, and the effects of these films and to the challenges and benefits of using computer techniques for these purposes.

Meike Uhrig is Research Associate at the Department of Media Studies at the University of Tuebingen, Germany. She worked as Visiting Researcher at the Department of Psychology at Stanford University, USA. In her dissertation project, she studied the "Representation, Reception, and Effects of Emotions in Film" (2014).

T0386586

Routledge Advances in Film Studies

For more information about this series, please visit: https://www.routledge.com

Emotion in Animated Films

Edited by
Meike Uhrig

Routledge
Taylor & Francis Group

NEW YORK AND LONDON

First published 2019
by Routledge
52 Vanderbilt Avenue, New York, NY 10017, USA

and by Routledge
2 Park Square, Milton Park, Abingdon, Oxon OX14 4RN

First issued in paperback 2020

*Routledge is an imprint of the Taylor & Francis Group, an
informa business*

© 2019 Taylor & Francis

The right of the editor to be identified as the author of the
editorial material, and of the authors for their individual
chapters, has been asserted in accordance with sections 77 and
78 of the Copyright, Designs and Patents Act 1988.

All rights reserved. No part of this book may be reprinted
or reproduced or utilised in any form or by any electronic,
mechanical, or other means, now known or hereafter invented,
including photocopying and recording, or in any information
storage or retrieval system, without permission in writing from
the publishers.

Trademark notice: Product or corporate names may be
trademarks or registered trademarks, and are used only for
identification and explanation without intent to infringe.

Library of Congress Cataloging-in-Publication Data
A catalogue record for this book has been requested.

ISBN 13: 978-0-367-58477-1 (pbk)
ISBN 13: 978-1-138-30328-7 (hbk)

Typeset in Sabon
by codeMantra

Contents

Foreword

When I began creating CGI-animated films in the early 1990s, I was working on intuition and hunches. At that time animation was experiencing a major upheaval, with *Jurassic Park* and *Toy Story* defining the sea change of that era. Many of my contemporaries – Bob Sabiston, Joan Staveley, Isaac Kerlow, Karl Sims, and others – were creating explosive animated content based on a jumble of intuition and hunches I was experiencing. In the new field of CGI animation, there was not yet a clear sense of the emotional power these works could have on audiences. It's really only with the hindsight of nearly three decades that I can now see a coherence, a sensibility to the exuberant chaos of the content we were making then.

It always seemed odd to me that over those past three decades, the media of animation was not receiving nearly the scholarly attention that other film content has received over the past century. There are truly unique patterns in that exuberant chaos in animation since the early 1990s that are only now being examined and revealed, through conferences such as the Society for Animation Studies and journals such as *Animation* and *Animation Studies*. Through the research presented in these conferences and journals, we're only now beginning to see many of these patterns, things that have in fact transformed the cultural landscape of films and audiences worldwide.

Norman McLaren asserted that in animated works, what happens between each frame is much more important than what exists on each frame. He's referring to something invisible and intangible, the stuff that will gobsmack audiences if it's understood by its creators. He's referring (in large part) to the invisible force in this visual media to evoke emotional response in its audiences between the frames. And this force is often a far different beast than the one that occupies what we call 'live-action content'.

Like a quantum particle or a brilliant joke, this beast will always evade encapsulation and definition, for as soon as we shine a light on it to examine it, it will transform away from us. Nonetheless, if that light is carefully used, that beast will show us patterns that we can understand (if only partially) and, we hope, extrapolate to new landscapes of emotion and imagination.

This book, *Emotion in Animated Films*, is an ambitious collection of essays that shines this light on the invisible stuff between the frames of a body of recent animated works. You will see new patterns in mainstream films like *Inside Out* and *Moana* and in more experimental works by Don Hertzfeldt, Signe Baumane, myself, and others – patterns that will lead you to better understand basic feelings we experience when watching these films–empathy, joy, anger, etc., as well as strange emotions like "Fago," a jumbled mix of love, compassion and sadness. And beyond animation, perhaps you will even better understand those elusive things in our common world, like quantum particles and good jokes.

Chris Landrteh
1 July 2018

Acknowledgments

This book would not have been possible without the support of many wonderful people whom I would like to thank sincerely.

First of all, I would like to thank Stephan Schwan, who encouraged me to "think big" and proceed with the idea to approach leading experts in film, cognitive, and animation studies and to actually put the project into practice, which seemed like just a pipe dream at first. Thanks also to Ed Tan, Maureen Furniss, and Jens Eder for providing their kind support along the way.

A big thank-you to all the wonderful authors and contributors, not only for submitting brilliant papers, interesting interviews and kind forewords but also for trusting me with the project from the beginning. Thanks also to the whole team from Routledge for their supportive adoption of the book.

Also, this book project would probably not have appeared in its present form if it hadn't been for the assistance of Luzie Kollinger, who accurately double-checked every detail. Thanks also to University of Tübingen for funding this work by awarding me the "Athene Program" as part of the University's Excellence Initiative.

Last but not least, I would like to thank my family, Denis, Klara, and Paula, for their support. Without their backing and patience, it would not have been possible to finish such a major project.

Thank you all! It has been a great pleasure.

Part I
Introduction

1 AnimOtion

Animating Emotions in the Digital Age

Meike Uhrig

Only decades ago, computer technology was regarded as "too cool and technical to be involved in artistic projects" and even labeled as an "invention of the devil" (Kerlow 2009: 16) by media artists. Thus, it seems paradoxical today that computer animation appears to be the first choice when it comes to creating emotional film contents and/or eliciting emotional reactions in recipients – especially as the potential irrationality and often subconscious character of emotions diametrically oppose computer technology's calculatory nature.

Some early pioneers, however, defied the predominant skepticism that shaped computer technology's early years. As one of the first artists, David Em created stills of fantastic planets based on NASA's jet propulsion theory (JPL) simulation "Voyager 2" in the late 1970s. In 1989, Loren Carpenter, Boeing employee and later cofounder and chief scientist of Pixar Animation, presented his adaption of fractal techniques for landscape animations in *Vol Libre*. Also, George Lucas' film team for his first *Star Wars* (1977) movie consisted mostly of members from New York Institute of Technology's Computer Graphics Research Group (for more details see Kerlow 2009; Isaacson 2011). Together these *techno-artists* started experimenting with the new art form and have played their part in promoting computer animation to its current status as a widely used, highly approved art form.

Furthermore, along with its technological development, computer animation began to unchain itself from its preliminary flaw of being suppressed by its technological restrictions and has begun to develop its potential as a technique offering various stylistic and aesthetic possibilities for media production. Ranging from blockbuster movies to experimental independent shorts to documentaries or educational videos, computer animation shapes a great part of media communication processes around the world.

Today, films are spread out on Internet platforms or via DVD collections (*Animation Show of Shows, Animation History*), provided by filmmakers themselves, by film schools, or by companies. Furthermore, they are presented at several hundred animation festivals worldwide – starting with the Annecy International Animated Film Festival in France that has taken place since 1962 – with some of them focusing on particular forms of animation such as the Scottish Puppet Animation Festival or on specific filmmakers as the Tricky Women Festival in Vienna. Also, special events such as the International Conference on Animation, Effects, VR, Games and Transmedia (FMX) in Stuttgart or the annual conferences of research societies for animated films (e.g., the Society for Animation Studies) display the artistic potential and spectrum of animation.

Computer animations are given special attention at the annual conference of the Association for Computing Machinery's (ACM) renowned Special Interest Group on Graphics and Interactive Techniques (SIGGRAPH). Here, animation artists such as Chris Landreth, Bob Sabiston, or Ton Roosendaal present their works, which comprise both technical innovation and artistic delicacy. It was at SIGGRAPH where John Lasseter presented Pixar's first short film *Luxo Jr.* in 1986 – a milestone in the history of computer-animated films.

Since the late 1990s, not only niche festivals or conferences honor the artistic potential of animated films; the Academy of Motion Picture Arts and Sciences (AMPAS) has also paid tribute to the art form by adding an award in 2001 for *Best Animated Feature* to the annual Academy Awards ceremony.[1] The reputation of animated films changed from margin to mainstream as today they make up a high percentage of the total amount of new releases in movie theatres.[2] Computer animation thus plays an increasing role in the area of popular blockbuster movies.

This increase of popular formats brought a specialization in content, claim, and effect. While animated films have been used for political, intellectual, and even subversive causes from the beginning, their popular mainstream variants show an increasing tendency to entertain a wide variety of viewers – including even specifically aiming at children and adolescents (see Chapter 10). Accordingly, popular computer-animated films bring their emotional impact into focus and use their artistic potential to elicit emotions and glue their diverse audience emotionally to their stories and characters. This tendency is also being mirrored in the list of genres represented in computer-animated films. Between 1995 and 2015, emotionally charged genres, like comedy (70%), adventure (70%), and fantasy (35%), make up the largest part of completely computer-generated films in movie theatres – while many films are categorized as meta genres, containing elements of more than three (emotionally diverse) genres at a time ('family' is being used as category in 82% of the films). In addition, science fiction, action, drama, romance, mystery, and thrillers are represented in computer-animated films as well, more or less frequently (ranging from 12% of sci-fi films and up to 2% of thrillers – with thrillers being categorized as romantic and comic at the same time).

Accordingly, typical overarching emotionally charged themes of (computer-) animated films include those connected to childhood and growing up and to friendship. However, loss and loneliness also build on experiences that almost every viewer can relate to on an emotional basis and that may elicit feelings such as nostalgia, sentimentality, or melancholy in almost every viewer (see Chapter 2).

Furthermore, these popular variants display specific characteristics that aim to elicit emotions that are often equated to a film's success – and thus its box office results. These characteristics include the film's focus on a story that tends to subordinate its style (that again supports the narration to allow for a maximum of its effective force; see Chapter 7), its specific dramaturgy (a film's most important means to manage and even intensify emotions; Eder 2007), and likable – even if often undefined – main characters (Uhrig 2014, 2018).

Along with these general characteristics of popular movies, computer-animated films use their specific freedom to push their creations to an extreme, that is, by designing likable characters that display accordingly likable characteristics. Here it is not only the freedom in the choice of the referent of a character itself – be it a human, a bug, a toaster, or even a fictive being – but also the design of the characters, along with the film's focus on their expressions, that especially supports emotional engagement with the heroes. These characters are designed to transport their inner lives – feelings, thoughts, intentions – by way of the effects caused by their symbolic and metaphoric quality and also by their physiques, their physiognomies, and their expressions. Primarily, the design of computer-animated characters seems to aim at their potential to elicit certain emotions by emphasizing faces in general and parts of the face particularly. Here, the eyes of a character appear to be a major elicitor, as they are central in displaying most of the eight basic emotions according to Paul Ekman's Facial Action Coding System approach. Conversely, the reception of eyes most notably find resonances in the viewers' mental reactions (see Chapter 6). More than ever, characters displaying baby schemata, featuring big eyes together with high foreheads and round cheeks, elicit empathic reactions directly on a biological level. Thus, characters with huge eyes seem to set a new status quo of face aesthetics in computer-animated films (Uhrig 2016, 2018). The special importance of the characters' faces as transporters of emotions over the exaggerated body language in traditionally animated films is mirrored in the camera work and editing with the films' use of close-up shots – so-called scenes of empathy (Plantinga 1999, referring to Balázs 1952; see Chapter 9).

The films' character designs, along with the cameras' focus on their emotional (facial) expressions, therefore allow the viewers to both (emotionally) comprehend and thus empathize with the characters' actions and involve themselves in the (often fantastic) adventures that they experience. The films' narrations are further supported by emotional cues that are transported by their formal elements such as music, editing, or their *mise-en-scène* (Smith 1999; Uhrig 2014). Basic principles of animated films that support emotional engagement have already been described by Frank Thomas and Ollie Johnston in the 1980s, who mentioned aspects such as exaggeration, anticipation, or staging to support the emotional impact of a scene. In their often more naturalistic approaches, where style seems subordinated to stories, popular computer animations inherit these aesthetic traditions by, at the same time, developing their generic characteristics with respect to the use of movement, music, or color (on the application of principles of traditional animation on computer animation see, e.g., Lasseter 1987; see Chapter 8).

Next to fictional (mainstream) variants of digital animation and next to (early) experimental and art house films that often thematize unpleasant emotions and complex, indirect, and even subversive messages and taboos (see Chapter 4), documentaries and educational videos provide emotional contents and effects. Due to the seeming directness of the events portrayed in documentaries, along with the capability of animation to show the otherwise impossible, animated documentaries possess the potential to display and cause intense effects while at the same time being able to soften sensitive or savage contents with the help of their generic artificiality (see Chapter 5). Furthermore, health campaign videos, displaying emotional contents and/or contents aiming for specific emotional effects, seem omnipresent (see Chapter 3). In the context of clinic autism studies, for example, the potential to control, manipulate, and alter representations of faces is being used in order to study the effects of facial expressions and/or to adapt computer-generated expressions to certain forms of the disorder to help patients learn to recognize emotions. Also, videos on emotional disorders such as depression are being widely used for both educational and therapeutic reasons, making use of the benefits of digital technology to display and elicit certain emotions.

Research in 'AnimOtion'

Films in general and animated films especially have been subject to emotion research from the beginning. Appearing already in the earliest theoretical approaches, early film theorists described the potential and possibilities of the moving image to transport and elicit emotions like no other art form (e.g., Arnheim 1932; Münsterberg 1916) and even adapted their theories to film projects (Eisenstein 1924) and experiments (Kuleshov 1921). In the 1980s, psychoanalytical film theory started including the viewers' dispositions and early childhood experiences in their approaches and concentrated on sexual and gender-related aspects (Metz 1977; Doane 1982; Studlar 1984; Baudry 1994; Mulvey 1999, etc.). These were further developed by phenomenological approaches that emphasized bodily aspects of cinematic sensations (Sobchack 1992,

2004; Marks 2000, 2002). Furthermore, film technology seems indispensable especially when it comes to experimental and implementation emotion research. A field of research that conducts studies that combine films as the scope of investigation and use films also as a means to elicit emotions is cognitive film studies. Here, approaches from areas such as psychology, philosophy, and film studies are combined in an interdisciplinary manner. Within the last years, computer-animated contents have gained special attention within the field (e.g., Tan 2005; Flückiger 2008; Visch and Tan 2009; Visch et al. 2010, etc.). However, systematic research on emotions and animated films is still missing. This is surprising as the artificiality of computer animation makes it ideal for various areas connected to emotions – be it the portrayal of emotional characters in moving films or the creation of controllable emotional stimuli in scientific contexts. With the ability to move beyond the constraints of the empirical 'real world,' animation allows for an immense freedom of the portrayed – its aesthetic covering the full spectrum from stylized or abstract to photorealistic. Thus, computer animations are a powerful tool for depicting, studying, and manipulating emotions.

An area of research that genuinely focuses on animation as an art form and uses animations as a point of departure for their studies (rather than as means to experimentally manipulate variables or to use animated content as an example among others) is the field of animation studies. A major part of animation studies is shaped by its interest in media, especially television and film contents. These media scientific approaches to animated films date back to the beginning of film history (e.g., Irzykowski 1924; Holtz 1940; Poncet 1952; see also Eisenstein 1986) and culminate in an ongoing attempt to establish an independent research field that systematically studies animated films. An increasing interest in research into animated art and its preservation in the late 1980s and 1990s helped to promote this field. In these years, the Society for Animation Studies was established (1987), and some renowned researchers created elementary standard works, including Paul Well's monograph *Understanding Animation* (1998) and Marueen Furniss' *Art in Motion* (1999). In addition, with *Animation Journal* (since 1991), *animation: an interdisciplinary journal* (since 2006), and *Animation Studies* (since 2006), some highly relevant (online) journals were established that further helped promote the unique nature of animated film art and its justification as an object of scientific investigation. Since then, numerous articles, papers, and books have been published. Standard works in the young but relevant field of animation studies include books dealing with potential definitions of animated films (e.g., Wells 1998, 2002) as well as anthologies comprising essays offering theoretical approaches (e.g., Cholodenko 1991, 2007; Feyersinger and Reinerth 2013; Holliday and Sergant 2018) and studies on specific films, filmmakers, or genres (e.g., Ward 2008, 2011 on animated documentaries).

The field of computer animation, however, is a rather young technology that is still at its very beginning, looking back on a rather short history. Books on computer-animated films therefore most often present film-historic (e.g., Dobson 2009; Cavalier 2011; Bendazzi 2016) or technical (e.g., Flückiger 2008; Kerlow 2009) overviews, instructions for film production (e.g., Williams 2001; Rall 2015; also, e.g., Pintoff 1998; Apodaca and Gritz 2000; Wilkins and Kazmier 2005) or studies on certain films or production companies (e.g., Kurti 1998; Weishar 2002; Paik 2007). Further, online periodicals such as the aforementioned *Animation Studies* (Dobson 2006–present) and the online blog *Animation Studies 2.0* (Dobson 2012–present) have a unique influence in the field.

This Volume

Bringing together the two areas that gave rise to the establishment of computer animation as the art form it is today, namely film production and science, this book deals with the topic of computer-animated emotions from an interdisciplinary perspective – one that it deserves and is truly needed.

Paul Wells presents an analysis of a variety of different animated films to illustrate different ways that animation prompts empathetic and compassionate understanding. Introducing Fago, the condition in which the emotions of love, compassion, and sadness are blurred and mixed, he draws upon tenets of constructed emotion theory, namely goal orientation, emotion communication, valence/arousal, and granularity, to show "how affect is produced and incites emotion in animated film."

The subsequent group of articles covers the specifics of different animated film genres to display and elicit emotions. Kathrin Fahlenbrach and Maike Sarah Reinerth present a comparison of emotion display in both popular movies and informative animated videos. Drawing on conceptual metaphor theory, they show the specific potential of animated content to both represent and elicit emotions in the form of emotion metaphors and metonymies.

Patrick Colm Hogan discusses the animation-specific application of alteration and specification principles to (emotion-defined) story prototypes in animated art house cinema, using the example of the Chinese animated feature film *The Butterfly Lovers* (Shanbo and Yingtai 2004). He presents their thematic and emotional function as well as the (emotional) consequences of the viewers' sensitivity to these theoretical principles.

Documentary forms of animation are covered by Paul Ward, who addresses the emotional effect of the "extent to which animated documentaries foreground their constructedness" on the viewers, an aspect that, according to Ward, has been neglected in approaches to animated documentaries until now. His presentation of three central aspects of animated documentary, namely reenactment, performativity, and engagement, leads to the conclusion that it is the recognition of the very nature of animated documentary being a "form of representation" that elicits a "specific form of engagement or emotional response."

Torben Grodal covers the specific features of the animated diegetic world and its perception. Analyzing elements of the aesthetic and cognitive structure of animated films as well as the importance of social communication in these films that is based on facial expressions and intentionality, he describes playing with "fundamental mental mechanisms" of the viewers and further focuses on "violations of ontological templates" using comic animation, cartoons, and horror animation as examples.

Narration and sound are the central aspects that Nichola Dobson focuses on in her chapter. Discussing the problem of hyperreal animation, she analyzes the extent to which different examples of contemporary cinematic and television animations apply to a classic, or Proppian narrative structure, and links the (emotional) success of an animated film to its use of narration and sound, referring to it as the "right balance" on a continuum comprising several filmic elements rather than just the film's degree of realism.

Kirsten Moana Thompson also discusses aesthetic cinematic features, focusing on material surface, (e)motion, and color. Using the example of Disney's feature film *Moana* (Musker and Clements 2016), she examines the film aesthetics' historical roots and argues that, while illuminated, scintillating light is a key component of animated (e)motion in general, animated light in motion is part of a transformation of the contemporary screen into a new generative site across multiple art forms.

Camera scope and editing in animated films are addressed by Katalin E. Bálint and Brendan Rooney, who focus on the influence of close-up shots on the emotional impact of animated content. Describing studies on the use of shot scale, they present their conclusions on the emotional effects of the frequency, sequential position, and content of close-up shots.

Sermin Ildirar Kirbas and Tim J. Smith consider the perception of animated film content, examining its effects on specific target groups of animation, namely babies and children. Presenting an overview of multiple studies conducted with children, they explain the specific potential of animated content for addressing a young audience.

An interview conducted with Felix Gönnert, filmmaker and professor of computer animation, gives insights into the practitioner's mindset, answering questions covering the meaning of emotions in animated films, their great potential to display and elicit emotions, and the benefits of academic studies on 'animOtion' for film production.

Notes

1 *Best Animated Short Film* has existed as a category at the Academy Awards since 1932.
2 In 2016, with *Finding Dory* (Stanton), *Zootopia* (Howard), and *The Secret Life of Pets* (Renaud), three films out of the top 10 were completely computer generated (boxofficemojo.com).

References

Apodaca, Anthony A. and Gritz Larry. *Advanced RenderMan: Creating CGI for Motion Pictures.* San Francisco: Morgan Kaufman Publishers, 2000.

Arnheim, Rudolf. "Film als Kunst." [Film as Art]. In: Albersmeier, Franz-Josef (Ed.). *Texte zur Theorie des Films.* Stuttgart: Reclam, 2003 [1932]: 176–200.

Balázs, Béla. *Theory of the Film: Character and Growth of a New Art.* New York: Dover Publications, 1970 [1952].

Baudry, Jean L. "Le Dispositif: Approches Métapsychologiques de l'Impression de Réalité." [The Apparatus: Metapsychological Approaches to the Impression of Reality]. *Communications 23, Psychanalyse et Cinéma.* Paris: Seuil, 1975.

Bendazzi, Ginalberto. *Animation. A World History III.* Boca Raton: CRC, 2016.

Cavalier, Steven. *The World History of Animation.* London: Aurum Press, 2011.

Cholodenko, Alan (Ed.). *The Illusion of Life.* Sydney: Power Institute of Fine Arts, 1991.

——— *The Illusion of Life II: More Essays on Animation.* Sydney: Power Institute of Fine Arts, 2007.

Doane, Mary A. "Film and the Masquerade: Theorising the Female Spectator." In: Doane, Mary A. (Ed.). *Femmes Fatales: Feminism, Film Theory, and Psychoanalysis.* New York/London: Routledge, 1982: 74–87.

Dobson, Nichola. *Animation Studies.* Online Journal. (2006–present): https://journal.animationstudies.org/terence-dobson-norman-mclaren-beyond-100

——— Historical Dictionary of Animation and Cartoons. Lanham: Rowman & Littlefield, 2009.

——— *Animation Studies 2.0* (2012–present): https://blog.animationstudies.org

Eder, Jens. Dramaturgie des populären Films: Drehbuchpraxis und Filmtheorie. [Dramaturgy of popular films]. Hamburg: LIT, 2007.

Eisenstein, Sergej. *Eisenstein on Disney.* Calcutta: Seagull, 1986.

——— "Montage of Film Attractions." *Eisenstein Reader.* London: British Film Institute, 1924.

Feyersinger, Erwin and Maike S. Reinerth (Eds.). "Animationsfilm." [Animated Film]. *Montage AV.* Marburg: Schüren, 2013.

Flückiger, Barbara. *Visual Effects.* Marburg: Schüren, 2008.

Furniss, Maureen. *Art in Motion: Animation Aesthetics.* Sydney: John Libbey, 1999.

Holliday, Christopher and Alexander Sergant (Eds.). *Fantasy/Animation: Connections between Media, Mediums and Genres.* London/New York: Routledge, 2017.

Holtz, Reinhold Johann. Die Phänomenologie und Psychologie des Trickfilms: Analytische Untersuchungen über die phänomenologischen, psychologischen und künstlerischen Strukturen der Trickfilmgruppe. [Phenomenology and Psychology of Trick Film]. Hamburg: Niemann & Moschinski, 1940.

Irzykowski, Karol. *Dziesiąta Muza. Zagadnienia Estetyczne Kina.* [The Tenth Muse: Aesthetic Problems of Cinema]. Warschau: Wydawnictwa Artystyczne i Filmowe, 1977 [1924].

Isaacson, Walter. *Steve Jobs*. München: Simon & Schuster, 2011.

Kerlow, Isaac V. The Art of 3D Computer Animation and Effects. Hoboken: Wiley, 2009.

Kurti, Jeff. A Bug's Life: The Art and Making of an Epic of Miniature Proportions. New York: Hyperion, 1998.

Lasseter, John. "Principles of Traditional Animation Applied to 3D Computer Animation." *ACM SIGGRAPH, Computer Graphics*, 21(4), 1987: 35–44.

Marks, Laura U. The Skin of the Film: Intercultural Cinema, Embodiment, and the Senses. Durham/London: Duke University Press, 2000.

—— *Touch. Sensuous Theory and Multisensory Media.* Minneapolis/London: University of Minnesota Press, 2002.

Metz, Christian. *The Imaginary Signifier: Psychoanalysis and the Cinema.* Bloomington: Indiana University Press, 1977.

Münsterberg, Hugo. *The Photoplay: A Psychological Study.* New York: Appleton, 1916.

Mulvey, Laura. "Visual Pleasure and Narrative Cinema." In: Cohen, Marshall and Leo Braudy (Eds.). *Film Theory and Criticism*. New York: Oxford University Press, 1999: 833–844.

Paik, Karen. To Infinity and Beyond! The Story of Pixar Animation Studios. London: Virgin Books, 2007.

Pintoff, Ernest. *Animation 101*. Studio City: Michael Wiese Productions, 1998.

Plantinga, Carl. "The Scene of Empathy and the Human Face on Film." In: Plantinga, Carl and Greg M. Smith (Eds.). *Passionate Views: Film, Cognition, and Emotion*. Baltimore/London: The Johns Hopkins University Press, 1999: 239–255.

Poncet, Marie-Thérèse. *L'Esthétique du dessin animé.* [The Aesthetics of Animated Design]. Paris: Librairie Nizet.

Rall, Hannes. *Animationsfilm: Konzept und Produktion.* [Animated Film. Concept and Production]. Konstanz: UVK, 2015.

Smith, Jeff. "Movie Music as Moving Music: Emotion, Cognition, and the Film Score." In: Plantinga, Carl and Greg M. Smith (Eds.). *Passionate Views: Film, Cognition, and Emotion*, 1999: 146–167.

Studlar, Gaylyn. "Masochism and the Perverse Pleasures of Cinema." *Quarterly Review of Film and Video*, 9(4), 1984: 267–282.

Sobchack, Vivian. *The Address of the Eye: A Phenomenology of Film Experience.* Princeton/NJ: Princeton University Press, 1992.

—— Carnal Thoughts: Embodiment and Moving Image Culture. Berkeley: University of California Press, 2004.

Tan, Ed S. H. "Gesichtsausdruck und Emotion in Comic und Film." [Facial Expression and Emotion in Comic and Film]. In: Brütsch, Matthias et al. (Eds.). *Kinogefühle: Emotionalität und Film*. Marburg: Schüren, 2005: 265–289.

Thomas, Frank and Ollie Johnston. *The Illusion of Life: Disney Animation*. New York: Walt Disney Production, 1981.

Uhrig, Meike. *Darstellung, Rezeption und Wirkung von Emotionen im Film: Eine interdisziplinäre Studie*. [Representation, Reception and Effects of Emotions in Film: An Interdisciplinary Study]. Wiesbaden: Springer VS, 2014.

———— "In Your Face, Princess: On the Physiognomic Features of the Disney Princess Archetype." *Blog.animationstudies.org*, 2016.

———— "In the Face of… Animated Fantasy Characters." In: Holliday, Christopher and Alexander Sergant (Eds.). *Fantasy/Animation. Connections between Media, Mediums and Genres*. London/New York: Routledge, 2018.

Visch, Valentijn T., Ed S. H. Tan, and Dylan Molenaar. "The Emotional and Cognitive Effect of Immersion in Film Viewing." *Cognition and Emotion*, 24(8), 2010: 1439–1445.

Visch, Valentijn T. and Ed S. H. Tan. "Categorizing Moving Objects into Film Genres: The Effect of Animacy Attribution, Emotional Response, and the Deviation from Non-Fiction." *Cognition*, 110(2), 2009: 265–272.

Ward, Paul. "Animated Realities: The Animated Film, Documentary, Realism." *Reconstruction*, 8(2), 2008.

———— "Animating With Facts: The Performative Process of Documentary Animation in the Ten Mark." *SAGE*, 6(3), 2011: 293–305.

Weishar, Peter. Blue Sky, the Art of Computer Animation, Featuring Ice Age and Bunny. New York: Harry N. Abrams, Inc., 2002.

Wells, Paul. *Understanding Animation*. New York: Routledge, 1998.

———— *Animation: Genre and Authorship*. London: Wallflower, 2002.

Wilkins, Mark R. and Chris Kazmier. *MEL Scripting for MAYA Animators*. San Francisco: Morgan Kaufman Publishers, 2005.

Williams, Richard. *The Animator's Survival Kit*. London: Faber and Faber Ltd., 2001.

Films

The Butterfly Lovers. Directed by Ming Chin Tsai. 2004; TWN: Central Motion Pictures.

Finding Dory. Directed by Andrew Stanton. 2016; USA: Disney/Pixar.

Luxo Jr. Directed by John Lasseter. 1986; USA: Pixar.

Moana. Directed by John Musker and Ron Clements. 2016; USA: Disney.

The Secret Life of Pets. Directed by Chris Renaud. 2016; USA: Universal Pictures/Illumination Entertainment.

Star Wars. Directed by George Lucas. 1977; USA: Lucasfilm/Twentieth Century Fox.

Zootopia. Directed by Byron Howard, Rich Moore, and Jared Bush. 2016; USA: Disney.

Part II
Emotion Theory and Animated Film

2 'Perfect Bridge over the Crocodiles'

Tacit Contracts, Listen Thieves, and Emotional Labor in the Animated Fago

Paul Wells

In the following discussion, I will draw upon a variety of definitions of 'emotion' in developing an address of how affect is produced and incites emotion in animated film. Some of these definitions are drawn from the debates that inform how emotion is defined and understood by scholars working in the fields of sociology, psychology, and neuroscience (Koestler 1970; Pinker 1997; Keltner et al. 2010; Feldman Barrett 2017), the emergent field of bioculturalism (Grodal 2009) and others that are drawn from wider cultural sources (Watt Smith 2015). All these definitions find particular expression in animation as it is an inherently *rhetorical* and *enunciative* form. Simply, animation's inherently *rhetorical* condition means that its construction is *always* a critical intervention and interrogation of the representation of the material world. Its artificial and illusionist status signifies its self-conscious presence as an interpretive form, and privilege its presence as an *enunciative* practice. In literally announcing its very 'difference' as a method, it affords the opportunity for practitioners to create a more nuanced and considered *performance* of visual ideas, concepts, and narratives. In this instance, I wish to offer an analysis of how the particular condition of animation is especially pertinent in speaking to the tenets of *Constructed Emotion Theory*, and specifically, the work of Lisa Feldman Barrett.

The dominant theoretical understanding of 'emotion,' essentially derived from Darwin's pioneering work in *The Expression of Emotions in Man and Animals*, is that emotion is universal and hardwired into the human condition, sharing common characteristics and genuinely embedded as a 'fingerprint' in the mind and body (see Grodal 2009: 18; Feldman Barrett 2017: ix–24). This is usually understood as *Basic Emotion* or *Classical Emotion Theory*, and is predicated predominantly on the facial and physical recognition of core emotions – happiness, sadness, anger, etc. *Constructed Emotion Theory* argues, however, that our emotions are neither hardwired nor universal, but that humankind shares the facility to create what Feldman Barrett calls "emotion concepts" (Feldman Barrett 2017: 30) that are actually similar to cognitive processes and perception, and are constructed based on previous experience (Feldman Barrett 2017: 34–35). The theory suggests emotion emerges with the same speed and immediacy but is merely processed in a different way, based on rapid predictions and projections that *simulate* the emotion as a response to the context and events in question.[1] *Constructed Emotion Theory* insists that humankind moves from a position of 'experiential blindness' extremely quickly, forming concepts about emotion that in essence make it a shared *situational* phenomenon rather than a common aspect of all human *experience per se*. I wish to suggest here, then, that *Constructed Emotion Theory* offers the best explanation for why animation is especially conducive to the construction and expression of emotion as well as why its rhetorical and enunciative condition enables audiences worldwide to construct common emotion concepts that enable narratives in one culture to translate more readily to another.[2]

Animation is first prominently encountered in childhood and as such is one of the key carriers and progenitors of the visualization of emotion concepts. These emotion concepts are normally contained within scenarios – predominantly in children's television animation but in early years features, too – that privilege optimism over pessimism, care over conflict, welfare over woe, collaboration over alienation, and helping over abandonment. Grodal has argued such texts speak to innate dispositions and notes, for example, "the care of offspring is central to the winning mammalian strategy, and the disposition to care is crucial both in children's tales and in love stories" (Grodal 2009: 9). I also wish to suggest, though, that within such texts children *learn* Fago. Watt Smith suggests,

> *Fago* is a unique emotional concept that blurs compassion, sadness and love together. It is a the pity felt for someone in need, which compels us to care for them, but is also haunted by the sense that one day we will lose them. *Fago* comes in those moments when our love for others, and their need for us, feels so unexpectedly overwhelming – and life so very fragile and temporary – that we well up.
>
> (Watt Smith 2015: 105)

The animated narratives that populate childhood foreground how love and compassion can address and arrest the causes of sadness, and there is a clear understanding that these emotions are inextricably linked. There is also a sense in which these emotions become embedded and embodied in animated texts accordingly. As life becomes more complex, and humans age, this simple yet complex dialectic between emotion concepts is problematized further. What might have been defined or mistaken as an 'essentialist' or even 'primal' construction of emotional life in childhood is actually a core currency of development and maturity and maintains its currency thereafter in animated forms. It is my contention here, then, that animation, in embodying Fago, essentially transports these emotion concepts into all its texts; what audiences consequently 'read' in those texts is a version of Fago that is constantly readdressing the relationship between love, sadness, and compassion in the light of an increasing realization and acceptance of mortality. It is this combination of emotion concepts, then, created and evinced in childhood animation texts, that becomes a foundational core for what has passed but what remains valuable and pertinent in the understanding of the human condition thereafter. With each more complex view of life comes a more complex view of emotion concepts and a more complex construction of those emotion concepts *in* animation. Each new animated text in essence reaches back to the touchstone of childhood Fago to reposition it contextually and culturally. What *Basic Emotion* or *Classical Emotion Theory* does is to merely help identify these emotions, but *Constructed Emotion Theory* offers the affordance of terms and processes that help with an understanding of animated texts as they further problematize (while continuing to reveal) the Fago. In the discussion that follows, then, I wish to use *Constructed Emotion Theory* to explore the expression of emotion in a number of ways that are culturally (and sometimes nationally) specific while also speaking to wider social definitions of emotional agency through the identification of Fago.

If Pixar's *Inside Out* (Pete Docter 2015) engages with the dominant emotions that take up the core Fago of childhood, *Garden of Words* (Makoto Shinkai 2013) looks at the Fago of growing up and maturing; British feature *Ethel and Ernest* (Roger Mainwood 2016) at the Fago of life lived in response to social change; and American independent feature *Anomalisa* (Duke Johnson and Charlie Kaufman 2015) at the Fago of life in the pursuit of meaning and purpose. *Constructed Emotion Theory* is evidenced in the address of Fago in these texts in specific and particular ways by engaging with the construction of emotion concepts. I wish to use *Inside Out*, in the first instance, as an example of understanding the shift from *Basic Emotion Theory* to *Constructed Emotion Theory*, thereafter looking in more detail at some of the tenets of *Constructed Emotion Theory* by addressing *goal orientation* and *emotion communication* in the Japanese feature *Garden of Words*; *valence* and *arousal* in *Ethel and Ernest*; and, importantly, *granularity* in *Anomalisa*. Further, a key aspect of *Constructed Emotion Theory* is that emotions function as a social reality, and as such I wish to also ground some of this analysis in more widely held cultural concepts, taking into account the principles of 'tacit contracts,' 'listen thieves,' and 'emotional labor' that inform how viewers are cued to understand both how the representation of emotion is being constructed in animation and how this prompts particular responses. Ultimately, it will become clear why animation offers 'the perfect bridge over the crocodiles.'

What Is Going on Inside Her Head?

At the beginning of Pixar's *Inside Out,* the question is posed of the baby, Riley, "What is going on inside her head?" – a pertinent starting place, then, for how humankind might understand how a person functions psychologically and emotionally. Though this is clearly an extraordinarily complex area, bound up with contested definitions of mind, consciousness, and the psychosomatic, Feldman Barrett argues

> Pixar's movies are impressive in how well they do not stick to the stereotypes. Even the characters in *Inside Out,* which is a thoroughly essentialist fantasy about emotions, show a broad range of subtle and fascinating facial and bodily configurations during emotional episodes.
>
> (Feldman Barrett 2017: 184)

Feldman Barrett inadvertently draws attention to the specificity of animation in the way that it necessarily *nuances* expression, because it has to construct and represent it – in essence *simulate* it – in small slowly accumulating increments. This echoes *Constructed Emotion Theory,* which argues humankind *simulates* its emotion concepts in small, rapidly accumulating increments. Animation may be understood therefore as a vehicle that is a very, very, very slow motion visualization process in the psychosomatic construction of emotional experience. I will relate this further to the concept of the "micro-narrative" later in my discussion.

Inside Out tells the story of 11-year-old Riley as she and her parents move from her previous home in Minnesota to San Francisco. All such moves can be affecting and sometimes traumatic for a child, and the film explores this idea by constructing the narrative from the point of view of the five core emotions in Riley's mind – joy, sadness, fear, disgust, and anger. The film is, in effect, a playing-out of *Classical Emotion Theory,* as it appears that Riley's emotions seem hardwired from her birth, and everything she experiences is an act of emotion.[3] These emotional events are then either translated into significant core memories, stored in long-term memory, come to reside in the subconscious, or are eventually consigned to the 'dump' in which things are ultimately forgotten. The pre-credit sequence sets up the premise of the film introducing the core emotions as the *innate* drivers of response to the world, where the default position is 'happiness,' or more precisely, 'contentment,' before this may be disrupted by 'sadness' (epitomized in crying), 'fear' (which operates to keep a child safe), 'disgust' (which prevents a child from consuming anything dangerous), and anger (which responds to issues of justice and fairness).[4] With these core drivers in place, Riley experiences the world and stores memories that help define 'islands of personality,' the distinctive constructs that determine the key preoccupations or behavior of the child. In this instance, Riley's islands are based on her relationships with her family, her friends, her sense of honesty (a version of 'conscience'), her playfulness and sense of humor (Goofball Island), and her investment in hockey (her interests or hobbies).

The narrative hereafter demonstrates how experience modifies and re-defines these emotions as Riley becomes increasingly sad about her move from Minnesota, and more and more destabilized from her established personality traits, growing distant from her family and friends, losing her playfulness, not wanting to play hockey, and even acting dishonestly. In principle, this is a portrayal of a minor breakdown, depicted more as an intrinsic state of inertia in Riley, while the characters of Joy and Sadness seek to reconcile their relationship in a journey that is actually the primary emotional arc of the film. Joy and Sadness move through the literal depiction of 'long-term memory' (meeting Riley's early-years imaginary friend, Bing Bong); 'abstract thought' (nonobjective frag-mentation, deconstruction, the nonfigurative, etc.); 'dream-states' and 'the imagination' (French Fry Forest, the House of Cards, imaginary boyfriends); the 'subconscious' (featuring her fears of a clown); the 'processes of thinking' (inductive reasoning, language processing); and crucially, 'recollection.' Interestingly, these memories are visually con-ceived as 'gazing balls,' spherical orbs that operate as 'containers' for emotional events but permit a certain level of contemplation and the potential revision of their meaning.[5] Ultimately, what is recollected and what is forgotten and how this is understood all serve to illustrate that memories can be both happy and sad, depending upon a range of chang-ing factors and the passing of time. Indeed, the film serves to suggest that all emotion becomes relative, sometimes operating with different degrees of intensity depending upon the perspective or the context in which it is experienced or viewed. It is in this that the film demonstrates the shift from *Basic Emotion Theory* to *Constructed Emotion Theory*. Riley's experience is not merely part of Riley growing up, but a princi-ple condition of maturation for everyone, and as such this prompts a particular kind of empathy in audiences. Crucially, though, *Inside Out* both *dramatizes* the emotion Riley experiences and offers *metaphors* by which to understand emotion concepts. This helps to define the au-dience's relationship to common feeling and understanding, and as such it is in these respects that it is possible to both identify Fago and look at *Constructed Emotion Theory* in more detail.

Animation *always* simultaneously offers this dramatization of emo-tion and the construction of emotion concepts that in effect 'teach' the audience the cues and connections that define their own emotional re-sponse. Riley 'blurs compassion, sadness, and love together' when she returns to her family (having planned to run away), admits to them that she is unhappy about the move from Minnesota, and breaks down, prompting the empathetic hug that reconciles the family once more.

The viewer has been offered the rhetorical and enunciative instruction in the personification of the emotional states *as* emotion concepts that compassion, love, and sadness are *simultaneously* bound up in the Fago Riley and her family feel, the complex 'mix' that the audience experiences, too. Like many animated texts principally aimed at children, *Inside Out* prioritizes the representation of *dominant* (or what might be argued are the most *obviously identifiable*) emotions. Within the context of an extensive metaphor of the mind, the narrative effectively places emphasis on the *mutuality* of these dominant emotions in their least nuanced but most affecting combination – what Grodal calls a "functional bundle" (Grodal 2009: 33). This is a principle in which a pertinent symbol or metaphor summates complex conjunctions of key emotions. This is normally a character like 'the evil witch' or 'the fairy godmother,' but in *Inside Out*, it is distilled in the emotional 'console' that seemingly manages Riley's behavior. As the film concludes, a new console is in place that is newly fitted for the demands of 'puberty' and the kinds of expression that will be likely in those formative years.

Ultimately, then, this defines emotion at its most emphatic and dramatic and draws attention to how animation can create Fago, because at one and the same time it can speak to the emotional concepts of 'love,' 'sadness,' and 'compassion' as the combination that best represents our acceptance and reconciliation of human experience. In its most profound sense, it is an acknowledgment of mortality in texts that are first principally encountered in childhood, and it serves to underpin how the increasing complexity of life is negotiated thereafter. *Inside Out* is a sophisticated narrative that calls upon a core discourse about the relationship between joy and sadness and the realization that that the things that make humankind 'happy' may also be the source of greatest unhappiness when they pass, are lost, or become subject to an alternative interpretation. *Constructed Emotion Theory* insists "an emotion is your brain's creation of what your bodily sensations mean, in relation to what is going on around you in the world" (Feldman Barrett 2017: 30) and thus locates emotion in the particularity of the way it rapidly processes "diverse instances" (*ibid.*: 23) of previous experience in order "to form concepts that make our physical sensations meaningful" (*ibid.*: 38). In this it *situates* emotion back 'in the moment' and begins to nuance the nature of emotion beyond 'headline' terms like 'anger' into more granular terms like 'annoyance,' 'resentment,' 'exasperation,' 'rage,' etc., which may by inflected by other kinds of powerful emotions like jealousy or grief (it is no accident that these are the underpinning emotions of the *Toy Story* trilogy). From the perspective of animation, there is a strong resemblance in breaking down the expression of emotion in this way and its self-consciously constructed, frame-by-frame representation as emotion concepts in a variety of techniques – drawing, using puppets, deploying materials and objects, employing computer generated imagery, etc. Simply, the necessity to break down the expression of what is portrayed as an emotion in animation into what I have elsewhere termed *micro-narratives* (see Wells 2010) – from the smallest gesture to the specific gradation of color and form – echoes and ultimately represents some of the particular conditions of *Constructed Emotion Theory*: *goal orientation and emotion communication, valence and arousal,* and *granularity.*

"I Was Learning to Walk as Well": Goal Orientation and Emotion Communication

> Emotion concepts are goal-based concepts. Instances of happiness, for example, are highly variable. You can smile in happiness, sob in happiness, scream in happiness, raise your arms in happiness, clench your fists in happiness, jump up and down doling out high fives in happiness, or even be stunned motionless in happiness. [...] To you, in the moment, however, these sets of physical changes are equivalent for some goal. Perhaps your goal is to feel accepted, to feel pleasure, to achieve an ambition, or to find meaning in life. [...] Emotions are not reactions *to* the world; they are your constructions of the world.
>
> (Feldman Barrett 2017: 92–104)

Feldman Barrett here provides a brief example of the ways in which a dominant emotion might be broken down into common, yet more nuanced forms of expression and argues that each attaches itself to a more abstract goal orientation. Emotion concepts are thus inherently 'meaningful' and develop, emerge, and impact in different ways for different people at different times, sometimes aligning, sometimes clashing, always informing relationships of all kinds. Ultimately, it is this that is the fundamental subject of most narratives, but, I have argued, it finds special currency in animation, because animation foregrounds, and rhetorically enunciates, the mechanism by which emotion concepts are dramatized and attain metaphorical abstract meanings.

Makoto Shinkai's *Garden of Words* takes up these ideas almost explicitly by creating a narrative in which Akizuki Takao, an earnest and mature 15-year-old, encounters a troubled 28-year-old school teacher, Yukari Yukino, on rainy days in the Shinjuku Gyoen National Garden. Many are versed with Japan's emotional concept of *mono no aware* – essentially the despair felt at the impermanence and transience of life, especially in its most satisfying moments – arguably another version of Fago; less well known is the emotional concept of *koi*, the Japanese conception of love as lonely sadness. Akizuki directly relates his emotions to the weather and the landscape and his deep desire to be a shoemaker, and on rainy days he skips school to sit and draw in the park. Ms. Yukino is also missing school; the victim of harassment by students, and still feeling the breakdown of a previous relationship, she sits in the park, also on rainy days, drinking and eating chocolate. The two strike up an unlikely bond, free of sentiment and informed by their own emotional intensities: Akizuki is able to express himself through designing shoes, on one occasion recalling a pair given to his mother, on another actually measuring Ms. Yukino's feet to make a pair; Ms. Yukino, struggling to express her feelings but communicating through *Man'yoshu* literature in a *tanka* she gives him. As is common in Shinkai's films, there is an inherent yearning implied in their relationship but also a conflicted space; the audience knows that there would be something improper and inappropriate in the consummation of their relationship while wishing for them both to find emotional resolution. The film then is concerned with the conflicting *goal orientation* the two experience – both experience love as lonely sadness that will not (cannot) be reconciled in each other.

Though they are 'stuck in the same place,' Akizuki resolves to make a pair of shoes that will 'make her want to walk.' The key metaphors that define emotion concepts in the film are feet/shoes and rain. They are intrinsic to the narrative because they help to illustrate and imply repressed emotion in characters that cannot freely express it in identifiably 'performative' ways common in most films, but, more importantly, because their emotions are 'abstract' in their complexity and feeling. Akizuki is mature enough to know that he cannot act on his feelings for Ms. Yukino because it will arrest his whole potential to succeed personally and professionally. Ms. Yukino is simply emotionally lost, admitting to herself that 'she was not any smarter at 27 than she was at 15.' When Akizuki actually finds out that Ms. Yukino is actually a teacher at his school, he partly plays out his confused emotions by trying and failing to beat up the third-years who have accused her of having affairs with students. This is dramatic irony for the viewer, as the audience knows she has not sought an affair with Akizuki and that her emotional state has been depicted by Shinkai as a struggle with herself, not selfish or manipulative, but incomplete and unfulfilled. To Akizuki, she is beautiful, well presented, polite, and invested in his maturity, and he falls in love with her. After a major rainstorm, the couple retreats to Ms. Yukino's flat, and Akizuki declares his love, which she politely deflects by asking him to call her by her formal name; he responds to this by thanking her for her hospitality and leaving. Shinkai places their goal orientation in direct opposition – Akizuki knows he must "walk on my own, even if I am barefoot," while Ms. Yukino falls silent. It is at this juncture that Shinkai deliberately moves from the repressed emotions embodied in the rainy landscapes and shoe imagery and the introspection of the two protagonists, permitting the overt *emotion communication* where the core emotional concepts of couple directly relate and reveal themselves. Ms. Yukino chases after Akizuki, finding him on the stairwell, but still unable to say what she feels. Akizuki, on the other hand, turns on her with a raging litany of shifting emotional perspectives – "I hate you," "I was just a kid, what's wrong with you?" "Humor the little kid," "I'll never measure up to my dreams," "Say something for a change," and ultimately, "You'll live all your life alone." He shifts between the emotion concepts of self-pity, embarrassment, disgust, bitterness, self-doubt, abuse, and cruel accusation, yet this is all expressed in the full knowledge of Akizuki, and the audience, that he loves her. Ms. Yukino finally breaks, moving from quiet tears of suffering and pain to profound physical emotional release in which she clings to Akizuki, and admits, "You saved me." Their goal orientation becomes aligned in the resolution of their desperate embrace, and the emotion concepts that defined them in 'lonely sadness' are resolved in the salvation of Fago.

The film concludes with the couple moving on, Akizuki leaving the shoes he made for Ms. Yukino in the park and his love for her as a spiritual guide for his future 'path,' as he concludes, "I was learning to walk as well." If the rain or love cannot be controlled or stopped, there are still many ways of walking through it. Shinkai readily demonstrates the complexity of emotions involved in love, in the situated circumstances of his narrative, and the characters he brings together. More, though: in investing objects and the environment with such core metaphoric purpose, he properly exploits the intrinsic condition of animation to speak to the micro and the macro simultaneously, and instead of the (voice) actors alone creating the 'performance' of emotion, the visualization of emotion concepts, permits the whole *mise-en-scène* to embody the Fago. Love, sadness, and compassion are embedded in nature and the passage of time itself and provide the situational context in the emotional lives of individuals as – at different stages in their maturation – both help each other to grow up. Shinkai, in essence, in revealing how a couple reach a state of self-awareness emotionally, equally enables his audience to empathize with that experience.

"We're in Clover!": Valence and Arousal

If *Inside Out* necessarily extended its metaphor in order to dramatize the impact of emotion, and *Garden of Words* used its metaphors to nuance emotional goals in relationships, *Ethel and Ernest* takes a more subtle view based in the observation of everyday behavior. *Ethel and Ernest* extends the idea that while humankind may be driven by emotions and feelings, it does not necessarily *express* them, either through words or dramatic gestures. Life is not one long act of laughing, crying, arguing, sickness, or fright but rather a complex negotiation of feelings in relation to context, and rarely are the expressions of joy, sadness, anger, disgust, or fear fully expressed as emphasized or exaggerated performances, instead playing out in more complex ways. *Constructed Emotion Theory* suggests, then, that the starting place in understanding how humankind expresses emotion with greater emphasis is to recognize that a body's first responsibility is to itself, and emotion is first grounded in the internal monitoring of normal mental and physical functioning – this is termed *interoception* (Feldman Barrett 2017: 66–73) – and using the 'body budget' of energy, feelings, and well-being to secure what might be viewed as a balanced or neutral model of emotional life. This is normally expressed in everyday life as functional behavior, neither troubled nor excessively cheerful but stable and able to execute tasks and required actions. Indeed, the emotional concepts that may be attached to these behavioral traits are those which determine their meaning, but these are normally only identified by the *affect* which occurs as events happen and interaction with people and the environment takes place or, of course, if the internal body is not in good health or invaded in some way.

Ethel and Ernest, based on the graphic novel by Raymond Briggs about his parents' lives from their first meeting in 1928 to their deaths in the early 1970s, is grounded first and foremost in the everyday ordinariness of existence. The animated film is faithful to the design and the narrative of the novel but, most importantly, bases its emotional arc on the oscillation between the more 'neutral' behavior of the main protagonists and the illustration of the emotional concept that comes with the *affect* of personal and social events as they impact upon the couple. Feldman Barrett notes that affect is composed of two aspects:

> the first is how pleasant or unpleasant you feel, which scientists call *valence*. The pleasantness of the sun on your skin, the deliciousness of your favorite food, and the discomfort of a stomachache or a pinch are all examples of affective *valence*. The second feature of affect is how calm or agitated you feel, which is called *arousal*. The energized feeling of anticipating good news, the jittery feeling after drinking too much coffee, the fatigue after a long run, and the weariness from lack of sleep are examples of high and low arousal.
>
> (Feldman Barrett 2017: 72)

This tends to render behavior as a model that moves in emotional degrees between serene and calm (pleasant valence, low arousal), effusive and upbeat (pleasant valence, high arousal), lethargic and low (unpleasant valence, low arousal), and upset and distressed (unpleasant valence, high arousal). These states of being are located in what Feldman Barrett calls the "affective niche," the psychosomatic context in which defines the particular reality of a situation and the emotional concept the mind simulates. *Ethel and Ernest*'s narrative moves imperceptibly from one 'affective niche' to another as each scene unfolds, drawing Ethel and Ernest's particular backgrounds, sensibilities, temperaments, and behavior into the same orbit over time. If *Inside Out* and *Garden of Words* essentially take place over about a year, *Ethel and Ernest* plays out over 40; more significantly, it foregrounds emotions as much as products of their social context as the inherent affect that emerges from an individual response to a situation.

Ethel and Ernest initially observe each other from afar, Ethel initially playing out the first display of affect with unpleasant valence and mild arousal, signaling disappointment that she does not see him pass her window. This is followed by an instance of pleasant valence and mild arousal when she is surprised by Ernest: He calls at the house at which she is a housemaid and presents her with flowers, asking her for a date. On the date, Ernest enjoys a pleasant valence and high arousal, playfully dancing to amuse Ethel. These are all understated scenes that resist overdramatizing their courtship and stress the gentle emergence of their affection for each other. This is not overtly expressed or urgent romantic love but a respectful exchange of care and warmth, underscored by the moral and social mores of the period and informed by the 'affective reality' of their social class and position. Ethel is happy to introduce Ernest to her parents, but Ernest resists the idea that she should meet his – the implication being he is a little fearful that they are not 'good enough' or that he is ashamed of his background. These exchanges implicitly suggest Ethel's aspirant middle-classness and conservatism set against Ernest's left-leaning working-classness, and this implicitly sets an emotional agenda. Ethel's employers display mild annoyance when Ethel leaves to marry Ernest, which at one level is an endorsement of their social compatibility, but at another, a mismatch of social ambition. The tone of the piece is reserved and conditional – all aspects of affect are played out through mild valence and arousal. Ethel is mildly amused or irritated by Ernest, never demonstrably emotional, more often quietly embarrassed by his behavior or by their social standing. When the couple gets a cooker, she exclaims, in what passes for pleasant valence, high arousal, "We're in clover!" She is celebrating the evidence of their material progress, but this is tempered by her response to Ernest's job as a milkman, when she says, "Do you think you'll ever be promoted?" As in many domestic and social exchanges, there is little performative excess in the expression of these emotions, but both the characters and the audience feel and perceive the emotional concept of an irreconcilable 'tension' that implicitly articulates their differences. (The tension in *Garden of Words* is partly concerned with unconsummated desire, irreconcilable through age difference, while *Ethel and Ernest* is about ignored – rather than reconciled – class tensions.) Significantly, though, their 'affective niche' is heightened when Ethel breaks down while looking at a picture of a baby she places above their bed. This symbolic act is one of affect again for both the characters and the audience, who feels sad that the couple has not yet been successful in having a child, something clearly longed for by Ethel. There is much greater narrative impact in this act of pain and anguish and in Ernest's attempt to comfort her. It is one of the rare instances in which there is the expression of physical affection, one that resonates further when Ethel cannot explicitly tell Ernest she is pregnant and only implies it. Throughout the film, Ernest suggests he has a broader sexual knowledge, but as in all else, this is understated, a marker of less liberal times. When Ethel nearly dies in childbirth, however, a potentially 'dramatic' act is rendered 'offstage,' and in response to Ernest's nervous anticipation, concern, and, ultimately, joy, the doctor asserts "There had better not be any more." Again, the doctor's tone is in some ways accusatory, as if Ernest had transgressed unwritten social rules in making love with his wife and having a family. This is not the sensual and emotional transcendence of sex implied in *Anomalisa*, which I will engage with later in my discussion, but a culturally imposed view of sex as a functional and not pleasurable act. Crucially, then, this concentration on affect as the predisposition for, or forerunner of, emotional experience serves to demonstrate the social construction of emotion as well as its personal expression.

Ernest is an avid newspaper reader and freely expresses his socialist leanings with the onset of World War II, while Ethel continues to assert her social aspiration in denying that the couple are 'working class.' Ethel becomes defined by three core emotions following the birth of Raymond – 'fear' for her child (she cries when he has his hair cut, is evacuated during the war, and when he is caught stealing); 'disgust' and 'embarrassment' at the falling domestic and social standards she perceives; and a certain backward-looking 'wistfulness' that combines nostalgia with disappointment as she ages. Ernest, on the other hand, is characterized by the ways he circumvents what he is required to socially repress – he expresses joy through song and in finally getting the car he has always wanted to drive out to the country and embrace the pastoral idyll which he has often dreamed about. Ernest is fundamentally changed, though, by the experience as a volunteer in the war, in a scene where Ernest is animated to physically communicate the subtle shifts in affect as he releases his emotion, shifting from the mild unpleasant valence and low arousal of tiredness, to the increased unpleasant valence and high arousal of bleak and depressive acceptance, and finally, to the profound unpleasant valence and very high arousal of breaking down into tears of desperate release at his recognition of witnessing death. This is all the more affecting for the audience because – as was socially customary – men like Ernest were not expected to cry or express their emotions at all, to any degree. The viewer witnesses him break down in the privacy of his home, but it is a powerfully public statement about the expression of despair. His emotion is an articulate physical statement that represents the rapid immediacy of escalating emotion concepts in response to extreme social circumstances. Such emotion concepts determine 'meaning' in experience and serve to define some of the complex and contradictory aspects of the human sensibility – a perspective addressed further in the direct representation of a psychosomatic condition in *Anomalisa*.

"I Feel Like an Anomaly": Granularity

Steven Pinker has argued,

> The problem with the emotions is not that they are untamed forces or vestiges of our animal past; it is that they were designed to propagate copies of the genes that built them rather than to promote happiness, wisdom, or moral values. We often call an act 'emotional' when it is harmful to the social group, damaging to the actor's happiness in the long run, uncontrollable and impervious to persuasion, or a product of self-delusion. Sad to say, these outcomes are not malfunctions but precisely what we would expect from well-engineered emotions.
>
> (Pinker 1997: 370)

Constructed Emotion Theory does not accept Pinker's view that emotions are hardwired and work in the service of genetic maintenance, nor that emotions work in opposition to reason, and are for the most part of a destructive order. Rather, the theory maintains that the simulation of emotion predicated on cascades of rapid predictions and projections based on previous experience is a highly specific response to a situation. This principle of emotional *granularity* is highly correspondent to the concept of the micro-narrative that informs the representational aspects of the minutiae in the construction of animated images. One look, one glance, one gesture, one sound, one point of expression can carry with it important indicators of affect and, ultimately, a particular emotional agency. The rhetorical and enunciative qualities of animation implicitly invite the audience to participate in the conditions it constructs for the perception of the overall narrative and its embedded micro-narratives. As a form, it is especially persuasive in illustrating interior states – dreams, memory, fantasies, solipsistic states of consciousness, etc. – sometimes literally and explicitly exemplified in films like *Inside Out*, but also in even more challenging works like Duke Johnson and Charlie Kaufman's *Anomalisa*.

The film is principally informed by a dramatization of the neuropsychiatric condition of Fregoli's Syndrome, in which a sufferer presumes everyone to be the same person, usually a person known to them, who, despite configuration in other bodies and disguises, constantly maintains their identity. Kaufman is not concerned with a literal depiction of the condition, however, and uses the *delusion* more as a metaphor for one man's emotional estrangement from the world until he is reengaged by the 'anomaly' of feeling love, passion, and desire, if only temporarily, once more. Kaufman's narrative is more complex than this, though, in that the *delusion* is reinforced by the *illusion* that all the protagonists (barring the central character, customer service guru Michael Stone, and his muse, Lisa) look and sound the same, and all the characters are not hiding their status as 'puppets' (reinforcing themes about conformity, banality, routine, and repetition). This statement of deliberate artifice despite the quasi-naturalistic behavior of the characters suggests that the material status of the events is in question and that the narrator is inherently unreliable. Rather than operating as the depiction of characters playing out emotion concepts, this is a narrative that defines and illustrates the framing and feeling of the emotion concept itself. In this it also demands something different of its audience, suggesting other ways in which the audience is being cued to embrace the perspective of the narrative. It is in this respect that animation can also speak to broader concepts of emotional life. Animation insists upon a *tacit contract* with its viewers that they should invest in the inner logic that the illusion is based on; this is predicated on becoming what the Swedish call *listen thieves* (Watt Smith 2015: 67) and conducting *emotional labor*, NOT "to control...feelings in order to influence those of others" (Watt Smith 2015: 44–47) but to understand *how* feelings are used to influence and direct others. 'Listen thieves' – the audience in this case gathers and accumulates 'intimate capital'. It secures knowledge about any one character and as such, is in a position to situate and anticipate what a character may feel, want or need. This is sometimes private or forbidden knowledge that is made available by the particular illusionist strategy that animation offers. In showing 'micro-narratives' of thoughts, private actions, shifts in behaviour unavailable to other characters, and unavailable in live action representation, a film like *Anomalisa* shows the relationship between emotion concepts, and the 'labor' required by the audience to perceive and understand them. This often requires high degrees of emotional empathy, and may define differences in audiences who do not necessarily have the emotional capacity or experience to properly relate.

This is what *Constructed Emotion Theory* insists is concerned with emotional *granularity* and as such begins with an act of listening at the beginning of *Anomalisa*, which is characterized by multiple voices speaking simultaneously. For 'listen thieves,' it is implied that this might be the cacophony of voices playing out in the mind of middle-aged British author Michael Stone on the eve of a Keynote address he is giving the next day in support of his book about customer service. All the people he engages with have the same voice and the same face, one of whom is an ex-lover, Bella Amarossi (not quite 'beautiful love?'). He met Bella 10 years before on a previous visit to Cincinnati, and he recalls her voice while on his flight as he scans an old love letter he has kept. This is genuinely 'intimate capital' in that it shows that Stone has had a clandestine affair but left Bella to return to his wife and son. It also helps to suggest the solipsistic air to the piece – this is an ordinary context 'made strange' by the film's highly concentrated and detailed focus on banal exchange and actions. Writing in the late 1960s, Koestler drew attention to theories on 'two kinds of emotion': one essentially 'preparatory,' in which there was a tendency to resist affect or stimulus that was predominantly unpleasurable, the other 'participatory,' in which there is a desire to maintain or even increase the affect or the stimulus that caused it (Koestler 1970: 333–334). In essence, all emotional life might be understood, therefore, as a tension between these two areas, but this is to insufficiently take into account the personal and social context. If Ethel and Ernest, in effect, stoically endure and occasionally enjoy the 'participatory model' of an 'ordinary' existence, for example, Stone is in a perpetual 'preparatory' state of resistance to it. As his narrative unfolds, he becomes consumed by the oppressiveness of the ordinary. While Ethel and Ernest move through different degrees of understated emotion, and occasionally, heightened emotion, the extended preoccupation with Stone's behavior becomes an emotion concept for his alienation. It seems as if he is beyond stoicism or resistance, and despite moments of mild, self-directed irritation, he cannot seem to feel anything. The narrative emphasizes the minutiae of Stone's conversation with his cab driver and the process of checking in at the Fregoli Hotel and being escorted to his room by a bellboy. In his hotel room, the audience witnesses the normally private sense of Stone's routine and habituation: going to the toilet; phoning for room service; calling home to speak to his wife and son, with nothing to say; smoking a cigarette; looking from his hotel window and seeing a man masturbate in another hotel room; briefly practicing his intended speech; going down the hotel corridor to the ice machine; and passing a man behaving aggressively towards and abusing his partner. This is an emotion concept for the audience too, as there is a clear intention to show that Stone can neither prepare nor participate as he is lost in his own solipsistic inertia.

He seeks to be proactive in changing his situation by phoning Bella in the hope that, after all the intervening years, they might be able to meet. Bella is unsurprisingly shocked by the call and only highlights Stone's own emotional regression by talking directly about how 'intense' the exchange is, how she is seeking emotional balance, and how she is self-conscious about her weight and looks. The audience again is a 'listen thief' in hearing the intimate capital of her response and is invested in the emotional labor that suspects that Stone's intentions, for all their grounding in emotional need, are actually sexual. Bella agrees to meet Stone; her awkwardness is visually played out in the way she withdraws her hands back within her long sleeves, her exasperation that Stone cannot explain why he left her, and ultimately, when she walks out suspecting Stone just wants to 'fuck.' Stone merely gets more drunk and takes to the night to go to a toy store that the cab driver says is open 24 hours in order to buy his son, Henry, a present. The store, though, only sells sex toys, and Stone finds himself intrigued by a Japanese sex doll, seemingly part simulacra of a geisha, part open mechanism, that exhibits unusual facial markings and sings songs. Though this sequence seems initially amusing, it takes on much greater significance at the end of the film, when it transpires Stone has bought the antique doll as a gift for his son. His wife notices what seems to be 'semen' emitting from the doll. Stone stares at it as it relentlessly sings its childlike refrain ("Momotaro's Song"). The doll, like the habituation routine, becomes an important emotion concept in symbolizing Stone's sexual drives and fantasies, and this helps to properly contextualize the key scenes that are at the heart of the narrative.

When Stone returns to his room from visiting the sex shop, the camera is stationed somewhat voyeuristically at the bathroom door as Stone comically negotiates the impact of the hot and cold feeds in his shower. As he gazes into the mirror, his face seems to break up and 'fast forward.' Upon hearing a different voice from voices that he has heard throughout the narrative, he hurriedly dresses to rush from his room to trace its source, knocking on hotel doors in manic fashion. Stone rapidly shifts into 'participatory' emotions; his affect is driven by highly pleasant valence and intense arousal. He finally finds Lisa, also in customer service, who is sharing a room with her colleague Emily. Both have come to attend Stone's talk and are immediately overwhelmed by the fact he is at their door and his celebrity in their field. They join him for drinks, and as the trio get drunk, Emily flirts with Stone, while Lisa continues to chatter nervously, but in Stone's ears, with 'a miraculous voice.' Though clearly Emily wishes to sleep with Stone, Stone asks Lisa for a nightcap and takes her to his room. It is important to keep in mind that this kind of interaction could have easily been achieved in live action, but the film's status as animation gives the scenes a hallucinatory, dreamlike feel, especially when Stone seduces Lisa. Lisa initially fears Stone is a 'pervert' or a 'chubby-chaser' because he wishes to kiss the scar near her eye that she hides beneath her fringe, and she thinks he is 'weird' because he asks her to sing her favorite Cindy Lauper song, "Girls Just Wanna Have Fun." Stone kisses her, and she admits, "I feel like an anomaly," to which Stone christens her 'Anomalisa,'. This is representative of a symbolic intervention in his life, which in itself is anomalous as it is characterized by participatory emotion, but more prosaically, within the overall narrative, is seemingly a powerful example of the act of falling in love. Stone undresses Lisa and performs cunnilingus and coitus, consummating not merely his physical desire but also his reengagement with feeling and emotion *per se*.

The film sets this scene into relief thereafter by playing out what it explicitly frames as a dream sequence in which Stone's paranoid anxiety is readily in evidence. The hotel manager, housed in a distant basement office, says he loves Stone; a pool of female administrative staff offers themselves to Stone, insisting "just not Lisa"; his puppet face falls off; Emily warns off Lisa, saying "Don't go with him, he's insane"; and he brings

Lisa to his room, telling her, "Everyone is one person but you and me," and claiming, "You are the only other person in the world." The couple then both awake, and this is all revealed as a dream. In the breakfast scene that follows, despite his declaration of love and commitment, Lisa begins to irritate and annoy Stone. He starts to hear her previously distinctive and magical voice dissipate back into the sound of the collective 'voice' he heard earlier. Stone then attends his speech engagement, and in front of his audience, appears to break down, mixing corporate speech (stressing to "look for what is special about each individual, focus on that") with a political rant and personal musings on the purpose of his life ("I've lost my love," "I have no one to talk to," "I need tears to let this nightmare escape," "I think there is something very, very wrong with me").

By this stage it is clear that the use of animation invests all these scenes with an ontological equivalence in which reality cannot be separated from illusion or fantasy and that the film operates as an extended expression of Stone's state of mind as he processes emotional concepts. The film's coda – a surprise party thrown by his wife, in which he gives Henry the Japanese doll – once more features everyone with the same face and voice, apart from a sequence in which Lisa is driving away with Emily, both of whom have their own faces, and in which Lisa voices a letter to Stone. She says she has looked up the word 'anomalisa' in her Japanese/English dictionary, and that it translates as 'goddess of heaven.' Though she had earlier mentioned a propensity for languages, there is no real reason why she might have chosen Japanese to translate the word. Further, there is no correspondent word in Japanese that is similar to 'Anomalisa.' It seems, then, that this is Stone's final fantasy, in which his sexual experience has been translated into a romantic projection. Lisa and the doll share facial transfiguration, auburn hair tones, and the same space of intimate capital in Stone's mind; his 'self-assertive' emotions are desperately seeking to be 'self-transcendent' emotions (Koestler 1970: 252), but ultimately the 'preparatory' becomes a mere substitute for the 'participatory.' This final aspect of the narrative then, may also be an exemplar of Georges Bataille's suggestion of the subject or object of affection and desire – Lisa – in being so self-consuming for Stone, renders his own identity subject only to his fantasy projection about Lisa and what she represents, but equally, subsumes the subject or object until they become mere 'aura' – an ephemeral feeling or affect that has no substance in itself, or reality, or even past memories (see Watt Smith 2015: 70–73). However read, though, *Constructed Emotion Theory* seems most fully evidenced in *Anomalisa*, referencing the solipsistic sometimes *as* the social, and as such demonstrating that emotional reality can also be understood as the *specific* mediator of experience and existence. The *granular* distinction of emotion concepts in the film further evidences the mutuality of love, sadness, and compassion in the animated Fago.

Conclusion: Perfect Bridge over the Crocodiles

Many years ago, I remember a history teacher quoting a speech of British Prime Minister, Winston Churchill about the idea of countries remaining neutral in war – "Each one hopes that if he feeds the crocodile enough the crocodile will eat him last." This set up a lasting impression of the danger of crocodiles in my mind, an enduring symbol for me of quiet, understated threat that, if roused, could cause devastating damage and death. For everyone, there is probably a phobia, fear, or anxiety that carries this emotional weight. The animated films I have addressed in this analysis have embraced emotions as emotion concepts, rapidly constructed psychosomatic outcomes that are predicated on the prediction and projection of known previous experience. I have aligned this construction with the construction of animated texts and suggested that as a consequence of the deep effect of childhood animation, any animated texts seen in adulthood transport the lost feelings of childhood into any later – and potentially more complex – animated texts and help to illustrate and prompt the feeling of Fago. *Constructed Emotion Theory* insists upon recognizing the ways in which humankind simulates rich and nuanced emotion categories to address the deep complexity of experience and, often, the highly relative nature of any one emotion. By looking at a variety of ways in which *Constructed Emotion Theory* helps to delineate the specificity of animation as a rhetorical and enunciative model that both dramatizes emotion and shows the conditions of its construction, it is possible to understand the shades and contradictions in these expressions of feeling. Earlier, Feldman Barrett noted the relativity of 'happiness' and how emotion concepts relate directly to goals. Watt Smith confirms this: "Because while for one person, happiness is an uninhibited groan of contentment, and for the next an eerie sense of everything being 'just right', and for a third a fluttering of excitement, it's also an emotion which feels dangerous and daring, a 'perfect bridge over the crocodiles'." (Watt Smith 2015: 131). I wish to suggest here, then, that the use of animated aesthetics to represent emotion concepts permits the deeper reconciliation of highly relative and evolving emotions as meaningful insights into the acceptance of existential challenge – indeed, a perfect bridge over the crocodiles.

Notes

1 This process of simulation should not be confused with the concept of *Simulcra and Simulation* (1981/1994) advanced by Jean Baudrillard, nor should it be confused with common usage of the word in describing something as false or misrepresentative. In this context, to simulate is to construct based on known evidence and experience in order to respond in the most genuine way.

2 Some of my remarks are inevitably informed by very direct experiences, which themselves suggest areas that require further exploration than the space or remit of this analysis permits – for example, the relationship between animation, emotion, and sound, particularly as it is expressed in the songs of yearning and aspiration in Disney's musical features. For me, this was powerfully witnessed when accompanying my daughter to a sing-along version of *Frozen* (Buck and Lee 2013) and watching a room principally full of women raising the roof to Idina Menzel's "Let It Go." At the same event, though, I also overheard conversations about Elsa as a point of focus for those young women with eating disorders or, more straightforwardly, what it was like to be at odds with your sister. Or the occasions in Zlin, Teblice or Prague, in which the Czechs have roared with delight at the singular Englishness of Aardman's *The Pirates* (Peter Lord and Newitt 2012). Or more complexly, when around the world dubbed versions of anything featuring *Wallace and Gromit* render crowds helpless with mirth. Or most poignantly, when observing a Japanese audience rendered silent and tearful when watching *Grave of the Fireflies* (Takahata 1988), or children standing up en masse in Poland and shouting with frustration at Scar in *The Lion King* (Allers and Minkoff 1994), after he causes Mufasa's death in the wildebeest stampede and then blames the fearful Simba. These observations inevitably prompt issues about the ways in which audiences engage with animated films, but equally prompt ideas about animation and its models of representation, identity politics and modes of address, especially when they are expressed through direct emotional responses.

3 This is intrinsically linked to the child's capacity to undertake *statistical learning* (see Feldman Barrett 2017: 94–99), in which the baby learns from repeated events and experiences and begins to project and predict on the basis of the probability and frequency with which things occur.

4 Grodal suggests that animated films like *Bambi* (Hand et al. 1942), *The Lion King, Finding Nemo* (Stanton and Unkrich 2003), and Spirited Away (Miyazaki 1991) have "very prominent emotional concerns" based on the "hazard-precaution system," "attachment to some parenting agency," "the creation of reciprocal relations," and "the urge for exploration and play," and while these emotions are "social constructions," he argues "the emotional dispositions to which they appeal are innate and represent the biological refinement of features found in other mammals" (see Grodal 2009: 27). This is a fundamental aspect of *Biocultural Theory* that differs markedly from *Constructed Emotion Theory*.

5 Gazing balls first emerged in thirteenth-century Venice as decorative ornaments and enjoyed a renaissance as Art Deco objects in the 1930s. They are used extensively in the work of American pop artist Jeff Koons as interventions in other objects in order that such objects may be rethought in the contemporary era.

References

Feldman Barrett, Lisa. *How Emotions Are Made: The Secret Life of the Brain*. New York: Houghton Mifflin Harcourt, 2017.

Grodal, Torben. *Embodied Visions: Evolution, Emotion, Culture and Film*. Oxford/London: Oxford University Press, 2009.

Keltner, Dacher, Jason Marsh, and Jeremy A. Smith (Eds.). *The Compassionate Instinct*. New York/London: WW Norton & Co, 2010.

Koestler, Arthur. *The Ghost in the Machine*. London: Pan Books Ltd., 1967.
Pinker, Steven. *How the Mind Works*. London: Allen Lane, 1997.
Watt Smith, Tiffany. *The Book of Human Emotions*. London: Profile Books, 2015.
Wells, Paul. "Boards, Beats, Binaries and Bricolage: Approaches to the Animated Script." In: Nelmes, Jill (Ed.). *Analysing the Screenplay*. London/New York: Routledge, 2010: 89–105.

Films

Anomalisa. Directed by Duke Johnson and Charlie Kaufman. 2015; USA: Harmonius Claptrap/Snoot Entertainment/Starburns Industries.
Bambi. Directed by David Hand et al. 1942; USA: Disney.
Ethel and Ernest. Directed by Roger Mainwood. 2016; UK: British Broadcasting Corporation (BBC)/British Film Institute (BFI).
Finding Nemo. Directed by Andrew Stanton and Lee Unkrich. 2003; USA: Disney/Pixar.
Frozen. Directed by Chris Buck and Jennifer Lee. 2013; USA: Disney.
Garden of Words. Directed by Makoto Shinkai. 2013; JP: CoMix Wave.
Grave of the Fireflies. Directed by Isao Takahata. 1988; JP: Shinchosha Company/Studio Ghibli.
Inside Out. Directed by Pete Docter. 2015; USA: Pixar.
The Lion King. Directed by Roger Allers and Rob Minkoff. 1994; USA: Disney.
The Pirates. Directed by Peter Lord and Jeff Newitt. 2012; UK/USA: Aardman Animations.
Spirited Away. Directed by Hayao Miyazaki. 2001; JP: Tokuma/Studio Ghibli/Nippon.

Part III

Genres

Popular Movies and Health
Campaign Videos

3 Audiovisual Metaphors and Metonymies of Emotions in Animated Moving Images

Kathrin Fahlenbrach and
Maike Sarah Reinerth

Introduction

The history of animation is full of inventive and powerful representations of emotions. Some of the very first animated films, like J. Stuart Blackton's *The Enchanted Drawing* (1900) or *Humorous Phases of Funny Faces* (1906), can essentially be described as sequences of exaggerated emotional expressions: stick men characters grinning, frowning, raising their eyebrows, gaping open-mouthed. In 1943, Walt Disney's World War II propaganda short *Reason and Emotion* (Roberts) takes a more elaborate route, displaying the workings of the mind 'from the inside' as two characters – 'Reason' and 'Emotion' – battle for the 'driver's seat' to control human behavior. Roughly 50 years later, when Bart Simpson, star of *The Simpsons* (Groening 1989–present) – one of, if not *the* most influential animated TV series – is told that his crush Laura Powers has a boyfriend, the emotional impact of this realization is shown by her literally ripping his heart out of his chest (S04E08 "New Kid on the Block" 1992). And to date, films like Matthew Johnstone's animated adaptation of his book *Living with a Black Dog: His Name Is Depression* (2006) or Don Hertzfeldt's *Everything Will Be OK* (2006), which can both be found on YouTube, as well as Signe Baumane's cinematic release *Rocks in My Pockets* (2014) personify the experience of complex mental and emotional states such as depression, schizophrenia, and other psychiatric diagnoses in representations of strange creatures that seem to appear and disappear at their own will.

This list, incomplete as it is, still gives a good first impression of the variety of aesthetic strategies animated moving pictures have employed to represent emotions throughout history and across different media. Animation may visually abstract, reduce, and exaggerate the bodily features of characters (see Feyersinger 2013, 2017) to distribute explicit emotional cues, create highly stylized, atmospherically thick and emotionally dense metaphorical spaces of the 'inside,' represent figurative emotional language verbatim (see Siebert 2005: 79–87), as well as personify, objectify, and *animate* – as in 'bring to life' – emotions, experiences, and inner states. In fact, animation, throughout its history, may be seen as a privileged mode for representing such complex emotional and mental states in striking and often unconventional ways that seem almost unconceivable in any other media form (see Buchan 1998; Wells 1998: 122–126, 2002: 71; Reinerth 2013: 339–340).

In this chapter, we seek to systematically explore how animated moving images in different media and genres tackle issues of inner states, such as emotions, experience, and subjectivity. We ask why animation provides such powerful ways for representing and eliciting these rather complex phenomena. Following conceptual metaphor theory (CMT), we claim that animation is especially prone – and extremely suited – to metaphoric and metonymic representations of inner states that are aesthetically inventive and, though sometimes challenging, deadpan precise. Animations develop emotional impact on the viewers by excessively building on the deep semantics of embodied notions and underlying concepts of emotions and the self. Our previous examples have already hinted at the fact that animated images display emotions in a variety of media formats. Despite their different contexts, they all share aesthetic characteristics that also play into the way they deal with emotion. We will thus begin our analysis with a brief introduction to our transmedial understanding of animation as moving images and some general thoughts on what we might call an 'aesthetic affinity' between *animation and emotions*. This is followed by a more theoretical section that focuses on two specific strategies of representing emotions, *audiovisual emotion metaphors, and metonymies*. While metaphorical and metonymic representations of emotions are not exclusive to animation, we will show that they seem to play a uniquely prominent role in all kinds of animated moving images. The last two thirds of the chapter will then be dedicated to *case study analyses* of emotion metaphors and metonymies in two very different forms of animated 'films': in informative animated videos distributed via YouTube and in the beloved animated movie *Ratatouille* (Bird and Hegarty 2007). A brief *conclusion* sums up our findings and puts them in context with our more general claims.

Animation and Emotions

Although the history of animation *in sensu stricti* is closely tied to the history of film, animation has always been a transmedial phenomenon (see Reinerth 2016). From pre-cinema devices such as the *laterna magica*, flipbooks, or the *phénakistiscope* to the GIFs, flash animations, or video game mods of today, animated images have often emphasized their kinship to different media such as paintings, sculptures, comic strips, magic tricks, TV, and digital media. Moreover, animation has been made available across all kinds of media formats and outlets, such as short and feature-length films distributed by cinemas, film festivals, or museums; kids' series, ads, idents, or even weather maps on TV; and tutorials, video game playthroughs, and other user-generated content on YouTube, Facebook, or Twitter.[1]

The production of animated images in any form or genre is characterized by a high level of control and allows for a precise attunement of colors, character, object, and camera movement as well as character and set design. In animation, everything an animator might imagine becomes representable because they, within the limits of their creative ability and the available technology, can control every pixel of every frame of their work. At the level of representation, laws of time and space may not apply, common realistic properties such as scale or the identity of objects over time may be invalidated, and there are principally no physical obstacles, such as walls or body limits, that cannot be overcome in animation. Although there are, of course, types of animated images that strive to imitate reality (for example, CGI in live action films, certain video games or training simulators), animation as an art form seems especially suited for representing intangible, invisible phenomena, such as abstract ideas and subjective experience, in an intersubjectively accessible, perceptible way.

On the one hand, this feeds into the popular view that "animation may be viewed as the most auteurist of film practices" (Wells 2002: 73), because – at least in its prototypical handmade and independently produced form – it meets the criteria of being able to faithfully convey an animator's or an animator collective's subjective 'worldview' or perspective, including *their* thoughts, ideas, feelings, dreams, etc., represented in their own "signature style" (*ibid.*: 103) or "handwriting" (Baumane 2017; see also Reinerth 2018). On the other hand, this tendency in animation can also more generally be understood as enabling "film-makers to more persuasively show *subjective reality*" (Wells 1998: 27, original emphasis) in and outside themselves, thus making all kinds of subjective experiences, including those of animated characters, some of the central thematic issues of animated films.[2]

Yet animation is not limited to capturing someone else's state of mind, emotion, and being. Animated moving pictures also generate highly emotional responses in their recipients. Consider, for example, the often fond and nostalgic memories of childhood viewing experiences like watching a Disney feature with your family over the holidays, being unable to stop laughing about a series of cartoons, or sobbing through Carl's flashback in *Up* (Docter and Peterson 2009). The emotional effects of animated films as compared to live-action movies still have to be studied in detail, but not only personal experience and anecdotal knowledge point to a high degree of emotional involvement with animated films. Again, the fact that every stimulus can be controlled and may be altered to meet the desired effect, makes it very likely that animation, at least in able hands, has great potential to effectively address and stimulate emotions in viewers.

In our chapter, we follow the premise that audiovisual metaphors and metonymies are among the most effective strategies to display *and* evoke emotions. As we will demonstrate, the especially stylized and densely composed images in fictional and nonfiction animation films make use of cognitively anchored metaphoric and metonymic thinking and feeling. In this they do not only represent diegetic emotions but, at times, also cue emotional viewer responses that are similar to those experienced by the animated characters.

Audiovisual Metaphors and Metonymies of Emotions

According to Cognitive Metaphor Theory (see Lakoff 1987; Kövecses 2003),[3] complex or abstract ideas, states, or feelings are cognitively understood and imagined by the use of embodied image schemata with distinct gestalt attributes, such as *force* (strong–weak), *container* (in–out), *balance* (steady–unsteady), or *path* (source–path–goal). Image schemata grow from our mundane bodily experiences (see Johnson 1987) and imply multisensory, affective, and cognitive associations. In metaphorical thinking and communicating, embodied image schemata (e.g., *container* or *force*) and correlated cognitive concepts (e.g., 'building' or 'storm') are activated to project them onto a concept that is more difficult to grasp and is part of a different experiential domain (e.g., 'society' or 'love'). By projecting the gestalt structure (e.g., in–out) of an embodied source domain (e.g., 'building': container) onto the semantic structure of the target domain (e.g., 'society'), a third metaphoric meaning is created (e.g., 'society is a house' → 'entering a society').

Moving images of different genres give embodied gestalt schemata a very concrete manifestation in image, sound, and movement, namely as metaphoric or metonymic sources (see Fahlenbrach 2010, 2016; Forceville 2011, 2017; Coëgnarts and Kravanja 2012). A key role of audiovisual metaphors lies in the display of emotions (see Fahlenbrach 2008, 2010, 2017; Bartsch 2010), drawing on emotion metaphors in our minds. Emotion metaphors are a specific category of *conceptual metaphors* that have emotions as their target domain (see Kövecses 2003). Audiovisual media use metaphors in order to intensify emotions on the screen and offer evaluative cues for the viewers by interpreting the invisible aspects of the emotional states in pictures, sound, and movement. They elaborate on an emotion by relating the depiction of prototypic emotion expressions to a different experiential domain using film style (e.g., in the use of color or camera perspective), characters (e.g., in personifications, see later in this chapter), and settings (e.g., the experience of 'feeling enclosed by a natural force' in the generic rain-metaphor, see later in this chapter). By such mappings, they convey a more complex inner state of a person or character which cannot be seen or heard by her emotion expression. Such invisible aspects include somatic states (e.g., arousal), affective appraisal (e.g., pleasant–unpleasant), moral cognition ('good vs. bad'), and the personal dimension of an emotion (e.g., traumatic memories or associations).

However, emotions in moving images are not only represented and evoked by metaphors but also, and sometimes even more pervasively, by metonymies (see Forceville 2009; Urios-Aparisi 2010). Metonymic depictions focus on external emotion expressions, highlighting single mimics or gestures as *pars pro toto* for the whole emotion state. Following Barcelona's general definition, a metonymy is "a conceptual projection whereby one experiential domain (the target) is partially understood in terms of another experiential domain (the source) included in the same common experiential domain" (Barcelona 2003: 4). Photographic and iconic representations of emotional expressions are *per se* metonymic: The facial expression is part of the emotion and can be conceptualized in the representation as a *pars pro toto* for an emotion (e.g., *angry facial expression stands for anger* in close shots of an enraged face). Hence, metonymic mappings abound in almost any kind of moving image. They act as hyperboles that emphasize certain aspects of emotional states but, in contrast to metaphors, *without* relating them to other experiential domains. Using close shots focusing on the emotional expressions of a character (e.g., crying eyes or a laughing mouth) their inner experience is put in the foreground of the viewer's attention in a saliently deictic manner. Such representations invite viewers not only to infer an inner state in an indexical manner; rather, they are confronted with a representation that is strongly guided by a certain deictic intention of the creators to emphasize somewhat specific characteristics of the depicted emotion (see Forceville 2009).

In contrast, audiovisual emotion metaphors not only create deictically structured symbolic performances of character emotions. They also address viewer emotions by providing them with multisensory scenarios, offering evaluative cues beyond what metonymy can do. While metonymies highlight significant aspects of an emotional reaction, audiovisual metaphors go further and exhibit cross-modal interpretations of intangible experiences and emotional states to affect viewers (see also Bartsch 2010).

Audiovisual Emotion Metaphors and Metonymies in Animation

As argued earlier, and as other contributions in this volume show, a key characteristic of animation lies in its boundless freedom to create audiovisual worlds, independent from pre-filmic reality and at the will of the animator(s). In this regard, the depiction of emotions is no exception; animation attempts to capture the whole spectrum of human emotions. And even more so: Human emotions are transferred to other beings, such as animals (as in *Steamboat Willie*, Iwerks and Disney 1928 or *Antz*, Darnell and Johnson 1998) and plants (as in *Alice in Wonderland*, Geronimi et al. 1951 or *One, Two, Tree*, Aronova 2015), even machines (as in *Kyvadlo, Jáma a Naděje*, Svankmajer 1984 or *Wall·E*, Stanton 2008) and other nonliving things, such as toys (*Toy Story*, Lasseter 1995), cars (*Cars*, Lasseter and Ranft 2006), or skeletons (*Coco*, Molina and Unkrich 2017). From the beginning of (animated) film history, this transfer of human emotions to nonhuman beings and things has demonstrated to be a most effective strategy by which to create popular characters: Wladislaw Starevicz endowed a married couple of embalmed beetles and their antagonists, a dragonfly and a grasshopper, with love, desire, jealousy, and rage in *Mest kinematograficheskogo operatora* (1912); Winsor McCay made his famous dinosaur lady *Gertie the Dinosaur* (1914) laugh and cry; and Walt Disney relied on anthropomorphic animal and machine characters well before his company's widely celebrated feature films, e.g., in the early *Laugh-O-Grams* (1921–1923), which he animated himself. Many animated characters are thus *per se* metaphorically and metonymically conceptualized because characteristic physical and psychological traits are made visible in their design, combining conceptual and affective meanings of different domains. This is most obvious when it comes to the display of emotions. Even more than live-action films, animated depictions of emotions make use of metaphorical and metonymic concepts that are anchored in culture and in the viewers' minds. Providing animated characters with prototypical emotional expressions in mimics, gestures, voices, and body movements is also an essential premise for making them accessible as 'human-like' beings viewers can relate to affectively and emotionally.

On the one hand, animations' potential to visually exaggerate and stylize facilitates metonymic representations of prototypical emotion expressions that convey the feelings of a character. Single parts of a body, such as an eye or a mouth, can be shown in extreme detail or in unrealistic proportions, transmitting the intensity of an emotion like fear or anger by their size: When in *Finding Nemo* (Stanton and Unkrich 2003), Bruce, a shark and recovering 'fishaholic,' attempts to attack the bleeding Dory, his fellow detoxing sharks look at each other in fright, their eyes growing and almost jumping out of their heads (*big, scared eye stands for great fear*) before intervening to save the naive blue tang. For metaphorical displays of emotions, on the other hand, animation benefits from its artistic license to design image schemata as source domains at will: The whole spectrum of visual, auditory, or audiovisual gestalts of image schemata are freely arranged in the design of characters and, even more so, in the whole setting of an emotional scene. In a striking moment that depicts the beginning of a depressive episode, *Rocks in My Pockets* shows the character Signe as being physically inhibited by an empty balloon-like shape with rotating razor blades. "Once or twice a year, a little needle pokes under the heart," she says in voice-over, before a disturbing, ear-hurting sound reminiscent of a very loud, very irritating tinnitus takes over the soundtrack (*depression is a moving force, – is an absorbing force, – is physical pain*). Like *Rocks in My Pockets*, the Japanese *anime* series *Haibane Renmei* (Abe 2002) deals with suicide, depression, and grief. In episode 8, grieving for her friend, the main character Rakka departs on a journey into the dark and abandoned woods (*grief is a dark forest, – is a deserted landscape*), that, at the same time, functions as a psychological self-discovery (*the search for identity is a journey*). Creating visual and aural gestalt elements related to mentally anchored image schemata is a common principle of different genres in animation (see Forceville and Jeulink 2011; Forceville 2017), creating lively as well as sensory and affectively convincing emotional scenarios. Some genre differences, however, might be discerned in metaphorical target domains to which these gestalts are related. In other words, the focus of metaphorical display differs in various genres and depends on the functions and contexts of animated moving images (see Fahlenbrach 2017).[4]

Cases Study I: Emotion Metaphors and Metonymies in Informative Animation Videos

In the following part, we present results from a comparative analysis of informative and entertaining animated films. Instead of focusing on single emotions or emotional states, we concentrate on examples that deal with a spectrum of emotions and the dynamics that emerge from their interplay. First, we are going to analyze a selection of three on-line video clips commissioned by institutions of psychology or education and distributed via YouTube that aim to explain the human emotion system. How do emotions arise? What characterizes their experience? What are strategies for coping with negative emotions? The second part of the analysis focuses on emotions in fictional animated films, mainly in Brad Bird's and Parick Hegarty's Pixar feature *Ratatouille*, whose animal protagonist, Remy, a rat, is endowed with human emotions and character traits that make him accessible and likeable, not only to other characters in the film but also to a human audience.

The first video, *Alfred & Shadow: A Short Story about Emotions* (Vassbø 2015), presents a couple of owls as subjects of human emotions. Their antagonist, a black shadow in the gestalt of a cat, confronts the brown owl several times in a threatening way, emerging from below and rising in size, sometimes fully enclosing the bird. Trying to reach her partner, the pink owl gives body signals that the other, however, does not seem to register (Figure 3.1).

The whole scenario is based on a general metaphoric concept: *emotion is a natural force – emotion is an animal*. The personification of

Figure 3.1 Emotion is an animal in *Alfred & Shadow: A Short Story about Emotions* (©Institute for Psychological Counseling/Sheriff Film Company).

emotions as 'animals' is a pervasive audiovisual metaphor in animation (see Fahlenbrach 2017). This allows many things to be rendered: the inner experience and the intensity of emotion states, automatic affective reactions, the shape of animals of different sizes, forces and behavioral characteristics. Hence, the choice of animals is not accidental in such metaphoric scenarios. In this case, two species have been chosen whose antagonistic relations are anchored in nature: bird vs. cat. The cat is a natural enemy of the bird and physically much stronger. By referring to our cognitive knowledge of animals, these general attributes are transferred to the display of emotions in the video: the cat as a predator, representing powerful negative emotions like fear or shame (*negative emotion is a strong animal, – is a cat*); in comparison, the owl may be perceived as a more defensive animal, typically hiding in the dark and, as contextualized by the narration in the video, as a subject confronted with negative, but also sometimes positive emotions (*the subject of emotions is a defensive animal*). More specifically, the variable shapes, sizes, and movement patterns of the animated characters provide concrete metaphoric images: *negative emotions are a growing black animal, – are a slowly enclosing black shadow*. The owl, experiencing and dealing with different emotions, is shown in different sizes: shrinking in the face of the huge shadowlike cat (e.g., *fear is a shrinking animal*) or growing bigger in pride or anger, when defending itself (*coping with negative emotions is a growing animal*). Other aspects of emotional dynamics are metaphorically displayed by the creation of movement patterns: The two owl characters move along a fixed horizontal path in a static image frame that they sometimes leave to the left or right. The flat images do not allow them any movement backward or forward. This gives the impression of subjects with only limited options to cope with their inner states (*emotion subjects are animals with limited mobility*). At the same time, being both stuck on the very same path puts their emotional interaction into the fore of the picture (*emotional interaction is moving together along a path*). However, the antagonistic and negative emotions, displayed by the shadowlike cat, are presented to possess much more mobility and variability regarding their shape and size. In the gestalt of the cat, anger, fear, and shame appear from below the brown owl's feet, growing bigger and bigger, surrounding it from behind and even filling out the whole screen with its black shape (*negative emotions are dark animals with high mobility, – with changing size, – with changing shape*).

As it is often the case with audiovisual metaphors, several conceptual mappings go together in single images and scenes (see Fahlenbrach 2016, 2017). An important part of this metaphorical network is that of metonymies. They play a key role in communicating to the viewers the emotions that are being displayed and the target of the related metaphors. As argued earlier, emotion metonymies isolate – visually or audiovisually – single characteristic expressions in an accentuated way, taking them as *pars pro toto* for the whole emotion. In animation this often happens in an exaggerated way, helping viewers to recognize human emotions in fictional and even nonhuman characters. In informative videos, this also helps to explain typical behavioral reactions and body signals of emotions to the viewers. In *Alfred & Shadow*, the filmmakers make frequent use of metonymies. Basically, the body of the owl is metaphorically taken as a *container* 'filled' with different emotions. While these are often written in words on its belly, its face and body posture show typical human expressions in a metonymic way. Shame is performed by the owl covering body and head with its wings (*covered body stands for shame*), fear by a shaking body and eyes wide open (*shaking body/wide-open eyes stands for fear*), sadness by slowly dropping its head (*dropped head stands for sadness*). Metonymies also play a key role in the display of emotional interactions. The video makes the case of different interactions between the brown owl as emotional protagonist and the pink owl as its caring and supporting friend or partner, who is sometimes repelled by the negative feelings of the other. Distance and closeness are used to give viewers an embodied idea of emotional dynamics between affected people, based on two basic metonymies: *bodily closeness stands for emotional bond* and *bodily distance stands for emotional distance*. On their horizontal path, the owls' proximity visually and spatially evidences the interpersonal effects of certain emotional coping strategies – e.g., to be 'filled' with sadness, but physically express anger, increases both bodily and emotional distance, as represented by the pink owl moving away and leaving the frame.

The second example, *Why Do We Lose Control of Our Emotions?* (2017), addresses children, helping them understand their emotions and cope with negative feelings like fear, shame, or anger. The video digitally emulates hand-drawn pictures that are shown in the very process of being made. Presenting them in these stylistically basic, though moving images, the clip supports the idea of emotions as processes in time while also stressing that they may be controlled by the subject who has (or draws) them (see Reinerth 2018). While the video uses mostly metonymies, showing a young boy with prototypical emotion expressions in different situations, it also implies two prominent emotion metaphors: *anger is hot fluid in a container* and *the emotional brain is a building*. The drawing of a pot with boiling water on a fireplace gives an embodied picture of anger as an intensely rising feeling that results in expressive body reactions. The body is metaphorically conceptualized as a 'container' that holds in this emotion and loses its closed shape by 'exploding' from an inner force. While this might be considered a metaphoric stereotype, the other is more original in its visual manifestation: In order to explain the complicated and invisible areas of the human emotional brain, the video shows it as a space with an upstairs and a downstairs. This is explained accordingly in the commentary and visualized by literal staircases going up and down, relating the cerebral cortex, midbrain, and the brainstem. Furthermore, two miniature characters are placed on the stairs, communicating through a tin can phone. Whenever one of the brain areas dominates, the communication between the homunculi is disconnected, and the little boy loses control of his emotions. Metaphoric personalization of emotional processes (*emotion is a person*) and the transfer of a complicated inner system into a spatial image (*the emotional brain is a building*) are used to explain the basic neurological underpinnings of emotions.

The third online clip, *What Causes Anxiety and Depression: Inside Out* (2016), inhabits an interesting space between educational video and fictional animation film. Focusing on the two eponymous negative emotional states, the clip explains how different emotions interact by compiling scenes from the acclaimed Pixar movie *Inside Out* (Docter and del Carmen 2015). These are contextualized by comments and more 'informative' explanations in the voice-over. *Inside Out*, the feature, is itself rather atypical because – in contrast to most other fictional films – it is grounded in emotion research and explains the complicated dynamics of emotional experiences in a reductive, though informative and entertaining, way. *What Causes Anxiety and Depression: Inside Out* uses some of *Inside Out*'s scenes and storylines to deal with causes and experiences of depression and anxiety as well as ways to cope with them. In *Inside Out*, Riley, a young girl, who had to move with her parents to another town, experiences depressive feelings due to the loss of her former friends and home and anxiety toward her new environment. Like *Why Do We Lose Control of Our Emotions?* the clip evokes the metaphor that *the emotional brain is a building*, but elaborates it further. The brain is conceptualized three-dimensionally as a factory with the emotional brain as its control room. This is the space where the different emotions – joy, sadness, anger, fear, and disgust – personified as humanlike characters, act and interact. The control room itself is a huge pink space equipped with a switchboard and tubes that transport glowing balls. These moving balls signify the energetic substance fueling the emotional brain. They contain Riley's memories, which become visible for the viewers when the camera zooms in on one of the balls, their color indicating its affective tone: blue for sad, yellow for joyful. Thus, the video creates several metaphors: *the emotional brain is a factory, emotions are persons, memories are glowing balls, – are substances in a factory, sadness is dark/blue, joy is light/yellow* (Figure 3.2).

The emotional brain is given the audiovisual gestalt of a complex system with a specific space, actors with different motivations and behaviors, as well as a substance that keeps it going. Emotional dynamics are shown to imply, on the one hand, automated processes jolted by the balls that sustain the 'factory,' but also, on the other hand, as a constant act of negotiation between individual emotions, personified by the homunculi and their struggles over who takes control. Building on preexisting material from an elaborate 90-minute feature film, the entertainment, suspense, and production value of *What Causes Anxiety and Depression: Inside Out* offers surpass that of the other two online video clips. Enjoyment, involvement, and admiration of the audiovisually stunning animation – as well as, possibly, preexisting knowledge about the film it is based on – feed into the reception of the otherwise informative clip. It is one that, compared to the other clips, not only displays and explains but probably also evokes emotions in the viewers. However, in contrast to the animated feature, its stripped online version

Figure 3.2 The emotional brain is a factory in *Inside Out* (©Disney/Pixar) and *What Causes Anxiety and Depression: Inside Out* (©MindSet).

is a mash-up that functions like a 'best of,' combining emotional scenes devoid of their narrative context in a rather forced way, united mainly by the voice-over.

Case Study II: Emotion Metaphors and Metonymies in Animated Movies

As explained earlier, the display of emotions plays a key role in creating vivid personalities for fictional – and often nonhuman – characters that viewers can still relate to affectively. Hence, in contrast to informative videos, the display of emotions has a strategic relevance for building entertaining and appealing characters in animated feature films. Even more so than in live-action films, densely composed audiovisual metaphors and metonymies help to create salient emotional scenarios for viewers, often aiming to intensify viewers' feelings toward the characters in an inexplicit way. In the following analysis, we will take a closer look at the specific uses and functions of metaphoric and metonymic displays of emotions in the Pixar film *Ratatouille*.

The film's protagonist, Remy, is a rat that becomes humanlike in several ways. First of all, and like all rats in *Ratatouille*, he is an anthropomorphic character that thinks, speaks, and acts similarly to human beings, one of the "ordinary lifeless objects, plants, beasts" that, according to Sergej Eisenstein, are "brought to life" in animation (1986: 43). However, Remy also has specific skills and attitudes that distinguish him from his conspecifics. He walks on two legs, dreams of being more than a furry food thief, and, most importantly, he is gifted with a highly sensitive sense of smell and taste. Accordingly, most of the waste-food his fellow rodents eat disgusts him. During the movie, Remy develops a deep passion for good food and cooking, inspired by a French TV cook whose show he follows secretly at the house of an old lady. When she discovers him, he is banished by force, so Remy escapes through the sewerage system and happens to arrive in Paris, the heart of the French Cuisine. By chance, he ends up at the former restaurant of his role model, gourmet chef Gusteau; the restaurant has, however, been taken over by an untalented and mean successor. Remy becomes involved in the problems of a young scullion, Linguini, who accidentally spoils a soup but, by the help of the rat, develops a remarkable talent for cooking. Notably, the film includes many scenes that are told from Remy's perspective and even temporarily adds his voice-over. From the very beginning, Remy is thus more than 'just' a rat – as the most distinguished in a pack of humanized rats, he offers enough common ground with the viewers for them to accept him as the story's protagonist. Equipping Remy with the ability to sense, think, act, and *feel* in a humanlike fashion is an important strategy to counter common, primarily negative, associations with rats as 'impure' animals eating human garbage and disseminating diseases. Typically, rats are objects of disgust. Yet by transferring human personality traits and emotions to the rats in the movie, and especially to Remy, viewers learn to put their reservations and negative feelings aside and develop sympathy and even empathy toward them.[5] Remy performs cognitively and emotionally like a human individual with personal interests, desires, and distinguished skills. Most significantly for our analysis, he expresses the full spectrum of emotions. This provides him with a distinctive psychological personality that viewers can relate to.

In an early scene, Remy discovers the taste of fresh strawberries combined with cheese. His face performs characteristic expressions of human joy, with a smiling mouth and eyes closed with pleasure. This expression is underlined verbally in the voice-over where Remy joyfully describes his sensations. Over the black background of the image, colorful graphics move in a synchronous rhythm with the accompanying jazz music, reminiscent of early abstract animations by Oskar Fischinger or Viking Eggeling. As Joseph Kickasola (2017) convincingly argues in his analysis of this scene, the joyful gustatory effects that Remy experiences are conveyed to the viewers by an audiovisual composition of pictures, movement, and sound that creates cross-modal, synesthetic associations. In response to the frequencies and melodic contours of the music, geometric forms pop up, move around and disappear, giving the harmony and intensity of the taste a cross-modal dimension. Through audiovisual metaphors, this scene communicates Remy's rich sensorial experience: *gustatory joy is seeing and hearing harmonious motions* and *gustatory joy is seeing colorful lines and circles in motion* (Figure 3.3).

As Kickasola observes, "experience is 'expressed' in an audiovisual form, and so the expression *also* crosses sensory boundaries, [...] the experience is portrayed as deeply meaningful (even to a rat)" (2017: 163,

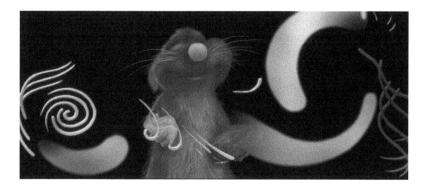

Figure 3.3 Gustatory joy is seeing and hearing harmonious motions in *Ratatouille* (©Disney/Pixar).

original emphasis). As is typical for metaphorical compositions, embodied memories and associations are transferred to more complex meanings, in this case, the understanding of a distinctive taste of food. Being positioned at the start of the movie, this crucial scene significantly contributes to establishing Remy as a sophisticated, individual character with remarkable sensibility and talent, which separates him from his conspecifics.

Another significant scene paints the dramatic escape of Remy and his clan from the angry old lady who discovers them inside her home. She hunts them with a gun, even after they have already left the house. At first, a rather stereotypical emotion metaphor is employed: *feeling intense emotion is being in heavy rain*. Emotional key scenes in many movies, animated or not, show protagonists overwhelmed by strong negative or positive emotions being exposed to heavy rain. The intensity of the rain, fully covering their bodies, conveys a loss of emotional control and protection, as well as the intensity of their feelings. Similarly, Remy and his family are fleeing in panic while rain pours down on them, thus metaphorically stressing their extreme fear (for their lives) and loss of protection (i.e., their home). Secondly, other metaphors for emotion are created when Remy also loses his family in the sewers. Now his individual fear is displayed by showing him alone in the huge tunnel. As in the previous example, the filmmakers' conceptual decision to put him in this specific spatial environment works to intensify empathy in viewers, combined with a meaningful understanding of his personality. In the tunnel, Remy stands on Gusteau's cooking book, which he took from the house and that now serves as a float. Hence, the book as part of his individual vocation and desire gives him the only stability in this existentially threatening situation, which also implies a metaphoric meaning (*identity is a ground*). Still, it is unstable ground and one that does not protect him from the torrent. However, losing balance and falling off his float is not the only reason for his anxiety. His physical instability furthermore conveys his (justified) fear of losing his family who are, as he later explains to his father, yet another grounding part of his identity. Desperately shouting at each other, Remy floats farther and farther apart from his family and into the unknown. Visually, this is captured by full shots of Remy alone in this dark, huge, and hostile space (Figure 3.4).

As soon as he is out of earshot of his family, the music stops and the soundtrack now focuses on the streaming water, the echo of his panicked breathing and paddling, together with rising atmospheric noise. He is flushed to a crossroad where the tunnel splits and, shortly after, falls into a descending canal, fully losing control of his path. In this scene, cinematography and sound work together to convey Remy's fears through a metaphoric scenario: *fear is losing control over movement, – is being transported by water, – is being transported through a huge container.* Water as a motif seems especially suited for metaphoric representations

Figure 3.4 Fear is being transported by water in *Ratatouille* (©Disney/Pixar).

of emotions, because it relates to the intensity and strength of feelings one loses control of or is overwhelmed by and it has been made use of in a variety of ways throughout film history (see Urios-Aparisi 2016).[6]

Conclusion

As we have shown, audiovisual metaphors and metonymies play an important role in animated representations of emotions and complex inner states. Relying on embodied image and gestalt schemata, they not only show what is otherwise invisible but also offer conceptual frames that make aspects of highly subjective experiences – such as emotions – intersubjectively recognizable and, more importantly, tangible and relatable for audiences. Although not exclusive to animation, animated moving images – from informative self-help or public health campaign videos to fictional short and feature films – are prone to such representations of subjectivity, and thereby make excessive and often quite exemplary use of metaphors and metonymies.

It seems no wonder that the tropes themselves as well as their audiovisual realizations share similarities in the use of image schemata across distinct genres. After all, they relate to basic semantics that universally structure human experiences. However, differences arise regarding more specific aesthetic elaborations, the functions and effects of metaphoric and metonymic emotional display. Contrasting online videos aimed to educate about mental health issues, treatment, and coping strategies, with examples from fictional feature films whose main goal it is to entertain, our analyses suggest they differ in at least three ways: (1) the degree of simplicity or complexity in the usage of metaphors and metonymies; (2) the level of narrative contextualization and elaboration; and (3) the ability to evoke feelings of sympathy and empathy in the audience.

Simplicity and Complexity

The short online videos discussed tended to use metaphors and metonymies to reduce complexity and highlight salient aspects in a sometimes playful, but still quite obvious way, often relying on rather simple or conventionalized 'go-to' metaphors for certain states of emotions. However, examples from *Ratatouille* proved to be more complex: Representing Remy's joyful experience of taste through multi- and cross-modal imagery seems to be a deliberate exploration of the senses, paralleling his gustatory sensations with the audience's aesthetic pleasures and aiming at a comprehensive understanding of his experience that not only covers the taste of cheese and strawberries but also his surprise, excitement, and enjoyment of novelty. The scene where Remy loses his family relies on common metaphorical notions surrounding the water motif, but uses it to refer to different (short-term and long-term, physical and psychological) dimensions of his momentary anxiety. The scenario is also enriched with other metaphors, such as *identity is a* (sometimes unstable) *ground*, linking it to Remy's and Linguini's search for their 'true' identity that serves as an underlying theme for the whole film. Additionally, Remy's ability to express the complete spectrum of human emotion also makes metonymical representations more nuanced: When he sniffs at a piece of goat cheese, his face goes from uncertainty to surprise to enjoyment to curiosity within seconds. However, Remy's big, exaggerated mouth and eyes (with hints of eyebrows), typical features of most animated characters, still ensure that all the emotions are discernible and recognizable (see Chapter 6). Without wanting to overstate them, these differences explore two distinct, yet not mutually exclusive potentials of animation: (a) the exaggeration of and reduction to a selection of prototypical features of an object and/or concept (as in the almost stick men-like drawings in *Why Do We Lose Control of Our Emotions?* that reduce the human face to mouth, eyes, eyebrows, and a tiny nose but also, less explicitly, in Remy's appearance as described earlier); and (b) the agglomeration of multiple stimuli, creating atmospherically dense, sensually rich, visually complex, and often cross-modal imagery that resonates as a holistic impression in the viewer (exemplified beautifully by the food tasting scene in *Ratatouille*). Both strategies can be put to good use in the metaphorical and metonymical externalization of inner states and feelings; neither should be considered 'better' than the other. Neither of the two is exclusive to either educative or entertaining media and in fact they are usually combined. *However the simplification of emotions to prototypical stimuli* seems to be in line with an overall goal of transparently distributing information while the *exploration of the complexity of emotions* seems more suited to invite viewers to imagine the represented emotions as if they were their own experiences.

Narrative Contextualization and Elaboration

Our analyses have shown that educative online videos seem to rely more strongly on visual exaggeration, abstraction, and reduction as means to enunciate unequivocal meaning, and often also employ conventionalized or 'simple' metaphors that require little effort on the side of the viewers. Given that the goal of these videos is to inform and educate a broad audience, this seems an effective strategy to communicate what the producers or clients of such videos deem most important within the very short time span of online videos. Fictional films, on the other hand, typically seek to offer aesthetic pleasure to their audience and strive for some sort of artistic value and deeper meaning. Narrative animated films like *Ratatouille* portray emotions not as an object of study or information but as the individual experience of their characters – exploring and 'experiencing' their emotions means getting to know them. Through variation, narrative elaboration of common, as well as the creation of new emotion metaphors, characters like Remy seem to become individual beings whose very own subjective feelings color the way the story is told by the filmmakers and perceived by the audience. We experience our own emotions as highly complex, multidimensional, often ambiguous, and as processes in time. As such characters like Remy seem more lifelike and humanlike than ones like the owls or the nameless boy in the online videos.

Sympathy and Empathy

This is also an essential precondition for feelings of sympathy or empathy toward characters (see Tan 2005). These feelings are ones that most narrative moving pictures (and not only fictional ones) want us to develop over the course of their (often feature-length) duration. Here, emotional metaphors highlight the characters' feelings at crucial points in the story, aligning us, the audience, with their state of mind and emotions and cueing hypotheses regarding their motivations for past and future actions. Metonymic expressions of emotions may involve basic processes of empathy originating from an activation of mirror neurons even devoid of narrative contextualization. Note, however, that informative videos like *Alfred & Shadow* often include micro-narratives, such as the action motivated by the changing inter-personal relationship between the two owls. These micro-narratives make the overall educative message somewhat more entertaining, co-herent, and relatable. While emotional metonymies typically express momentary states and are immediately understood, especially complex emotional metaphors may also resonate with viewers more deeply, giv-ing them the feeling of sharing an atmospheric, emotional space with the character or hinting at dimensions of meaning which are larger than (the character's) life.

Summary

On a basic level, then, animated moving images in any format, context, or genre, share the same aesthetic potentials for displaying emotions. We have highlighted audiovisual metaphors and metonymies as strategies that significantly contribute not only to the representation of emotions but also to their bodily and emotional reception and experience by the viewers. Both are realized effectively in combination with animation's potential to, on the one hand, isolate and accentuate salient aspects of emotions and, on the other, accumulate and seamlessly interweave dif-ferent stimuli to explore the complexity of feeling and 'being.' Given the immense liberty of creating embodied gestalt forms and image sche-mata at will, animated moving images are able to invent quite original metaphoric and metonymic depictions of emotions, even when they are grounded in seemingly simple primary schemata. However, the extent as well as level of complexity and originality with which individual ani-mated films employ such strategies of representing emotions depends on their respective goals that often coincide with production, distribution, and viewing contexts (e.g., art film festival vs. self-help YouTube chan-nel) and genre expectations (e.g., information vs. immersion). While acknowledging these apparent aesthetic and thematic tendencies, they should not be overstated as categorical differences. Today, as the lim-its between animation and live-action films, as well as between tradi-tional genres such as 'information' and 'entertainment,' tend to blur, these forms of expression can rather be expected to migrate increasingly across ever more media, genres, and modes of production of moving images – a phenomenon that invites further research.

Notes

1 While not all of these examples qualify as films in the narrow – and by now outdated – sense of the continuous projection of a series of single frame images onto a screen, they belong without question to what Lev Manovich

and others have subsumed under the umbrella term "moving images" (see Manovich 1995; Feyersinger 2007), a term we adopt and use interchangeably with "moving pictures" and "film." In our paper, the focus lies on fictional feature length films as well as online videos distributed via platforms like YouTube. These are also 'film-like' in that, although being digitally produced, they have no interactive or live elements, typically comprise of a story or statement, and address a public audience. However, we believe that many of our results also apply to other forms of animated moving images and a closer look at the use of emotional metaphors in pre-cinematic animation, video games, or animated private communication (GIFs, animojis), to name but a few, should prove them to be promising research areas.

2 For Paul Wells, animation's preoccupation with "internal space[s]" and "the invisible" (1998, 122) even comes close to being a genuine mode or genre in animation that he calls "penetration" (*ibid.*) or "primal" (2002, 71).

3 The following introduction of CMT and audiovisual metaphors is based on Fahlenbrach (2016b, 2017).

4 In a study on audiovisual emotion metaphors of depression in informative YouTube videos, Fahlenbrach showed that a strong focus of these videos, often mandated by mental health organizations, is advice on how to deal with depression as a mental health issue. Here the personification of 'depression' as 'an animal to cope with' is the most frequent metaphor: *coping with depression is taming an animal, – is getting an animal exhausted* (e.g., by physical activity), or – *is hugging an animal* (see Fahlenbrach 2017).

5 Incidentally, the DVD and Blu-ray release of *Ratatouille* includes the short film *Your Friend the Rat* (Capobianco 2007). In this animated 'documentary-style' bonus clip, Remy and his brother Emile address the audience directly, attempting to present nothing less than a history of the relationship between man and rat with the goal of reducing such prejudice and stereotypes.

6 Powerful *animated* metaphoric scenarios dealing with emotions and involving water are, e.g., the aforementioned "water spirit" linked to depression in *Rocks in My Pockets* (see also Baumane 2017); Roddy, the mouse, being *Flushed Away* (Bowers and Fell 2010) through the toilet in a scenario not unlike the one in *Ratatouille*; and – not surprisingly – many scenes from both *Finding Nemo* and *Finding Dory* (Stanton and MacLane 2016).

References

Barcelona, Antonio. "Introduction. The Cognitive Theory of Metaphor and Metonymy." In: Barcelona, Antonio (Ed.). *Metaphor and Metonymies at the Crossroads*. Berlin/New York: De Gruyter Mouton, 2003: 1–30.

Bartsch, Anne. "Vivid Abstractions: On the Role of Emotion Metaphors in Film Viewers' Search for Deeper Insight and Meaning." *Midwest Studies in Philosophy*, 34(1), 2010: 240–260.

Baumane, Signe. *Interview with Maike Sarah Reinerth*. Skype interview. Hamburg/Brooklyn, September 25, 2017.

Buchan, Suzanne. "Graphic and Literary Metamorphosis; Animation Technique and James Joyce's *Ulysses*." *Animation Journal*, 7(1), 1998: 21–34.

Coëgnarts, Marten and Peter Kravanja. "Embodied Visual Meaning: Image Schemas in Film." *Projections. The Journal of Movies and Mind*, 6(2), 2012: 84–101.

Eisenstein, Sergej. *Eisenstein on Disney*. Jay Leyda (Ed.). Calcutta: Seagull, 1986.

Fahlenbrach, Kathrin. "Emotions in Sound. Audiovisual Metaphors in the Sound Design of Narrative Films." *Projections. Journal for Movies & Mind*, 2(2), 2008: 85–103.

——— *Audiovisuelle Metaphern. Zur Körper- und Affektästhetik in Film und Fernsehen* [Audiovisual Metaphors. Embodied and Affective Aesthetics of Film and Television]. Marburg: Schüren, 2010.

——— "Audiovisual Metaphors as Embodied Narratives in Moving Images." In: Fahlenbrach, Kathrin (Ed.). *Embodied Metaphors in Film, Television, and Video Games: Cognitive Approaches*. London/New York: Routledge, 2016: 33–50.

——— "Audiovisual Metaphors and Metonymies of Emotions and Depression in Moving Images." In: Ervas, Francesca, Elisabetta Gola, and Maria Grazia Rossi (Eds.). *Metaphor in Communication, Science and Education*. Berlin/Boston: De Gruyter, 2017: 95–118.

Feyersinger, Erwin. "Diegetische Kurzschlüsse wandelbarer Welten: Die Metalepse im Animationsfilm." [Diegetic Short Circuits of Changeable Worlds: Metalepsis in Animated Films]. *Montage AV*, 16(2), 2007: 113–130.

——— "Von sich streckenden Strichen und hüpfenden Hühnern. Erkundungen des Kontinuums zwischen Abstraktion und Realismus." [Of Stretching Stripes and Hopping Hens. Explorations of the Continuum between Abstraction and Realism]. *Montage AV*, 22(2), 2013: 33–44.

——— "Visuelle Abstraktion in narrativen Filmen und Serien, wissenschaftlichen Visualisierungen und experimenteller Animation." [Visual Abstraction in Narrative Films and Series', Scientific Visualizations, and Experimental Animation]. In: Bruckner, Franziska et al. (Eds.). *In Bewegung setzen … Beiträge zur deutschsprachigen Animationsforschung*. Wiesbaden: Springer VS, 2017: 169–188.

Forceville, Charles. "Metonymy in Visual and Audiovisual Discourse." In: Ventola, Eija and Arsenio Jésus Moya Guijarro (Eds.). *The World Told and the World Shown: Issues in Multisemiotics*. Basingstoke: Palgrave, 2009: 56–74.

——— "The Source-Path-Goal Schema in Agnès Varda's Les Glaneurs et la Glaneuse and Deux Ans Après." In: Fludernik, Monika (Ed.). *Beyond Cognitive Metaphor Theory: Perspectives on Literary Metaphor*. London: Routledge, 2011: 281–297.

——— "From Image Schema to Metaphor in Discourse: The FORCE Schemas in Animation Films." In: Hampe, Beate (Ed.). *Metaphor. Embodied Cognition and Discourse*. Cambridge: Cambridge University Press, 2017: 239–256.

Forceville, Charles and Marloes Jeulink. "The Flesh and Blood of Embodied Understanding: The Source-Path-Goal Schema in Animation Film." *Pragmatics & Cognition*, 19(1), 2011: 37–59.

Grodal, Torben. "Aesthetics and Psychology of Animated Films." In: Uhrig, Meike (Ed.). *Emotion in Animated Films*. London/New York: Routledge, 2019.

Johnson, Mark. *The Body in the Mind. The Bodily Basis of Meaning, Imagination, and Reason*. Chicago: Chicago University Press, 1987: xic–xvi.

Kickasola, Joseph. "Metaphor without an Answer: Cross-Modal Experience and Embodied Meaning in the Cinema." In: Fahlenbrach, Kathrin (Ed.). *Embodied Metaphors in Film, Television, and Video Games: Cognitive Approaches.* London/New York: Routledge, 2016: 162–182.

Kövecses, Zóltan. *Metaphor and Emotion: Language, Culture, and Body in Human Feeling.* Cambridge: Cambridge University Press, 2003.

Lakoff, George. *Women, Fire, and Dangerous Things. What Categories Reveal about the Mind.* Chicago: Chicago University Press, 1987.

Manovich, Lev. "What is Digital Cinema?" *Manovich.net,* 1995: http://manovich.net/content/04-projects/009-what-is-digital-cinema/07_article_1995.pdf (25.09.2017).

Reinerth, Maike Sarah. "Animationsfilm." [Animated Film]. In: Kuhn, Markus, Irina Scheidgen, and Nicola Valeska Weber (Eds.). *Filmwissenschaftliche Genreanalyse. Eine Einführung.* Berlin/Boston: De Gruyter, 2013: 319–341.

——— "Animation – transgenerisch und intermedial." [Animation – Transgeneric and Intermedial]. In: Ritzer, Ivo and Peter W. Schulze (Eds.). *Transmediale Genre-Passagen.* Wiesbaden: Springer VS, 2016: 461–478.

——— "Entirely (Self-)Made Up! Animierte Imaginationsdarstellungen in Realspielfilmen." [Entirely (Self-)Made Up! Animated Representations of Imagination in Live Action Films]. In: Backe, Hans-Joachim et al. (Eds.). *Ästhetik des Gemachten. Interdisziplinäre Beiträge zur Animations- und Comicforschung.* Berlin/Boston: De Gruyter, 2018: 231–256 (in print).

Siebert, Jan. *Flexible Figuren. Medienreflexive Komik im Zeichentrickfilm* [Flexible Characters. Media-Reflexive Comedy in Animated Films]. Bielefeld: Aisthesis, 2005.

Tan, E. S. "Three Views of Facial Expression and Its Understanding in the Cinema." In: Anderson, Joseph D. and Barbara Fisher Anderson (Eds.). *Moving Image Theory. Ecological Considerations.* Carbondale: Southern Illinois University Press, 2005: 107–128.

Urios-Aparisi, Eduardo. "The Body of Love in Almodóvar's Cinema: Metaphor and Metonymy of the Body and Body Parts." *Metaphor and Symbol,* 25(3), 2010: 181–203.

——— "Stormy Weather: An Intercultural Approach to the Water Principles in Cinema." In: Fahlenbrach, Kathrin (Ed.). *Embodied Metaphors in Film, Television, and Video Games. Cognitive Approaches.* London/New York: Routledge, 2016: 67–81.

Wells, Paul. *Understanding Animation.* London/New York: Routledge, 1998.

——— *Animation: Genre and Authorship.* London/New York: Wallflower, 2002.

Films & TV Series

Alfred & Shadow: A Short Story about Emotions. Idea and script by Anne Hilde Vassbø, Animation by Christoffer Gundersen. Institute for Psychological Counseling/Sheriff Film Company, 2015: https://youtu.be/SJOjpprbfeE (13.12.2017).

Alice in Wonderland. Directed by Clyde Geronimi, Wilfred Jackson, and Hamilton Luske. 1951; USA: Disney.

Antz. Directed by Eric Darnell and Tim Johnson. 1998; USA: DreamWorks/ Pacific Data Images.

Cars. Directed by John Lasseter and Joe Ranft. 2006; USA: Disney/Pixar.

Coco. Directed by Adrian Molina and Lee Unkrich. 2017; USA: Disney/Pixar.

The Enchanted Drawing. Directed by J. Stuart Blackton. 1900; USA: Edison.

Everything Will Be OK. Directed by Don Hertzfeldt. 2006; USA: Bitter Films: https://youtu.be/1IUX0Qy-IDM (13.12.2017).

Finding Dory. Directed by Andrew Stanton and Angus MacLane. 2016; USA: Disney/Pixar.

Finding Nemo. Directed by Andrew Stanton and Lee Unkrich. 2003; USA: Disney/Pixar.

Flushed Away. Directed by David Bowers and Sam Fell. 2010; UK/USA: Aardman/DreamWorks.

Gertie the Dinosaur. Directed by Winsor McCay. 1914; USA: McCay/Vitagraph.

Haibane Renmei: JP 2002, Fuji Television, created by Yoshitoshi Abe.

Humorous Phases of Funny Faces. Directed by Stuart Blackton. 1906; USA: Vitagraph.

Inside Out. Directed by Pete Docter and Ronnie del Carmen. 2015; USA: Disney/Pixar.

Kyvadlo, Jáma a Naděje [The Pit, the Pendulum and Hope]. Directed by Jan Svankmajer. 1984; CS: Krátký Film.

Living with a Black Dog: His Name Is Depression. Written, Illustrated, and Narrated by Matthew Johnstone. 2006; USA: World Health Organization/ Matthew Johnstone: https://youtu.be/XiCrniLQGYc (13.12.2017).

Mest kinematograficheskogo operatora [The Cameraman's Revenge]. Directed by Wladislaw Starevicz. 1912; RU: Khanzhonkov.

One, Two, Tree. Directed by Yulia Aronova. 2015; FR: Folimage/Nadasdy Film.

Ratatouille. Directed by Brad Bird and Patrick Hegarty. 2007; USA: Disney/ Pixar.

Reason and Emotion. Directed by Bill Roberts. 1943; USA: Disney.

Rocks in My Pockets. Directed by Signe Baumane. 2014; LV/USA: Rocks in My Pockets/Locomotive.

The Simpsons. 1989–present; USA, FOX, created by Matt Groening.

Steamboat Willie. Directed by Ub Iwerks and Walt Disney. 1928; USA: Disney.

Toy Story. Directed by John Lasseter. 1995; USA: Disney/Pixar.

Up. Directed by Pete Docter and Bob Peterson. 2009; USA: Disney/Pixar.

Wall·E. Directed by Andrew Stanton. 2008; USA: FortyFour/Disney/Pixar.

Walt Disney's Laugh-O-Grams. Directed by Walt Disney. 1921–1923; USA: Laugh-O-Gram Films.

What Causes Anxiety and Depression: Inside Out. 2016; Mind Set. Guided Meditations, Informations, Thoughts: https://youtu.be/tNsTy-j_sQs (13.12.2017).

Why Do We Lose Control of Our Emotions? 2017; Kids Want to Know: https:// youtu.be/3bKuoH8CkFc (13.12.2017).

Your Friend the Rat. Directed by Jim Capobianco. 2007; USA: Disney/Pixar.

Art House Cinema

4 *The Butterfly Lovers*

Sex, Gender, and Emotion-Based Story Prototypes

Patrick Colm Hogan

The Butterfly Lovers, a 2004 animated feature film from Taiwan by Ming Chin Tsai, is an instance of the romantic prototype. Its realization as a particular story results from alterations and specifications – some specific to animation – that foreground thematic issues relating to sexual orientation and gender identity. Both thematic concerns become particularly apparent through a cognitive analysis, incorporating a distinction between global and local interpretation.

In earlier work, I have argued that story development can be partially modeled as the application of alteration and specification principles to story prototypes. Some of these principles are a function of the communication medium of the new work, since the prototypes are generally medium-neutral; other principles are independent of the medium. The most important story prototypes are the cross-cultural genres, including romantic tragicomedy. These prototypical genres are generated from the goals defined by emotion systems. The alteration and specification of the prototypes serve two functions – the fostering of emotions and the communication of themes, which is often itself integrated with the fostering of emotions.

Beginning from these premises, which have both theoretical and interpretive consequences, the following essay considers Ming Chin Tsai's 2004 animated feature film *The Butterfly Lovers*. A popular tale, the story of Liang Shanbo and Zhu Yingtai (the *Butterfly Lovers*) has been retold many times over the centuries in Chinese literature. Its basic plot is a prototypical romantic tragicomedy. However, it includes some fascinating alterations and some unusual specifications, across versions and in this particular adaptation. For example, it often happens in romantic stories that the lovers are prevented from being united because they belong to socially opposed identity groups (e.g., feuding families in the well-known case of *Romeo and Juliet*), though they might not initially realize this. In *The Butterfly Lovers*, Yingtai and Shanbo are prevented from being united in part due to one of them mistakenly believing that they do not belong to the right identity groups. Specifically, Shanbo believes that they are both male, though in fact Yingtai is female. This and other aspects of the film, including some that are specific to animation, make the thematic concerns of sex and gender identity – and sex and gender identity presentation – particularly salient. The result is a film that in effect challenges standard views of sex and gender identity for its young target audience. The film furthers its thematic points through emotional appeal. That emotional appeal includes the development of empathic attachment feelings by the use of animated figures that are recognizably agentive, but also clearly not real humans, a recurring but little understood aspect of our attachment response.

In sum, *The Butterfly Lovers* neatly illustrates the development of a specific story from a (emotion-defined) prototype through alteration and specification principles, some bearing particularly on animation. It also presents us with a clear case of the thematic and emotional function of such alteration and specification. At the same time, our awareness of these theoretical principles helps us to recognize and articulate some of the thematic and emotional depth of this film.

A Model of Story Production: Development Principles

In *How Authors' Minds Make Stories* (2013a), I argue that particular or "realized" stories – what we actually read, watch, or listen to – may be understood in part as the result of applying specifiable development principles to more abstract story structures, generally prototypes. For example, authors and readers share a (comic) romantic prototype of roughly the following form. Two people fall in love; they encounter obstacles to their union (e.g., parental opposition); they are separated; they recruit help to overcome the initial obstacles; they overcome those obstacles and are united. One simple development principle is merely to give particular dispositions to the main characters. Another is to place them in particular circumstances. For example, suppose one author makes the male lover mercurial in his temper, while another makes him melancholic. That very simple difference will have broad ramifications for just how the individual stories work themselves out. Similarly, suppose one puts the lovers in an occupied city during wartime, while another places them in a beach resort during their colleges' spring break. These differences in setting have ramifications for the rest of the story's realization.

This is not to say that the authors think self-consciously that they are going to specify a prototype. Rather, an important cognitive operation is simulation, our imagination of particular causal sequences.[1] Simulation operates as we are experiencing some sequence of events. For example, our social interactions involve ongoing, unselfconscious simulations of our interlocutors' intentions, beliefs, perspectively limited perceptions, and so on, as well as possible outcomes of events, possible precedents, and other aspects of the situation. Even more obviously, simulation operates when we engage in hypothetical or counterfactual thinking, that is, when we envision how something might play out ("What might happen if I suggest that the department head nominate me for a university award?") or when we consider how something might have gone differently ("How might I have done better in that interview?"). In hypothetical and counterfactual thinking, we necessarily vary limited features of the real world as we understand it. That 'parametric variation' is a crucial part of the flexibility of simulation and thus of its adaptive value. In other words, it is part of what enabled the evolution of our simulative capacities. The evolved capacity for parametric variation in simulation includes the ability to change the circumstances and dispositions of simulated agents. Indeed, circumstances and dispositions are probably the key causal factors in our understanding and explanation of individual human action, thus fundamental parameters for our social simulation.

As this indicates, development principles in the production of stories are simply a form of the routines that operate in simulation. We may further elaborate on these principles by distinguishing 'specification principles' and 'alteration principles.' Specification principles provide means of particularizing prototypical (or other) structures. Thus, one might specify characters, settings, or events (among other things); these constitute the 'targets' of specification. The means of such specification are various, but most obviously involve one's own particular experiences. For example, an author might locate a story in a particular city with which he or she is familiar. Of course, this use of 'exemplars' (or instances) need not be singular. An author is free to combine several exemplars. For example, we may simulate an ideal job candidate by drawing on dispositional features of several acquaintances. The same points hold for an author's simulation of a character in a story.

Clearly, particular stories involve specification. However, they involve more than that. For example, romantic stories differ not only by their details. They differ in structure also. Indeed, the point about prototypes – as opposed to more fixed schemas or templates – is that there is variation in the structures, even if there are also central tendencies. Alteration principles may apply to the prototype alone. For example, one alteration principle is intensification. The separation of the lovers may be intensified into their death, sometimes producing tragedy rather than comedy. I say 'sometimes' because intensification may apply to the helper character as well, leading to saintly or divine intervention, which may lead to the resurrection of the dead lovers or their union in an afterlife. Other alterations of the prototype alone would include the division or fusion of character roles, which is to say, the parts characters play in the development of the action. For example, the parents might initially operate as blocking agents, but then repent and serve as helpers for the lovers.

In terms of our categories of development rules, many of these cases are equivocal. We might consider at least some instances of the preceding sorts to be a matter of specification. For example, in making the helper character divine, intensification is a form of character particularization.

The distinction between specification and alteration is clearer in cases of principles that bear on more than one abstract structure. Specifically, some alterations involve integration of different structures, such as different prototypes, or a prototype and an exemplar. For example, *Romeo and Juliet* is fundamentally a romantic tragedy. However, it embeds a brief revenge narrative in the middle of the work, complicating and intensifying the separation of the lovers by making Romeo guilty of the death of Tybalt and arguably in part responsible for the death of Mercutio as well (itself an alteration of the revenge prototype). Note that this is not simply a separate story, say a tale recounted by a character, but an integral part of the romantic plot itself. Moreover, that romantic plot is itself embedded in an encompassing sacrificial narrative in which social devastation (of civil conflict) is ended only through the sacrificial deaths of the lovers – perhaps particularly the death of the innocent Juliet.

Whether the development is a matter of specification or alteration, the function of story developments is constant. As attested by a long history of literary criticism – famously summarized in Horace's assertion that poetry should be both sweet and useful (1998: 75) – authors produce works and readers take up works for both emotional and ethical or political (more generally, thematic) purposes. In keeping with this, development principles serve ultimately to contribute to the thematic orientation of a work (e.g., its political point) or to enhance its emotional impact – or to combine the two in motivating political or ethical action through intensified emotional force.

A Model of Story Production: Medium Specificity

Prototypes are generally neutral with respect to medium, economic context (e.g., mode of distribution), mode of production (e.g., individual versus collective), and other material conditions of the new or 'realized' work. Moreover, most development principles are neutral regarding these conditions as well. However, some aspects of development are a function of material factors. This is true in two senses. First, some material conditions require certain sorts of development; these developments may be considered partially medium specific. For example, visual media require a range of specifications that are not required in purely linguistic media. To take an obvious case, a novel may not specify a character's clothing; a film generally must do so. Second, some material conditions foster or enable certain sorts of development principles, though these principles are not particularly tied to those conditions. For example, the mode of distribution of a work may make it more likely that developments will be comic or tragic (e.g., as a function of audience preferences, especially as these bear on investment decisions and production costs).

The point applies in obvious ways to animated films. These are visual media, with the usual implications for required development, such as the particularization of visual features and the definition of an optical point of view for the visual narration. They are collective products, with the usual consequences for the distribution of development across participants. This may involve a hierarchy in which some individuals (e.g., actors) produce numerous possible specifications (in different takes) and other individuals (e.g., the director) select which will be part of the film. It is also a medium that enables a certain degree of leeway in constraints of plausibility. For example, relative to other visual media, it is often easier for animated works to represent catastrophes as innocuous (as when a piano falls on a character's head, flattening him or her into a disk, before he or she pops out again, as good as new). This is in part the result of the way animated film has developed historically, but it is also due to the representational quality of animation, as the figures are both recognizably human and nonhuman, and to its representational scope, since it is easy to turn a character into a disk then back into a human. These aspects of animation have important emotional consequences as well, as we will discuss later.

Target audience also figures here. Animated film may of course be directed toward adults or children. However, relative to live-action films, there is clearly a greater tendency for animation to be aimed at children. Target audience clearly has consequences for story development independent of medium – (for example, in the depiction of sexuality), but medium may bias development toward certain target audiences rather than others.

A Model of Story Production: Prototypes

Up to now, I have been speaking of prototypes as structures that we have in mind in creating and responding to literary works. I have said nothing about their variability or derivation. It is important, however, that some story prototypes recur across a wide range of unrelated literary traditions. These are generally the most common and most important structures for story production (see Hogan 2003, 2011a for the prototypes themselves and evidence for their cross-cultural recurrence). Thus, very often the prototypes at issue in specification and alteration are the cross-cultural genres of romantic, heroic, sacrificial, and other tragicomedies.

The romantic genre is perhaps the most common of even the major cross-cultural genres. It follows the basic sequence sketched earlier. Two people fall in love. They face some sort of social opposition, often from parents, and often due to some conflict in identity categories. It sometimes happens that they fall in love in ignorance of this identity opposition, though they may also realize that they are violating social norms. The 'blocking' characters (prototypically parents) often prefer a rival for one or both of the lovers. This embeds a love triangle plot in the social conflict plot. The lovers are separated, sometimes with one exiled and one confined. They may communicate through some intermediary. The separation may involve imagery of death or false reports of death (or actual death, in tragic versions). With the aid of some helper, sometimes one with a degree of social authority, they manage to defeat the rival and be united. Sometimes this involves a change in identity categories (e.g., a discovery that the wealthy child's beloved is not actually a slave but an aristocrat separated from his or her family in childhood). Sometimes it involves an alteration of the identity opposition (e.g., a change in social norms). The lovers' ultimate union is commonly connected with family reconciliations and a sort of utopian vision, which is characteristic of the endings of the main prototypical genres in their comic form.

This and other prototypes recur across cultures not because they are innate or somehow archetypal. They recur rather because they are generated by standard simulative processes. Specifically, a story is first of all a particular causal sequence, thus the sort of thing we simulate. We are most fully emotionally engaged by such sequences when they bear on human subjects, and such human sequences occur most significantly when human agents pursue goals. Thus, given the operation of simulation, we would expect stories to arise in which human agents pursue goals. Those goals are necessarily things that the agents believe will make them happy (or relieve them from unhappiness). Happiness is a function of emotional satisfaction, which is in turn defined by emotion systems. The sexual desire system sets sexual relations as a goal; the hunger system, consumption of tasty food; the attachment system, proximity to and affectionate interaction with the attachment object. Thus, the emotion systems define goals that guide sequences of human action. The cross-cultural genres are defined first of all by such goals. In other words, the cross-cultural genres derive from emotion systems.

Before explaining how the prototypes are generated from these goals, I need to mention two complications. First, although these goals are most often narrowly egoistic, they have social forms as well. In their social forms, they still bear on individual feelings, but they extend the scope of the goals to other members of an identity category. Thus, Jones may be proud of his or her own achievements or of those of his or her nation or sports team. This is important for the genres themselves and for their political implications. For example, the heroic prototype involves two narrative sequences. One concerns the fall of a legitimate leader or a loyal defender, thus an individual humiliation. The other concerns the defeat of the home society by an enemy, thus a social humiliation.

The second complication concerns the relation of the emotion systems to goals. Emotion systems of course generate goals individually. However, most genres combine emotion systems and goals, presumably because human life and human agency involve the combination of goals. Moreover, our most important social emotions, such as romantic love, combine different emotion systems. Thus, the romantic genre sets romantic union as the goal of the hero and heroine. Romantic union is defined as a goal by romantic love. But romantic love is itself a combination of attachment bonding, sexual desire, and what might be called "reward dependency," the dependency of one's reward system on a particular object (for this account of romantic love, see chapter three of Hogan 2011b). The reward system is the system that drives "wanting" and manifests "liking" or pleasure (see Chatterjee 2014: 309). Reward dependency occurs when someone's wanting and liking become contingent on the availability of one target (e.g., a particular drug in addiction, or the beloved in intense forms of romantic love). This is why the loss of one's beloved may give rise to depression and may lead to suicide, in life and in stories.

The basic orientation of a genre is, again, given by some emotion-defined happiness goal. The fuller prototype is first of all the result of applying general principles of emotion intensification to the causal trajectory of goal pursuit. For example, outcome emotions are strongly affected by prior expectations and associated emotions. When I anticipate an award and do not receive it, I feel sad. But that is not due simply to not receiving the award. There are all sorts of awards I don't receive, and that doesn't affect me in the least. It is rather the happy anticipation of the social esteem, warm praise, and prospects for yet more future advancement, that leads me to view the neutral outcome – being in the same state as before the award announcement – as a loss. Thus, the happiness of the lovers' comic union is intensified by their separation. Moreover, that separation is itself intensified by the imagery or rumor of death. Other principles of intensification include the exacerbation of the pain of conflict when it is with an attachment figure rather than some stranger. It is more hurtful to have one's happiness blocked by a parent than by some indifferent social authority – hence the prototypical role of parents in the romantic prototype (of course, here the fact that parents are often in conflict with their children over marriage enters as well). Attachment feelings bear not only on people but also on places. Thus, the spatial arrangement of a story will have emotional consequences insofar as it bears on place attachment – which enters with the motif of exile.

The Butterfly Lovers: Overview of the Story Prototype

The Butterfly Lovers (*Liang Shanbo yu Zhu Yingtai*) is a 2004 animated, feature-length film directed by Ming Chin Tsai and scripted by Ya-Yan Teng and Ming Chin Tsai. This film adapts a much older story, with many versions. Indeed, the tale of Liang Shanbo and Zhu Yingtai is "among the most widely circulated and most often rehearsed topics of folk literature in China and beyond, in much of East and South East Asia" (Altenburger 2005: 166; on the range of ancient and modern versions, see Idema 2011: 504). The basic story, mostly shared by the various retellings, is a fairly prototypical romantic narrative. Yingtai and Shanbo fall in love. There is social interference leading to a love triangle as the powerful Ma family wishes to have Yingtai as a bride for their son. The lovers die, but are reunited after death, transformed into butterflies, sometimes being reborn as human and achieving worldly success (see *Newly Compiled* 2008).

Some distinctive developments of the romantic prototype are shared by the different versions of the Yingtai-Shanbo story. Indeed, those distinctive developments are what mark these as versions of one story and not simply as different romantic narratives. In consequence, we may speak of prototypical features of the Yingtai-Shanbo story, which is a partial specification or development of the romantic prototype. More generally, we may refer to the 'genre prototype' (e.g., romantic tragicomedy), the 'story prototype' (e.g., the Yingtai-Shanbo romantic tragicomedy), and the 'realized story' (e.g., the Ming Chin Tsai film). Authors rewriting the Yingtai-Shanbo story then are responding to at least two prototypes – the more general romantic (genre) prototype and the more specific Yingtai-Shanbo (story) prototype.

There are two aspects of the story prototype that are most obviously distinctive of the Yingtai-Shanbo story and that in effect serve to mark off the identity of this particular, realized story. In other words, these are the features that most clearly make retellings count as versions of one story rather than merely cases of the romantic genre. These obtrusively distinctive components are found at the beginning and the end of the realized story. The first occurs in the material that serves as a sort of preface to the prototypical story – the circumstances that lead to the meeting of the lovers and their falling in love. In the genre more generally, such prefatory material is highly variable and thus generally falls outside the definition of the prototype.

The Yingtai-Shanbo story begins with Yingtai wishing to continue her studies, despite the fact that she is female. The solution to her dilemma is to dress in male clothing and attend a school for boys. Considered in relation to the romantic prototype, this is merely background to the meeting of the lovers. It is simply a means for establishing the romance, which will engage the readers or viewers in wishing for their union. It does serve that purpose well, since it fosters the recipients' sense of the warm attachment between the lovers by making them close friends. In keeping with this, the motif of the lovers as schoolmates is not unknown in romantic literature elsewhere. For example, we find it in at least some versions of the most prominent love story of the Arabic and Persian traditions – Layla and Majnun – including in the most famous version of that story, written by Nizami (1966). However, in this case, the prefatory material is thematically central to at least many versions of the story. Moreover, these thematic concerns bear on the emotion of the story in that the individual, realized works seek to recruit recipient emotion toward their thematic ends (e.g., they may direct our fondness for Yingtai toward support for women's education). These thematic concerns often bear on gender or sexuality, and they are elaborately developed in the course of the story.

The theme of sexuality is especially relevant to a more subtle development of the story prototype, one that constitutes an alteration of the romantic prototype rather than a mere specification of its prefatory material. From the start of their acquaintance, there is clearly a deep attachment between the Yingtai and Shanbo. The bond is straightforwardly romantic on Yingtai's part, but there may be hints that it is romantic on Shanbo's part as well. The difficulty here is that Shanbo is unaware that Yingtai is a woman. Thus, we find that one of the lovers is ignorant of the identity category of the other lover. This takes up a common motif, as we have seen, but it reverses the usual operation of the motif, since Shanbo thinks that Yingtai falls into a socially excluded category. This is significant because the suggestion of this motif is usually that the lovers might have discounted one another as possible love objects had they realized each other's group identity. For example, Juliet laments that she has learned Romeo's identity "too late" (I.iv.263 of Shakespeare 2009) to prevent her from falling in love with him. The implication is that proper category knowledge would have been sufficient to forestall her romantic response. If the process were the same in Shanbo's case, then he should have discounted Yingtai as a possible love object, given that he mistakenly believes she is male, but this appears not to occur. We will return to the consequences of this point.

The other obviously distinctive feature of the story prototype occurs at the end of the realized story. First, the lovers die, their separation intensified to actual demise. This is so common that it cannot count as an alteration, only as a slightly less prototypical variant of the separation. However, it is related to a more distinctive change – the postmortem metamorphosis of the lovers into butterflies. What appears to have happened here is a sort of literalization of metaphor, itself partially prototypical but specified in a somewhat distinctive way. As conceptual metaphor theorists have shown, there is a common tendency for metaphors to link positive emotions with the direction up (see Lakoff and Johnson 1980: 18 on "HAPPY IS UP"). In keeping with this, literary imagery for the joy of united lovers often involves flight or creatures that fly, prominently birds. Such imagery is indeed prototypical for romantic love (on cross-cultural patterns in imagery, see Hogan 2005). Here, the image is altered slightly from birds to butterflies. Then, as just noted, it is literalized. Rather than lovers being associated with the direction 'up' and flying creatures (here, butterflies) in imagery, or being both identified with and differentiated from such creatures in simile or metaphor, they are directly presented as butterflies – often before becoming human again.

The Butterfly Lovers: A Realized Story
(Prefatory Material)

The Butterfly Lovers begins with a text and voice-over setting the scene in the Eastern Jin dynasty (the third to fifth centuries of the common era) and explaining that, at the time, women were 'second-class citizens' who could not attend school. The text and voice-over also explain that the different socioeconomic classes did not intermingle. This clearly orients the viewers toward some thematic concerns of the film, implicitly 'criticizing the present by pointing to the past,' as the saying has it. Though this is a Taiwanese work, the didacticism recalls the use of traditional stories in the pre-Deng period of the People's Republic – though there is also a strong didactic component in some of the prerevolutionary versions of these stories.

The prefatory text ends by introducing a special girl. We then cut to a pencil sketching a face. As a figure appears, the narrator asks "Shi ta?" ("Is this him/her?"). A series of sketched portraits follows, each accompanied by the question, "Shi ta?" Finally, we come to a figure who is not merely a static portrait but an animated character. She moves between white sheets, suggesting life beyond the paper on which she is sketched. This introduction is important for several reasons. First, it stresses the thematic importance of identity. The film is deeply concerned with our identification of individuals as such and as members of groups. This opening question, "Shi ta?" (with its repeated answer, "Bu shi," "It is not") highlights the topic of identity. This fits with other aspects of the story as well, for identity is clearly central to the thematic concerns articulated in the prefatory text (about education), and to the romantic prototype generally.

Not being a Chinese speaker, I am perhaps unusually sensitive to the linguistic features of this part of the opening. But the shift from text to purely spoken Chinese makes me particularly aware of the gender issue. The gender difference in the third person pronoun (he/she) is encoded in written Chinese, but not in spoken Chinese. The pronoun 'ta' refers equally to males and females. Moreover, the name 'Yingtai' is not confined to one sex (subsequently, Yingtai does not change her name when masquerading as a boy). Awareness of this may encourage the viewers to attend to issues of gender marking in the film as well.

It is also important to note that the film begins by foregrounding the fact that Yingtai is a representation, a drawing. This self-referentiality is obviously enabled by the medium, which allows the filmmakers to sketch a pencil that is itself sketching Yingtai. It may at first seem that this distances us from the character, producing an "alienation effect" (see Brecht 1974). However, it is far from clear that this is how it operates in this film. The foregrounding of the constructedness of the representation has many possible sources and many possible consequences (the film is less obviously suggestive of experimental drama than of other popular animations, such as those produced by Disney Studios, including the old television program, *The Wonderful World of Disney*; it playfully depicts the process of animation and perhaps engages young viewers more fully with the character by that means). Here, the technique might most plausibly be seen to converge with the thematic concerns of the film to stress the constructedness of gender presentation. Indeed, Yingtai arguably seems *more* real as she is in a sense liberated from the constraints of the sketch papers, especially when the narrator invites her to come out from behind them, as if from concealment in the home.

The introduction of Yingtai ends with a brief sequence in which she interacts with a single butterfly. This introduces the image that is so characteristic of the story prototype. It also provides a bridge or transition from the self-referential frame of the story (the 'meta-discursive' paper and pencil) to the storyworld in which the characters live and interact. Specifically, Yingtai chases the butterfly out of the paper into a scene of both nature and society. The narration provides a basic character sketch of Yingtai, focusing on gender characteristics. Specifically, the narrator explains that Yingtai has the personality features associated with boys. This prepares us for the following scene in which Yingtai implores her father to allow her to attend school. The scene is presented in silhouette, with the mother motionless and the father interacting somewhat stiffly with his very lively and animated daughter. When the father agrees, Yingtai's joy is palpable. More importantly, the scene appeals to the attachment feelings of the viewers by ending with Yingtai's warm expression of affection and gratitude.

I take it that the film is appealing to the attachment feelings of parents in the audience. In doing this, it makes use of a little-understood aspect of attachment response – the enhancement of our feelings of tenderness for some clearly unreal, but nonetheless recognizably human or human-like targets. Obvious cases of this include the stuffed animals of which children are so fond, but they also include cartoons. In his summary of empirical studies bearing on the topic, Plamper explains that, in both still and moving representations (e.g., stuffed animals and robots), the recipients' empathy increases with increasing realism, but only up to a certain point. If the target (e.g., a robot) becomes "too much like a human being, all empathy vanishes and is replaced by disgust" (2015: 27). Plamper illustrates the point by reference to the animated feature *Shrek* (Adamson and Jenson 2001). He cites the film's production team as asserting that they had to make Princess Fiona "less anthropomorphic" because "she was beginning to look too real, and the effect was getting distinctly unpleasant" (Plamper 2015: 27–28, quoting Misselhorn 2009: 103).

The existence of attachment feelings for what psychoanalytic writers call "transitional objects" (see chapter one of Winnicott 2005) would seem to have two obvious sources. First, we may have some innate tendency toward such attachment feelings; this is a plausible factor given the widespread occurrence of transitional objects and their function in attenuating separation anxiety and facilitating independence. Second, many of us have specific childhood experiences that connect human-like objects with attachment, from stuffed animals to cartoons. In any case, the film draws on attachment sensitivities to features that are partially characteristic of the medium. It does so here, in connection with the father–daughter relationship, and it will do so subsequently in the Yingtai-Shanbo relationship. This fostering of attachment feelings serves the emotional purposes of the realized story in obvious ways, but it bears no less on the thematic concerns, both relating to gender and, as we will see, sexuality.

The following scene returns Yingtai to the abstract space of the opening (she actually runs back in the direction from which she left that space at the beginning, thus preserving a sort of spatial continuity). Brought to a halt by the narrator's call, Yingtai stands before a patterned screen, looking out at the viewers and the narrator. Here, the viewers may realize for the first time that they are given the point of view of the narrator, who is also the artist. We see the pencil stretch out before us as the narrator explains that Yingtai cannot go to school in her female clothing. The eraser removes all parts of Yingtai – clothing and hair – other than her face. The pencil is then flipped around and Yingtai is re-sketched with new clothing, but of course the same face. The sequence graphically portrays a radical change in gender presentation combined with constancy in individual identity (represented by Yingtai's face). In consequence, it suggests the general point that a person's gender presentation can vary vastly without him or her ceasing to be the same person by violating some putative gender essence – a point that to some extent resists the pervasive gender ideology in most children's everyday experience (for some nonobvious cases of this, see Fine 2010: 189–206).

It is just after Yingtai's physical transformation into a boy that the titles appear with an indication that the story proper is beginning – the story proper being defined by the romantic prototype. In keeping with this, the following scene introduces Shanbo and the swift sympathy and affection experienced by the lovers. There is a small amount of further prefatory material as Yingtai and her servant sit and discuss boys and men who are passing by. This scene has a couple of purposes. One is to present an idealized portrait of interclass relations, taking up the class issue announced in the opening text. Another is to establish the sexual and romantic interests of the female characters (e.g., in Yingtai's references to the physical appeal of the various male passersby).

Finally, Shanbo arrives on the scene. Yingtai is overwhelmed with feelings for this beautiful youth. Interestingly, Shanbo's response seems only slightly less dramatic, despite the fact that he believes Yingtai is male. There is a directly parallel interaction between Yingtai's servant,

Yenzing, and Shanbo's servant, Sei Gao – a relation that Yingtai characterizes as moving 'fast' (kuai). Though the film is very decorous, it does
have some indications of mild sexuality, which are more explicit with
the servants. For example, when the two women finally confess their sex
to the two men, it is the servants who fall behind the bushes, kissing,
then draw fantastical curtains, suggesting that they have retreated to a
private room. This is already hinted at in the "fast" quality of their relationship. Moreover, Yingtai generalizes their character of being "kuai,"
noting that it applies to young people generally – presumably including
Yingtai and Shanbo themselves.

After Yingtai and Shanbo introduce themselves (with, again, no
change of names), we learn of a third couple. These are two birds, one
associated with Shanbo and one associated with Yingtai. They are actually engaged in courting. This clearly draws on the cross-cultural image
pattern noted earlier. But the parallel also makes clear the nature of the
relations between Yingtai and Shanbo as well as those between the two
servants. Yingtai then characterizes the relations between the birds as
even more "kuai" than those between the servants. This is relatively
banal from the perspective of the women, since they are aware that their
relations with the men are heterosexual. But it is not banal from the perspective of the men, for whom any parallel bond would be homoerotic.

Should the point about homoeroticism seem to be a matter of overint-
erpretation, it is followed by Shanbo praying that he and Yingtai would
be bound together even to the extent of sharing a pillow for 100 years.
Yingtai actually faces him with the question of whether the poem he
has just recited does not refer to a man and a woman, thus a sexual or
romantic bond. Shanbo replies that their bond will be even stronger than
that of 'nan' and 'nü,' male and female.

The scene ends quickly after this, and we shift setting to the school.
The first event at the school is the introduction of the rival, the heir of
the wealthy Ma family. This has several purposes, some having to do
with the class concerns of the film; others take up the romantic plot. For
our purposes, perhaps the most interesting is the song that accompanies
his introduction, with its repeated questioning of "Ta shi shei?" (Who
is he/she?) and "Wo shi shei?" (Who am I?). In this way, the filmmakers
once again stress the issue of identity, making its thematic and emotional
importance salient.

Gender and Sexuality: Two Ways of Reading

There is no need to attend to subsequent scenes in as great detail. They
largely develop the viewers' sympathy for the lovers or their antipathy
for the rival. Here, it is important to consider just how we might interpret the film, both emotionally and thematically. There are in fact many
ways in which the film might be approached – considering, for example,

its treatment of class. However, the most salient concerns of the film are gender and sexuality. Moreover, these two thematic concerns are brought out by slightly different ways of looking at the film, ways that have implications for the study of literature and film beyond this particular work.

Specifically, there is a difference between the implications of the film as they develop *globally* and as they appear *locally*. Consider, for example, Shanbo's expression of almost marital attachment to Yingtai. Globally, in the context of the film as a whole, this is the expression of romantic attachment between a man and a woman. However, considered solely in its local context, it is the expression of romantic attachment of a man for (someone he considers to be) another man. Or consider Yingtai's character. Globally, she is literally a woman who has adopted the gender presentation of a man to escape discriminatory social constraints. Locally, however, she may be understood as a person whose experience of sexual identity is at odds with her social identity. Another way of thinking about the global versus local distinction is in terms of knowledge. The global construal is omniscient and objective; it brings into account the entire situation of the storyworld. The local construal, in contrast, is perspectival and subjective; it limits the interpretation to the understanding and related response of a particular character in isolation at a particular moment.

The global versus local difference suggests two distinct, albeit related complexes of thematic and emotional concerns in the film – or, indeed, in many versions of the story. Globally, the film – and the story prototype – treat gender, understood as the complex of capacities and behaviors that are socially considered to be a function of sex, but are not directly a matter of reproductive biology. For example, gender involves such concerns as putative male–female differences in intellectual capacity, empathy, and emotional control. The obvious thematic and emotional focus of the film, and of the story prototype, concerns the intellectual capacities and interests of boys and girls. Specifically, it addresses the under-education of girls, indicating that boys and girls have similar interests and capacities and fostering the viewers' sympathy for the girl who wants to engage in advanced study. In some ways, the film may seem less progressive on this issue than some other versions of the Yingtai-Shanbo story. For example, *The Newly Compiled Tale of the Golden Butterflies* (an eighteenth-century version) presents Yingtai as the superior student (2011: 513), which is not the case in the film (on the other hand, the filmmakers faced the difficulty that they presumably did not wish to discourage boys from being diligent students and wished to give them a positive role model to contrast with the unstudious Ma).

The gender theme is introduced at the start as Yingtai pleads with her parents for the opportunity to study. The fact that she can take on the male masquerade with such ease suggests that gender is superficial.

It is not a fundamental and determinative identity, but little more than a matter of what clothes one puts on. In terms of the scene with the artist's pencil, it is not a result of what one is – the face that cannot be erased without a loss of personal identity (through the disappearance of the character into mere blank space). It is, rather, just a matter of what happens to be sketched around that face and presents that personal identity to the world.

These thematic and emotional concerns are further developed in the course of the film, most obviously and most explicitly when the students at the school perform a play, *The River God Seeks a Wife*, a sacrificial narrative embedded in the romantic narrative of the film as a whole. *The River God* concerns a village devastated by floods. Under the guidance of an 'evil witch,' the villagers engage in human sacrifices – offering young women as wife to the River God – in order to protect their society. Yingtai plays the role of the woman who is to be sacrificed. Thus, in a Shakespearean touch, we have a woman pretending to be a man, who is in turn pretending to be a woman. When Yingtai approaches the water where she is to be drowned, the witch indicates that, as a woman, her "greatest purpose in life" is to sacrifice herself in this marriage. The witch goes on to criticize both women and the lower classes. This provokes the ire of Yingtai, who delivers a little speech on the equality of men and women and denouncing women's treatment as second-class citizens. The witch responds that 'xiaoshuo' or novels present women as inferior. Yingtai asserts that these writings are wrong, and the filmmakers thereby suggest that some progressive literature – including this film – shows us something else. Yingtai ends her speech by referring to exemplary women of the past. Shanbo exclaims, "Shuo de tai hao!" ("Well spoken"), and the entire audience applauds – thereby apparently ending the student play with an assertion of gender equality rather than female self-sacrifice.

This is not to say that the film rejects all aspects of gender. Yingtai is clearly more 'feminine' in her bearing and gestures. But the film indicates that gender-defined properties are limited and socially inconsequential. One possible exception to this would be the bravery shown by Shanbo when he and Yingtai first encounter Ma and his goons, but this is equivocal. Specifically, Yingtai calls out to Ma that he should stop some bullying behavior. Ma hears the admonition, but does not know if it comes from Yingtai or Shanbo. Shanbo takes the blame, thereby in effect offering to defend Yingtai against the goons. This suggests Shanbo's masculine bravery. However, this difference is not consistently developed in the rest of the film. Indeed, immediately after Shanbo stands up to Ma, the latter is attacked by two birds – one male (blue in color) and one female (pink in color). Moreover, Shanbo subsequently does confront the goons and is badly beaten, suggesting that he is not in fact much better at physical self-defense than Yingtai would have been. Indeed, Yingtai shows her own bravery at various points in the film, including her public defiance of gender inequality before an audience of men (an audience that includes only one other woman). Virtually the only gender differences that remain are purely physical – the men being on the whole larger than the women. The point should be both obvious and emotionally effective for viewers, including the young target audience.

But viewers' sense of the gender concerns of the film, their largely self-conscious processing of the ongoing conditions and explicit themes, is not all there is to response and understanding. Viewers also process the film locally, moment to moment, and a great deal of that local development is equivocal. Specifically, the local development of the film is regularly open to interpretation in terms of gay sexuality or transgendering. Put differently, the film does not literally treat homosexuality or transgendering, if we understand the film globally. But it does suggest both concerns and arguably prepares its target audience to have a more positive response to both than might be encouraged by some more conservative social tendencies. This aspect of the story prototype has led to that story prototype being "claimed as a charter by the Chinese queer movement" (Idema 2011: 504). Indeed, it is possible to read the story of Yingtai and Shanbo as an indirect representation of homoerotic bonding, given a veneer of heterosexuality in order to make it socially acceptable, or to allow for plausible deniability.

To explore the thematic and emotional topic of sexuality in the film, we might reconsider the students' play and the immediately preceding scene. After Yingtai and Shanbo meet Ma, the film shifts to the class of students, contrasting the classical knowledge of the lovers with the ignorance of Ma and his henchmen. After a brief transition, we accompany Yingtai and Shanbo to an Edenic natural scene where they are alone together. Yingtai asks Shanbo if he has a girlfriend (nüpengyou). Shanbo answers that he does not. Yingtai expresses delight, then goes on to say (evidently to herself) that it is good for her. Two butterflies, fluttering in spirals around one another, follow immediately. Subsequently, Yingtai and Shanbo are caught in the rain and must take shelter. As they crouch together beneath the foliage, we see pairs of frogs, butterflies, and ducks, suggesting that Yingtai and Shanbo form as natural a pair as any of these. It is important to note that, unlike the birds introduced earlier in the film, there is nothing that marks the members of these couples as male and female. The scene ends with a transition to the school play. Shanbo tells Yingtai that he will be playing the role of her husband. Yingtai responds – this time, not under her breath – that she wishes it were true.

For our purposes, what is perhaps most crucial about this scene is that, in and of itself, it is most obviously interpreted as the tentative romantic initiatives of a gay couple. Without the global information about Yingtai's sex, the scene would suggest that she is delighted over Shanbo's

lack of a girlfriend as it may suggest something about his sexual preference. A parallel point holds for her concluding wish that he could be her
husband. Moreover, this is all consistent with Shanbo's earlier wish that
the two would share the same pillow.

The following scene only enhances these suggestions. Yingtai appears
on stage accoutered as a woman, and the men in the audience respond
with obvious sexual interest, despite the fact that they 'know' she is a
man. When Shanbo and Yingtai appear as husband and wife, Yingtai
gives Shanbo a romantic kiss. Audience members remark on its realism.
Two aspects of this kiss are especially noteworthy for the local reading. First, Shanbo appears surprised, but he does not resist or recoil. He
seems confused, but not displeased by kissing someone he believes to be
a boy dressed as a girl. Second, male members of the audience call out
to be kissed similarly.

Though it is perhaps less fully elaborated, both scenes seem com-
patible with a transgendered interpretation as well. When the teacher
(laoshi) says that perhaps Yingtai really is a girl, the global suggestion is
that we have an anatomical female masquerading as a man (who is im-
itating a woman), but locally, the idea is consistent with an anatomical
male experiencing gender dysphoria and feeling that, though anatomi-
cally male, she is more properly considered female. In this reading, her
ability to play the woman's role does not come from her biology, but
from her identification as a woman. The point may also help to explain
the somewhat odd fact that, even when her gender presentation is male,
Yingtai appears to be wearing lipstick.

The Butterfly Lovers: Return to the Prototypes

Both the gender and sexuality concerns diminish as the story progresses
and becomes a more prototypical romantic tragicomedy. Indeed, a little
before the middle of the film, Yingtai reveals her secret – first, inadvertently, to Ma and then, intentionally, to Shanbo, but this does not mean
that the remainder of the film is without interest, beyond being one more
particularization of the genre and story prototypes. For example, gender remains an implicit topic, as when we see both the men and women
weeping over separation. Perhaps the most striking aspect of the second
half of the film is the way that it incorporates the sacrificial plot into
the romantic narrative. The viewers have been prepared for this by the
student play in that the play should prime the sacrificial prototype in
viewers' minds, making them more sensitive to sacrificial elements in
what follows.

Specifically, the powerful Ma family threatens Yingtai's parents and,
perhaps more importantly, Shanbo. This leads to a variation on the romantic plot in which one of the lovers blocks the union, foregoing her
own happiness to assure the life of the other. This is of course a form of

sacrifice, though it does not closely follow the sacrificial plot, where a devastated society requires the death of an innocent person to restore the beneficence and equilibrium of nature (as in the student play). Threatened by Ma's goons, Shanbo makes no attempt at escape and allows himself to be beaten brutally, fending off death only long enough to convey once more his love to the virtually imprisoned Yingtai. This death is also a sacrifice, in this case to free Yingtai from the need to marry Ma. But again, it is not really a sacrifice in the manner of the narrative prototype.

Faced with the death of Shanbo, Yingtai dresses in her wedding clothes and goes to Shanbo's grave, in effect to commit suicide and thus to make herself Shanbo's bride in death. This directly and clearly recalls the student play. There, Yingtai's character was supposed to commit suicide to marry the River God in order to protect the village. We can now see that this is in a sense what she was doing in agreeing to marry Ma. Yingtai's feminist response to that play undermined the case for that sort of sacrifice and the play was not completed. Similarly, her sacrifice for her family and for Shanbo (i.e., the marriage to Ma) was not completed. The film suggests that such a sacrifice would have been wrong. Certainly, the emotional force of the film goes against her marrying Ma, something that few if any viewers must desire. With respect to that part of the story, then, the film substitutes another sort of sacrifice – Shanbo's acceptance of death at the hands of Ma's goons. The suggestion is that society is in fact endangered, but the danger is from the cruel selfishness of the powerful. Sacrifices that give the powerful what they demand will not restore social good. They will only continue an oppressive status quo. Shanbo's self-sacrifice out of attachment and loyalty to Yingtai opposes this oppressive situation.

At Shanbo's grave, Yingtai weeps until Shanbo appears in a beam of light to take her with him. Yingtai's family calls out to her, but she goes with Shanbo anyway. The scene literally develops as a sort of bodily assumption into heaven. But the unspoken implication is that she has died, presumably through suicide. The calls of the family suggest attempts to revive someone who is recently deceased. The lovers then disappear and the immediate result is the withdrawal of the Ma family. The patriarch of the family in effect repudiates his earlier demands and chides his son for pursuing Yingtai. Though hardly utopian, a sort of social equilibrium has been reestablished, and Yingtai's family is out of danger. At this point, the two butterflies appear, twirling about one another in the air above everyone present. Yingtai's mother calls out to one of them, "Yingtai!" indicating that the butterflies are the metamorphosed souls of the lovers. In keeping the cross-cultural imagery patterns noted earlier, the appearance of the lovers as butterflies is triggered by the calls of the two birds who have accompanied them throughout the film. The film ends with the culmination of the sacrificial story. In the sacrificial prototype, social devastation is often a matter of the withering of nature (e.g., in famine). Shanbo's grave is fittingly located in a rather desolate place. As the butterflies spiral about one another and pass over the landscape, verdure springs up and flowers blossom everywhere.

The thematic implication here is somewhat different from the thematic concerns we considered earlier. It involves an affirmation of the ethical and social importance of individual attachment. On the other hand, this complements the gender concerns as it continues the opposition to women's marital self-sacrifice, an opposition introduced through Yingtai's extemporized argument in the student play. The emotional force of this concluding development is to encourage the viewers' empathy with the bond of the lovers as equal and parallel. The revival of nature suggests an attempt to foster optimism and support on the part of the audience.

Conclusion

We have considered general, theoretical points and specific interpretive issues. As to the former, we may partially model the production of realized stories (the fully particularized stories that we read, view, or listen to) as a process of applying development principles to prototypes. The prototypes are often the cross-cultural genres, which are the product of human emotion systems. However, there are also culturally specified genre prototypes and story prototypes (prototypes that define a collection of realized stories as versions of the same general story). The development principles may be loosely divided into specification and alteration principles, some of which are medium-neutral while others are medium-specific. In each case, the development serves the purposes of articulating and conveying thematic concerns or guiding emotional response.

Also at a general, theoretical level, we may distinguish two aspects of reception. A work may differ in its global implications and in the more local, moment-by-moment suggestions and resonances. Thus, recipients' unfolding (often more spontaneous) response to parts of a work may sometimes be quite different from their overall (often more self-conscious or modulated) response to the work as a whole. This may have interpretive as well as thematic and emotional consequences.

Ming Chin Tsai's *The Butterfly Lovers* illustrates these points and is illuminated by analysis in these terms. Globally, it treats the theme of gender, encouraging the viewers to understand gender as a superficial and malleable matter and fostering emotional responses consistent with this orientation. Locally, however, it suggests a thematic concern with sexuality. Specifically, the film may be understood as cultivating empathic sensitivity to the attachment needs of gay and transsexual youths or at least as preparing viewers to be open to developing such sensitivity.

In both its global and local aspects, the film draws on and develops the cross-cultural romantic prototype, as well as the Yingtai-Shanbo story prototype, which is itself a development of the romantic prototype. In creating this film, the filmmakers have taken up specification and alteration principles that result in the particular 'profile of ambiguity' and 'profile of ambivalence' that constitute its complex global and local implications and resonances. The profile of ambiguity is the range of interpretations – including thematic interpretations – enabled by a work. The profile of ambivalence is the range of emotional responses fostered by a work (on these ideas, see Hogan 2013b: 13–14 and 57).

In many cases, these development principles apply across material conditions of medium, production, and reception. Such general principles include the integration of genres, evident in this film through its combination of romantic and sacrificial prototypes. In some cases, however, the alterations and specifications are of particular relevance to the medium of the work. These medium-oriented developments serve the usual thematic and emotional functions.

There is no doubt that many aspects of animation bear on alteration and specification principles. Some of these are shared with other visual media, such as live-action film. For example, both animation and live-action film require the specification of some visual details that are not required by purely verbal media. On the other hand, some relevant aspects of animation are more distinctive. A number of these concern the required level of realism. For example, with respect to specification, animated characters may readily be drawn with no setting. Similarly, aspects of clothing or bodily features may be incomplete, as when an animal character is shown with a necktie, but no other clothing or distinctive physical properties (the necktie serving as a signal that this is a male animal). The point extends to just what can happen in animation and with what consequences. For instance, it is easy to resurrect an animated character from what would undoubtedly be a fatal accident in real life (e.g., being crushed by a falling piano).[2]

But what are the consequences or functions of this limitation on required realism? As we saw, animated figures are more appealing if they are largely, but not entirely realistic. Perhaps the appeal of limited realism is that it facilitates our experience of animation (as well as dolls and related representations) as more akin to our simulation of stories than to our encounters with real life. Our experience of simulation involves a range of ordinary emotions. However, in comparison with parallel experiences in the real world, such simulation is much less likely to become strongly aversive (on the reward system component of simulation and the experience of fiction, see the first chapter of Hogan 2013a). Moreover, animation and related forms of limited realism – as in transitional objects, such as dolls – appear particularly well suited to evoking attachment system responses. This is presumably in part due to innate inclinations, perhaps a matter of enhanced sensitivity to particular sorts of facial or bodily features bearing on childhood, as, for example, Haidt has discussed in relating "cuteness," transitional object dolls, and attachment or "Care" (2012: 155; cf. the operation of such sensitivity in bonding with pets; see Borgi and Cirulli 2016; Chapter 6 has also discussed animated characters' specific bodily features). The relation of animation and attachment is almost certainly connected with many viewers' childhood experiences of cartoons as well. In keeping with these points, animation is particularly likely to be oriented toward a target audience of children.

In these respects, then, animation involves medium-specific development principles or features bearing on such principles, including partial visualization, limited realism, attachment elicitation, and increased (though by no means exclusive) orientation toward a younger audience. Future research should help us to identify a greater range of such principles and features. It should also help us to further refine and more definitively explain those we have just considered.

Notes

1 For a representative selection of work on simulation, see Markman et al. (2009). On the relation of simulation and literature, see my *How Authors' Minds* (2013a) and Keith Oatley's *Such Stuff as Dreams* (2011), especially chapter one.
2 For qualifications to the opposition between animation and non-animated films, emphasizing the "continuum" between "mimesis" and "abstraction" that characterizes different sorts of live-action film, animation, and combinations or transitional cases, see Furniss (1998: 5).

References

Altenburger, Roland. "Is It Clothes That Make the Man? Cross-Dressing, Gender, and Sex in Pre-Twentieth-Century Zhu Yingtai Lore." *Asian Folklore Studies,* 64, 2005: 165–205.
Borgi, Marta and Francesca Cirulli. "Pet Face: Mechanisms Underlying Human-Animal Relationships." *Frontiers in Psychology*, 7(8), 2016. Available online at https://doi.org/10.3389/fpsyg.2016.00298 (accessed 1 August 2018).
Brecht, Bertolt. "Alienation Effects in Chinese Acting." In: Willett, John (Ed.). *Brecht on Theatre: The Development of an Aesthetic.* London: Methuen, 1974: 91–99.
Chatterjee, Anjan. "Neuroaesthetics: Growing Pains of a New Discipline." In: Shimamura, Arthur and Stephen Palmer (Eds.). *Aesthetic Science: Connecting Minds, Brains, and Experience.* Oxford: Oxford University Press, 2014: 299–317.
Fine, Cordelia. *Delusions of Gender: How Our Minds, Society, and Neurosexism Create Difference.* New York: Norton, 2010.

Furniss, Maureen. *Art in Motion: Animation Aesthetics*. Sidney: John Libbey, 1998.

Grodal, Torben. "Aesthetics and Psychology of Animated Films." In: Uhrig, Meike (Ed.). *Emotion in Animated Films*. London/New York: Routledge, 2019.

Haidt, Jonathan. *The Righteous Mind: Why Good People Are Divided by Politics and Religion*. New York: Pantheon, 2012.

Hogan, Patrick Colm. *The Mind and Its Stories: Narrative Universals and Human Emotion*. Cambridge: Cambridge University Press, 2003.

——— "Literary Universals and Their Cultural Traditions: The Case of Poetic Imagery." *Consciousness, Literature, and the Arts*, 6(2), August 2005: https://blackboard.lincoln.ac.uk/bbcswebdav/users/dmeyerdinkgrafe/archive/hogan.html.

——— *Affective Narratology: The Emotional Structure of Stories*. Lincoln: University of Nebraska Press, 2011a.

——— *What Literature Teaches Us about Emotion*. Cambridge: Cambridge University Press, 2011b.

——— *How Authors' Minds Make Stories*. Cambridge: Cambridge University Press, 2013a.

——— *Narrative Discourse: Authors and Narrators in Literature, Film, and Art*. Columbus: Ohio State University Press, 2013b.

Horace. "The Art of Poetry." Translated by Burton Raffel. In: Richter, David (Ed.). *The Critical Tradition: Classic Texts and Contemporary Trends*. Boston: Bedford Books, 1998: 68–77.

Idema, Wilt. "An Eighteenth-Century Version of 'Liang Shanbo and Zhu Yingtai' from Suzhou." In: Mair, Victor and Mark Bender (Eds.). *The Columbia Anthology of Chinese Folk and Popular Literature*. New York: Columbia University Press, 2011: 503–505.

Lakoff, George and Mark Johnson. *Metaphors We Live By*. Chicago, IL: University of Chicago Press, 1980.

Markman, Keith, William Klein, and Julie Suhr (Eds.). *Handbook of Imagination and Mental Simulation*. New York: Psychology Press, 2009.

Misselhorn, Catrin. "Empathy and Dyspathy with Androids: Philosophical, Fictional and (Neuro-) Psychological Perspectives." *Konturen*, 2, 2009: 101–123.

"The Newly Compiled Tale of the Golden Butterflies." Translated by Wilt Idema. In: Mair, Victor and Mark Bender (Eds.). *The Columbia Anthology of Chinese Folk and Popular Literature*. New York: Columbia University Press, 2011: 505–551.

Nizami. *The Story of Layla and Majnun*. Translated by Rudolf Gelpke. Final chapter translated by Zia Inayat Khan and Omid Safi. New Lebanon: Omega Publications, 1966.

Oatley, Keith. *Such Stuff as Dreams: The Psychology of Fiction*. Malden: Wiley-Blackwell, 2011.

Plamper, Jan. *The History of Emotions: An Introduction*. Translated by Keith Tribe. Oxford: Oxford University Press, 2015.

Shakespeare, William. *Romeo and Juliet*. Jonathan Bate and Eric Rasmussen (Eds.). New York: Modern Library, 2009.

Winnicott, Donald W. *Playing and Reality*. New York: Routledge, 2005.

Films

The Butterfly Lovers. Directed by Ming Chin Tsai. 2004; TWN: Central Motion Pictures.

Shrek. Directed by Andrew Adamson and Vicky Jenson. 2001; USA: DreamWorks/Pacific Data Images.

Documentaries

5 Animated Documentary

Viewer Engagement, Emotion, and Performativity

Paul Ward

Introduction

Although there has been a marked increase over the past two decades in the research and scholarship devoted to animated documentary,[1] how viewers are 'engaged' or 'addressed' by animated documentary – and specifically how they respond emotionally – has been somewhat overlooked. One of the central points underlying this chapter is the extent to which animated documentaries foreground their constructedness and the emotional effect this has on the viewers. It seems to be axiomatic that *all* animation is, by its very nature, making us acutely aware of its construction – the frame-by-frame process, the explicit use of drawings, puppets, and other representational forms: in short, it seems impossible to watch an animated film and *not* be aware of that constructedness. Clearly part of what I am arguing therefore falls into a tradition of thought where broadly 'realist' theories (where artworks are understood to function mimetically and show us the world) clash with broadly 'formalist' theories (where artworks are understood to use specific formal strategies to engage their viewers and reveal things that might otherwise be hidden from view).[2] Central to any theory of how animated documentary shows us the world in any meaningful way is an understanding of the ways in which animation can be said to 'knowingly' represent, or – to use a term that will become important presently – reenact, scenes that are from everyday life or otherwise show us real people or events.[3]

Central to my argument is the ways in which we can understand animated documentary *performatively* (Ward 2011), and then understand the types of emotional engagement that this entails. To this end, I will draw together a number of other people's arguments to propose a new way to think about animated documentary. First of all, I will examine the ways in which animated documentary can be thought through as a type of reenactment, one where the original real people and their actions are reinscribed through animation of various kinds. Any kind of reenactment inflects performance in specific directions, making us think about the relationship of the original action or scene to its reenacted counterpart. But in the case of what I am calling animated reenactment, there is an amplifying of certain performative aspects, complex relationships between the actions we see and hear onscreen and those actions that are 'behind-the-scenes,' namely, those of the animator. Donald Crafton's influential notion of 'performance in' and 'performance of' animation will be important here because it usefully plays upon the tension between these onscreen and off-screen ideas of performance and, crucially, how viewers negotiate and interpret them. It is this set of interrelationships that is pivotal in my discussion because I want to examine how animated documentary communicates ideas and knowledge, and elicits particular types of response from viewers – and the way it does this, I would argue, is through a highly self-conscious foregrounding of the interplay between animat*or* and animat*ed*, with the status of the animated being further complicated by its reenacted relationship vis-à-vis the real world.

This performativity of animated documentary will also be linked to a discussion of some of the ideas of John L. Austin, who argued that certain types of speech act were 'performative' in the sense that the speaker actually *did something*, or *performed an act* by saying what they did. Austin argued that speech acts had different intentions and outcomes – what he variously termed the "illocutionary force" of saying something in a certain way and the "perlocutionary act" that follows on as a consequence once someone has taken up or interpreted what was said in a certain way. My underlying argument is that animated documentary is a very specific type of performative act, so we need to understand animated documentaries by thinking about them performatively. Although some other scholars (Scheibler 1993; Bruzzi 2006) have previously touched upon some of Austin's ideas and the notion of the 'performative' in their discussion of certain (live-action) documentary filmmakers' work, I think there is a nuance to how these concepts function in relation to animated documentary that warrants further discussion.

Threaded through this complex interplay of ideas are assumptions about how viewers 'recognize' the status of what they are looking at and listening to – in other words, the way in which they might be said to 'identify' with something. Murray Smith's work on viewer engagement will be adapted here. Although Smith's sole focus is on live-action, fictional film, and he does not consider animation or animated documentary, his model is useful to help make a conceptual link between the 'work' that viewers do and the performative processes already noted. Insofar as animated documentary is clearly making assertive claims about real people and *the world* of actuality – as opposed to simply 'creating' or 'projecting' *a world* – we need to understand it from a documentary perspective. But, as Annabelle Honess Roe notes in her discussion of Bob Sabiston's animated interview films (something I return to below): "the films are liminal, discursive texts that negotiate tensions between reality and make-believe, observation and interpretation, and presence and absence" (2012: 25). The ways in which animated documentary films play out some of our emotional tensions in relation to how and why we believe (or make-believe) in what we see and hear are the foundation on which the rest of the chapter is built.

Animated Documentary as a Form of 'Reenacted Scene'

As noted above, I propose that one of the more useful ways to understand animated documentary is as a form of *reenactment*. I have written at length elsewhere about this (Ward 2018), but it is worth dwelling on the matter here because it is intimately linked to the arguments I would like to extend about how animated documentary – as a type of communicative act, and as a performative act – has an *emotional* impact on viewers. Steve Fore (2011), one of the few scholars who has previously directly addressed the idea of animated documentary as a form of reenactment, only refers in passing to how such representational strategies might elicit an emotional response from the viewers. However, Fore does clearly identify the foundations on which any such responses are built: in animated documentary, he argues, "the trope of reflexivity is [...] a pre-requisite component of the form" (2011: 288). It is this reflexivity, I will argue, that prompts a very specific type of emotional engagement.

Reenactments are, by definition, a type of communication that self-consciously 'replays' something that has already been 'enacted.' As Jonathan Kahana points out (2009: 53), in one of the more astute discussions of the status of reenactment in documentary, certain forms of enactment require or rest on "a rhetorical or mimetic effect dependent upon another's belief in or reaction to the act-ing in question" – in other words, for something to be "enacted," there has to be someone for whom the enactment *means something*. Enactment, and reenactment after it, are therefore performative, and performances always imply (and rely upon) an audience.

Although the prefix 're-' in 'reenactment' (or the related term used a lot in documentary: 'reconstruction') suggests a simple enough state of affairs – some action that has been repeated – it is clear that there are far deeper nuances. As Bill Nichols has noted about reenactment, it has a 'fantasmatic' power that is predicated on it being "recognised as a representation of a prior event while also signalling that [it is] not a representation of a contemporaneous event" (2008: 73): the temporal shifting implied by that 'recognition' and that 'signaling' underpinning the emotional resonance of reenacted or reconstructed scenes. We are, in effect, folded into the depicted events by their (re)enacted immediacy, while being held at arm's length by the recognition of a temporal schism, or lack of immediacy. The other level of recognition at play is one of the viewers explicitly recognizing that there is a form of performance going on – not simply by 'actors playing a role' in any reenacted scenes (though this may of course be occurring), but also in the sense of the filmmaker performing particular rhetorical (or technical, or aesthetic) maneuvers in order to engage viewers. In order for reenactment to work, there has to be a high level of audience recognition.

Clearly, then, reenactment is not as simple as it might first appear; but the idea of animated documentary being a form of reenactment should give us even more pause and requires that we understand how animation is functioning when trying to communicate something about the real world. Annabelle Honess Roe (2013) usefully proposes a tripartite model for understanding how and why animation might be used in animated documentary: mimetic substitution, nonmimetic substitution, and evocation. All three modes use animation differently in relation to the represented scenes and actions, but each acknowledges that the animation acts as a kind of 'stand-in' or substitute for absent (live-action) footage.[4] In the case of mimetic substitution, the animation acts as a substitute and attempts to *mimic* the look and feel of the real scenario, people, and actions. In the case of nonmimetic substitution, the animation acts a substitute, but makes no attempt at such mimicry (so, for example, real interviewees may be represented as anthropomorphized animals rather than animated humans). With evocation, things are different in the sense that the animation is not being used to *re*present something (either mimetically or nonmimetically) but is rather being used to evoke something that is otherwise impossible to film (for example, a mental state, the texture of a memory, or some other intangible phenomenon). In the case of evocation, then, footage does not exist because the thing-being-evoked is unfilmable in the first place – hence the use of animation.[5]

One interesting variant of animation-as-mimetic-substitution can be seen in Bob Sabiston's Rotoshopped 'interview' films, *Project Incognito* (1997), *Roadhead* (1998), *Snack and Drink* (1999), *Grasshopper* (2003), and *The Even More Fun Trip* (2007), which offer the viewers an animated documentary view of a specific person or group of people. Sabiston's process involves filming the interview/interaction using live-action video, converting the video files, and then using his own Rotoshop program in order to 'animate over' the existing footage (see Ward 2004; Honess Roe 2012; Ruddell 2012). One of the general effects or consequences of rotoscoped animation is an eerie sense for the viewers of being simultaneously in the presence of both the original live-action footage *and* the subsequent animation. This is one of the reasons why 'classical' rotoscoped animation has such a vexed reputation: it is characterized as 'cheating' or 'not proper animation' or as inhibiting the performance and action, but it is in the 'clash' or obvious commingling of live action and animated ontologies that rotoscoping does (or does not) work.

A hitherto underexplored sense of how this very specific form of animation functions is as a reinscribing of a preexisting performance or set of actions, or – to phrase it in terms that make more sense in a discussion of documentary – as a *reenactment*. When we watch *Snack and Drink*, for example, we are seeing an animated version of an encounter between Sabiston and the subject of the documentary, Ryan Power, an encounter that was filmed in live action by Tommy Pallotta and then Rotoshopped by Sabiston and his team of animators.[6] There is a clear sense of the emotional resonance of the film residing, to a great extent, in the way in which this 'on the hoof' encounter (it is actually a bit of a misnomer to call it an 'interview') is flamboyantly reinterpreted by the rotoscoped animation. Indeed, *Snack and Drink* (and some of the other early experiments in Rotoshopped animated documentary) appears to openly revel in the tension or interplay between how the animation can directly resemble what it is representing (i.e., be 'mimetic') and the more imaginative (or 'nonmimetic') flights of fancy in certain scenes, notably the one where Ryan stands at the drink dispenser in the convenience store, and the machine has multiple eyes and waving arms. Arguably, *Snack and Drink* exists in a liminal space that draws together (broadly) mimetic, nonmimetic, and even evocative types of animation (in the sense that it is an animated film that tries to evoke – as well as more straightforwardly show or 'document' – what it is like to have Asperger's syndrome).

Honess Roe (2012) has accurately captured the sense in which Sabiston's animated interviews offer us what she calls an "uncanny index". This is characterized by a paradoxical commingling of absence (of the original interviewee) and an "excessive" presence (of the stylized animation). The 'doubled' type of engagement we see in these Rotoshopped animations – of being simultaneously in the presence of the original encounter/footage *and* its creative reinterpretation or reenactment via animation – is arguably something that manifests itself in how viewers engage with *all* animated documentary. As Honess Roe notes: "Viewers of all animated documentaries find themselves in a strange epistemological and phenomenological position, of knowing that what they hear and see is at once a depiction of reality and a creation by the animator's […] hand" (2012: 27). Underlying any documentary, animated or otherwise, is an *assertive* stance – that is, we view something we *know* to be a documentary through a lens of *knowing* the filmmaker is asserting something about the real world.[7] In essence, then, documentaries are about – and are structured by – (real world) knowledge. They are also about – and are structured by – the act of asserting certain knowledge claims. In the case of animated documentaries, these knowledge claims are filtered or doubly mediated by an additional 'layer' of knowledge: that of 'knowing about,' or at least being 'aware of,' the hand of the animator. As Honess Roe makes clear, this places the viewers in a strange position in terms of the engagement they feel, and this resonates across two poles, what we might call the cognitive/known (or 'epistemological') and the emotional/felt (or 'phenomenological').

In certain key respects, Sabiston's animated documentary films are 'limit cases' that one could argue are not characteristic of the category in general. Due to their obvious live-action basis (i.e., the live-action footage that is subsequently rotoscoped, and that is still eerily 'present' in the films), they have a very particular relationship to the real people and events they are representing. Not all animated documentaries have the same kind of relationship between the actuality (the world) and the creative treatment (the animation), though I would agree with Steve Fore that central to all animated documentaries is the 'reflexive' dimension noted earlier, and it is this that underpins the audience's engagement. Such reflexivity can take various forms. For example, a science-oriented television series like *Walking with Dinosaurs* (Haines 1999) uses photorealistic animation in order to represent the dinosaurs in what we could call a 'scientific best guess' or hypothesis – this is arguably a 'reenactment,' albeit one that is speculatively based on paleontological evidence. Honess Roe, in her discussion of the series (2013: 45–55), notes that the program makers use various techniques to emphasize the authenticity of what is onscreen. She borrows Philip Rosen's term 'markers of indexicality' to highlight the ways in which animated documentaries like *Walking with Dinosaurs* will use certain 'strategies of visual and aural authentication' (camera and editing techniques, for example) to mimic what it would have been like if cameras had been present to film the dinosaurs.[8] The interesting point here is that such 'authenticating' 'markers of indexicality,' in the context of an animated series like *Walking with Dinosaurs*, become part of the repertoire of reflexive strategies that openly draw attention to the 'reenacted' status of the animation. This has the effect of simultaneously *drawing the viewer into* the represented world – by using perceptual cues (see Prince 2012) that make it a highly convincing approximation of the real world – while at the same time *holding the viewer outside* the represented world – by using strategies that clearly signal the constructed nature of the images. In many ways, then, the virtuosity of the animation leads to an emotional engagement that is inherently paradoxical: it both *engages* and *disengages* the viewers in relation to the world and events portrayed.

The Performativity of Animated Documentary: The Performance in/of Animation

Now that we have examined some of the ways in which we can understand some animated documentary films as a form of *reenacted* scene, and the potential complexity of the viewers' response to this, I want to link this to notions of performativity inherent to the reenactment. Donald Crafton's influential work on performance in (and performance of) animation is important here. Crafton asserts:

> The cartoon performance [i.e., performance *in* animation] occurs in the real time and space of exhibition, but the performance *of* animation is a composite phenomenon of mind and material that happens in

a common space to which animators and audiences have read-write access. I call this zone of fascination and fantasy the *Tooniverse*. Paradoxically it inducts and repels us while asserting and disavowing its existence by calling attention to its constructedness.

(Crafton 2013: 22)

Although Crafton's focus, as his use of the term 'Tooniverse' suggests, is almost exclusively on what we might call paradigmatic cases of 'animated cartoons' – i.e., (Hollywood) studio-produced animated shorts – and he does not discuss any examples that one might define as an 'animated documentary,' the underlying conceptual framework of what he is saying about animation as a performative process is something I want to pursue in my discussion of animated documentary and viewer engagement.

Central to this, as already noted, is the fact that the initial 'engagement' is driven by a recognition of the ontological status of the animated images. That is, that they are patently not simple and straightforward recorded footage of the people and events in question, but a frame-by-frame intervention/representation, performed by the animator, that – to echo Crafton again – simultaneously 'inducts and repels us' as viewers. This level of recognition – of the performative dimension of what we are looking at – means that it is necessary to have a more nuanced understanding of how performance functions in animation. Crafton's notion of animation consisting of 'figurative' and 'embodied' performances is important here. Put simply, 'figurative' performances are 'extroverted' and imply a certain 'use' of animation tropes like fantastical transformations or deformations; 'embodied' performances are 'introverted' and imply what we might call 'inner depth' or psychological roundness. 'Embodied' performance is linked to a 'more realistic' sense of character (specifically seen in the shift seen at Disney studios in the late 1930s onward, but by no means limited to 'Disney animation' as a style). What interests me here is the potential tension between these two tendencies and how it manifests in audience engagement with animated documentaries. This is especially interesting in relation to the aforementioned idea of the performance *in* and performance *of* animation. Performance *in* animation seems straightforward enough – the idea of specific characters having performative agency in the animated world. But performance *of* animation does not just simply refer to the animator 'performing' certain actions to get the animated world on the screen, it also refers to the ways in which the audience contributes here, how they take up or emotionally respond to the animated world. In the words of Malcolm Cook, in his review of Crafton's book:

The audience [can be said to perform the animation] in a number of ways: by deploying [...] belief [...] [in the characters and world] during the immediate viewing of an animated film; by bringing to bear historical and cultural specificities in their understanding; by imagining the production of the animated cartoon; by speculating about the onscreen characters beyond the film frame.

(Cook 2013: 305)

This seems to be the crux of the matter – the extent to which viewers 'believe' in what they see on screen and also the ways in which they speculate or imagine things about the characters 'beyond the frame.' In the case of the animated cartoons that Crafton focuses on (i.e., ones that can in no way, shape or form be called animated documentaries), it is true enough (as he argues) that the world, the performance, the characters (and their movement) *only exist at the point of projection.* Crafton quotes Alexander Sesonske: "there is no past time at which these events [in an animation] either did occur or purport to have occurred" (17). Yet this is not simply and straightforwardly the case for animated documentaries: we are experiencing something that *does* really exist (or that *did* really happen) but is being represented (or, to use the term I discuss above: reenacted) via the obvious artifice of animation. The mode of representation (and therefore the mode of engagement) is more complex as a result.[9]

For example, Chris Landreth's celebrated animated documentary *Ryan* (2004), about animator Ryan Larkin, takes the form of an interview, including some flashbacks, between Landreth and Larkin. Although the two animated characters clearly resemble the two real men, the animation falls into what Landreth has termed "psychorealism," where certain elements of the visual design are exaggerated to signify mental or psychological damage. These are in fact real people but represented via animated characters or artifacts. But it is the way in which the character performances in *Ryan* walk a tightrope between Crafton's notions of 'figurative' and 'embodied' performance that is really interesting. For, there's a sense that *Ryan*, as an animated documentary, offers us a 'dialogue' between the idea of 'extroverted'/figurative animation and 'introverted'/embodied animation: for example, the exaggerated head-half-missing designs of the characters can arguably be seen as an extroverted and figuratively stylized use of animated performance; at the same time, such flamboyant technique affords us as viewers an insight into the psychological make-up of these real people. In short, the animation 'embodies' them in performance terms, and anchors them as real people. This 'dialogue' between the 'figurative' and the 'embodied' therefore highlights the complexity of what happens when we, as viewers, engage with such an animated film.

One of the complications underpinning animated documentary and the response elicited from viewers is fundamentally based on how viewers recognize the ontological status of what they are seeing and hearing.

In the case of *Ryan*, the dissonance caused by the meeting (or clash) of two different categories – animation and documentary – is amplified by a kind of 'ontological uncertainty' or ambivalence. I have already argued that this is something that is an essential part of all animated documentary. There is a deliberate 'playing out' of the differences between the 'animated' and 'documentary' modes, something which is built on how artifacts are presented to us, to use Noel Carroll's term, 'indexed' beforehand (2003b: 169–70). As Carroll argues, we do not usually watch something and need to determine what kind of film it is while watching it – we come to it 'primed' by other discourses that contribute to the 'indexing' of the film before the act of watching it. So, we watch certain films with a 'fictive' stance – we 'already know' that we are meant to take them up as fictions. Similarly, we watch certain other films with an 'assertive' stance – these films are indexed in a way that means we understand we are meant to view them as asserting things about the real world, i.e., as documentaries. Clearly, there are some films that exist at what we might call the 'meeting point' of different 'stances' – the various forms of dramatized documentary, for example – and others that deliberately 'miscue' the viewers into believing they are watching one type of film when it is actually another. The important thing is that any of these stances – and the confusion deliberately engendered by such 'miscuing' – are based on indexing and recognition of prior cultural categories. In the case of animated documentary, though, I think something more pronounced is taking place because there is a deliberate foregrounding of animation as a performative process. This is where the audience can also be said to be contributing, by "imagining the production," to use Cook's phrasing again – as previously argued, the manifest 'constructedness' of animation means that reflecting in this way (a form of 'wondering how it was done') is fundamental to the form.

The Performativity of Animated Documentary: The 'Illocutionary Force' and 'Perlocutionary Act'

The idea of animated documentary as a *performed re-enactment*, as a specific kind of expressive act, is something I would now like to connect to a discussion of philosopher and linguist John L. Austin's concepts of the 'illocutionary' and the 'perlocutionary' in his 'performative' (or 'speech act') theory of language. Austin's initial thinking (in the lecture series that went on to be published as his 1962 book *How to Do Things with Words*) was around a distinction between what he called 'constative' and 'performative' utterances. Constative utterances simply describe (or 'constate') a thing or state of affairs; they assert something that can be said to be either true or false (a common example given is "The cat is on the mat"). Performative utterances, by contrast, do not simply describe something, they actually constitute the performing of an action in making the utterance (common examples here are statements such as "I name this ship..." or "You're fired"). According to Chantelle Warner, performative utterances "not only... describe a given reality, [they] actively change the social reality that they are describing" (2014: 365).

The illocutionary and perlocutionary elements of a speech act, terms that Austin developed later in the lecture series, are concerned with intention and effect: they point not only to what something *means* but also, crucially, to what you mean *by saying it* (in the way that you do) and the *consequences or outcomes* of saying it in that way. I would argue that animated documentary's power, and its ability to elicit a particular (albeit complex and paradoxical) emotional response, can therefore be more deeply understood by thinking about it in relation to these 'performative' and 'speech act' concepts. This is not to say that animated documentary *is* a form of 'speech act,' but that we can develop our understanding of *how* animated documentaries communicate and evoke emotions by reference to these theories. Central to the deeper understanding of animated documentary proposed by this chapter, therefore, is an interrogation of how the emotional 'charge' of viewing something we know to be real-yet-fabricated is underpinned by a series of paradoxes that are built on performance, belief, emotion, and affect.

In her book *New Documentary: A Critical Introduction*, Stella Bruzzi adapts elements of Austin's thinking and notes:

> [T]he performative documentary [...] – whether built around the intrusive presence of the filmmaker or self-conscious performances by its subjects – is the enactment of the notion that a documentary only comes into being as it is performed [...] although its factual basis (or document) can pre-date any recording or representation of it, the film itself is necessarily performative because it is given meaning by the interaction between performance and reality.
>
> (Bruzzi 2000: 154)

Susan Scheibler also discusses Austin's concepts in relation to documentary, when she talks about how the constative and the performative have different relationships to the reality with which they engage. According to Scheibler, when thinking about these terms in relation to an audiovisual form like documentary, the constative needs to be "defined by its dependence on a belief in the possibility of a knowledge that is able to guarantee the actuality and presence, the facticity, of its observations and remarks" (1993: 139) – in other words, it would appear to be simple, straightforward, descriptive, and referential to an externally verifiable state of affairs. The constative is concerned with "authenticity and authority" (ibid.). The performative in documentary, on the other hand, "demystifies the illusion that the thing at stake is truth or falsity

[and] [...] confront[s] the constative with its own assumptions of author-ity, authenticity, veracity, verifiability" (ibid.: 140). Scheibler also quotes Austin, when noting that the performative functions "not to inform or to describe but to carry out a performance, to accomplish an act through the very process of its enunciation" (ibid.).

As previously argued, animated documentary's harnessing of the viewers' emotional responses is fundamentally linked to how the per-formance of the animator, in 'reenacting' the real scene, is recognized *as a specific type of action*. The self-conscious inscription of process, the 'drawing-attention-to' that ensues when watching an animated documentary, can therefore be better understood by thinking about it through the lens of Austin's notion of 'performative' language, 'illo-cutionary force,' and 'perlocutionary' acts. In discussing illocutionary force and how it functions, Oliver Burkeman gives the following every-day example: you arrive home, say hello to your partner, look around the messy room and state, entirely factually and apparently descriptively, "It's untidy in here." Burkeman explains:

> "It's untidy in here" may *describe* the situation accurately. But my *intention* – the "illocutionary force", in Austin's jargon – is to try to make you feel bad, or get you to tidy up. On one hand, there's what the sentence *means*; on the other, there's what you *mean by saying it*.

As Yan Huang points out in *The Oxford Dictionary of Pragmatics*, "[t]he illocutionary force of a speech act is the effect a speech act is intended to have by a speaker" (2012: 147). Now, the *intended* effect, what is *meant* by the speaker, does not *automatically equate* with what the person listening takes (or mistakes) the speech act to mean.

When it comes to the relationship between the illocutionary force of a statement and the perlocutionary act that follows as a consequence, a useful example and commentary appears in Garren Hochstetler's blog "Words, Ideas, and Things":

JOHN: "Darling, do you want to go out to the show tonight?"
LAURA: "I'm feeling ill."
JOHN: "That's ok. You stay there and I'll make soup."

> Notice how Laura *didn't* respond to John's question by saying, "No, I don't want to go out to the show tonight." What she actu-ally said – her locutionary act – was "I'm feeling ill." An illocution-ary act is what a person does *in saying* something else. Locution is speech. In-locution (in speaking) becomes il-locution through pho-netic assimilation. In saying that she feels ill, Laura was telling John that she doesn't want go out. Beyond communicating the state of her health and the answer to John's question, Laura accomplished

one more thing *through saying* "I'm feeling ill." She got John to make her some soup. A perlocutionary act (per-locutionary, through speaking) is focused on the response others have to a speech act.[10]

In many ways, then, my central concern here is with the *perlocutionary* aspect of how animated documentary functions: in other words, the ways in which a specific type of communicative act – using animation, with all of its performative complexity, to 'document' something – emotionally engages the viewers and elicits a certain kind of response. Annette Hill has talked about documentary 'modes of engagement' and how viewers will "draw on the referential integrity and the aesthetic value of documentary at the same time" (2008: 226). On one level, this is merely a restating of John Grierson's famous definition of documentary as "the creative treatment of actuality" (Grierson 1933: 8), where documentaries (including those that are animated) are a fine and somewhat precarious balance between realism (or referential integrity) and artistry (or aesthetic value). I have written elsewhere (2011) about the phenomenological experience viewers might have when encountering an animated world they know not to exist – a form of the 'paradox of fiction' first written about by Colin Radford (1975). The question then is how might this phenomenological engagement be modified when viewers are experiencing a 'paradox of *non*fiction' – which is to say, a *real world* that we know exists (or exist*ed*) in some shape or form but not in the (animated) form in which we are directly experiencing it at that moment? There is a strange complexity to how viewers emotionally identify with these sorts of worlds, one structured by the tensions implied in what Hill says about documentary modes of engagement.

Animated Documentary, Engagement, and Emotion

Underlying my argument in this chapter is a really very simple question: how do animated documentaries *engage* their viewers? Another way of putting this is to ask: how might animated documentaries elicit an emotional response from an audience member? What I am interested in is identifying some of the ways in which aspects of the audience's emotional response might be *specific to or qualitatively different for* animated forms, due to the ways in which animation orients viewers in particular ways. Simply put, if we are engaged by drawings, computer graphics, puppets, or other things we know not to have a straightforwardly real world existence,[11] then in some ways this is a strange form of engagement. Furthermore, it is an *even stranger form of engagement* when the animation is asking us to engage (emotionally, politically, conceptually) with something in the *real world* (a theme, an issue, a real person's story) – i.e., when we are talking about *animated documentary*. All animation cues us in particular ways, to see things as a specific kind of constructed or enunciative act (see Chapter 2) and this is amplified when the animation is representing real people and real situations. As noted above, a useful concept for understanding how viewers engage emotionally with animation is the 'paradox of fiction' – clearly, we are conditioned as viewers to be able to empathize with characters and events that we know are fictional. It is likewise true that we are cued to emotionally connect with a range of nonhuman, anthropomorphized characters; so much so, in fact, that what I am calling a 'strange form of engagement' could be said to be not so strange after all. This complex range of responses is something Carl Plantinga summarizes well when he notes:

> [f]ictions [...] generate affective and emotional responses independent of belief, while at the same time eliciting higher-order cognitive and emotional responses that prevent viewers from responding as though the fictions were actual events.
>
> (Plantinga 2009: 66)

It seems to me that animated documentary as a form problematizes this in some very interesting ways. Due to the *asserted* nature of what is said/shown in an animated documentary (in other words, the events are proposed to have *actually* happened), the affective and emotional responses cannot therefore be 'independent of belief': we have to believe in them.[12] Yet, at the same time, the 'higher-order cognitive and emotional responses' that Plantinga refers to are also in operation – but in relation to animated documentary, they are not there to prevent us responding 'inappropriately' (i.e., to fictions as if they were actual) but are really working in recognition of the animatedness, the constructedness, which is an important part of the performative nature and perlocutionary force of the form.

Plantinga argues "emotions [...] [are] mental states that are often accompanied by subjective feelings, psychological arousal, and action tendencies" (2009: 55). He borrows Robert C. Roberts' term "concern-based construals" to further define emotions – noting on the one hand that "to construe" something does not necessarily mean to reflect upon or carefully consider (so they can be based on *impressions* and how things *immediately appear* to someone, rather than a rationalized position) and on the other hand that "concern" means that such mental activity is directed toward an object or a desired outcome. Emotions, as Plantinga argues, are *intentional* mental states, they are directed toward something. Clearly, documentaries, animated or otherwise, can evoke emotional responses from their audiences, such as anger, sadness, or sympathy, but my focus is more broadly on how animated documentaries orient their viewers to the knowledge they represent. The "emotional response," in this sense, is more to do with how viewers "take up" and understand the animation in relation to the real world events and people.

For some people, this might seem less to do with *emotion* per se and more to do with a *cognitive act*, an act of intellection where someone "thinks through" their viewing experience. As Plantinga notes, though, emotions are far from clear-cut phenomena and come accompanied by other feelings. The way in which viewers take up animated documentary material is a far-from-simple cognitive process and it is the paradoxical and conflicting thought processes and stances that characterize how we engage with this vibrant field – thought processes that are driven by the performative aspects of animation discussed earlier.

Murray Smith's discussion of how (fictional) characters in films 'engage' viewers – how we can be said to 'identify' with them in the course of the narrative – is a useful reference point here. However, we have to think carefully about how well Smith's model – devised for fictional (live-action?) films – works in relation to nonfictional (animated) films. What does it actually mean to 'identify' with a real person, talking about real things, but in an animated world? Smith usefully distinguishes between three levels of complexity in what is commonly called 'identification' with a character: 'recognition,' 'alignment,' and 'allegiance.'[13] Simply put: 'recognition' is when we can discern a specific presence, e.g., a 'main character' in a film, or when we 'recognize' people at a straightforward phenomenological level; 'alignment' is when the film gives us a form of 'access' to the character, e.g., via editing or dialogue or other elements, we are made aware of a character's subjective state; and 'allegiance' is when the film encourages us to emotionally engage with a character through a moral evaluation of their actions and outlook (though not necessarily to 'take their side' in what they say and do or, indeed, simply 'feel what they are shown to be feeling'). Smith's concepts of 'recognition,' 'alignment,' and 'allegiance' (instead of, simply, 'identification') are therefore a useful intervention in understanding viewers' relationships with – and emotional attachments to – *fictional characters and scenarios*. But how might they help us in understanding *nonfictional* (and, further, *animated documentary*) scenarios? There have been some recent attempts to apply Smith's schema to nonfictional films (see Ayisi and Brylla, 2013; Canet and Perez, 2016), but no one, to my knowledge, has examined how audience engagement (what Smith calls the 'structure of sympathy') functions in relation to animated documentary.

Fernando Canet and Hector Perez (2016) have applied Smith's concepts to their reading of documentary – their focus is on how the *documentary filmmaker* engages with their subject (either explicitly onscreen as part of the documentary process, or implicitly in the way they orient themselves to their subject matter). For them, it is this engagement which structures how viewers will respond. At one point, they quote celebrated ethnographic filmmaker David MacDougall I: "[f]ilming […] produces an object in which the filmmaker's interaction with the film subject is explicitly inscribed" (1998: 56 [page 217 in Canet and Perez]). Animation is of course a mode of production where the animator's "interaction" with their subject is "explicitly inscribed," frame-by-frame, and MacDougal's point in many ways echoes some of the tenets of Crafton's arguments about the performance in/performance of animation.

If we return for a moment to Landreth's *Ryan* as an example, we can see that Smith's schema is complicated by the animated form. 'Recognition' arguably functions in a similar way to that outlined by Smith, in the sense that we are cued to understand who the main characters are (and clearly, it obviously helps that, for much of its duration, *Ryan* is a two-way conversation between Larkin and Landreth). However, Smith notes of recognition that it is structured around the "spectator's construction of the character: the perception of a set of textual elements, in film typically cohering around the image of a body, as an individuated and continuous human agent" (Smith: 82). The peculiar 'damaged' aesthetic of *Ryan* problematizes this notion of 'coherent' embodiment, especially the idea of the real people in the film being 'individuated and continuous human agent[s].' The alignment in the film is similarly skewed by the ways in which animation enables bizarre flights of fancy and also how we, as viewers, are aligned to both the animated characters *and* the animator (in *Ryan*'s case, there is a further layer of complexity by an animated version of Landreth appearing in his own film). Clearly, we are meant to be emotionally engaged by Larkin (and Landreth) in the film, but our alignment (in Smith's specific meaning of that term), in terms of access to someone's subjective state, is clearly and explicitly 'filtered' via Landreth-as-animator. The 'mode of engagement,' to use Hill's term again, is one that we are conscious of as a kind of performative reenactment by Landreth, as he is 'inscribed' in every frame as well as in every design decision relating to the characters and layouts. Allegiance is something else again: it is not simply a case of us feeling what Larkin or Landreth are feeling, but of us understanding (and evaluating) what they are feeling (and saying) and responding accordingly. So, Larkin's evident struggles with drugs and alcohol might make him feel angry or despondent; our response as viewers might well be pity, sorrow, or empathy, or some other form of moral judgment. However, there is also the strange feeling we have in knowing about Landreth-as-animator: the illocutionary force in representing Larkin (and himself) in the way that he does is linked to his intention to elicit a certain response from the viewers. Of course, this could be said of any artist: They want to elicit a response. But I would argue that the animation complicates the emotional resonance felt by the viewers, due to the complex and overlapping commingling of the actual and the artificial.

I write elsewhere (2018) about Dennis Stein-Schomburg's film *Andersartig* (2011) and the fantasmatic nature of the kind of animated reimagining of actual events we see in that film. It tells the true story of a young girl (now an old woman, reflecting back on the past) who survived a bombing raid on an orphanage during World War II, a raid in which all of the other children were killed. Toward the film's conclusion, we see a representation of a (rotoscoped) photograph, showing the group of children, posed as if for the proverbial 'class photo.' All of the figures in the image gradually fade away, leaving just one girl: our narrator. In the case of the animated photograph in *Andersartig* one could argue: (1) it represents a *specific* photograph that actually exists[14]; (2) it symbolizes the trauma of a *particular event*; (3) it perfectly captures both the *indelibility* and *fleetingness* of memory; and (4) it embodies all that is powerful and unique about animation's ability to represent the real world. It is not just *showing* us something – a straightforward fact, this thing that happened during WWII – but it has the intention of making us *think and feel* about that something and the *way* in which it has been communicated to us. Carla Mackinnon (forthcoming) writes astutely about a very different type of film, the short student animation *Model Childhood* (Mercier 2017). The film is concerned with the director's abuse as a child, using a heightened, performative approach to stop motion where the puppet character (Mercier-as-child) sometimes enters into a self-conscious dialogue with Mercier-as-director. It is obvious that this animated documentary is reflexively mobilizing reconstruction and re-enactment of past events, but it is not simply trying to 'show us the past'; it is a performative process, a catharsis for the director, and an attempt to actively intervene and change the (perception of the) reality being represented. The emotional range and complexity of viewer engagement demonstrates the power that animated documentary can wield, but also shows that in order to understand the form, we need to fully engage with theories of performance, the idea of (animated) language as 'performative,' and the emotional resonances and paradoxes that can stem from animation's attempts to represent the real world.

Conclusion

The ways in which we can talk about animation as a communicative act are inherently linked to its explicitness, its constructedness, the fact that (so to speak) everything that is stated in animation comes with the unavoidable 'speech marks' around it. In short, we cannot avoid or miss the intervention of the animator(s) and the role they play in communicating to us. I have argued in this chapter that focusing on such constructedness helps us to understand animated documentary, but only if we see it in the light of theories of performance and how animation can itself be seen as a performative process. This, in turn, needs to be linked to the idea of the performative in language – the ways in which certain forms of communication do not merely (con)state or describe something, but they actually *do* something. And, in doing something, they elicit a specific form of engagement or emotional response – one that is inextricably linked to a recognition of the doubled nature of animated documentary as a form of representation.

Acknowledgment

The author would like to thank Annabelle Honess Roe for her very helpful comments on a draft of this chapter.

Notes

1 Within the term "animated documentary," we can or should see tendencies and nuances: a sense that it potentially covers a huge and slippery area where anything perceived to be "animated" meets anything that might be perceived to be "documentary," thus: documentaries that are completely animated; live action documentary films that contain animated scenes; animated films that have some sort of documentary tone or intention, but may be addressing related (and complex) areas such as memory, trauma, and personal identity. All of these could fall under this elastic term – though we might then more properly come up with (subtly) different but related terms such as "documentary animation" or "documentary with animation," or even neologisms such as "documation" or "animdocs." What all of these have in common is an attempt to communicate something about the *real world*, but they do so via animated images – frame by frame, manipulated moving images of whatever kind.
2 On the 'realist' side, see, for example, the work of André Bazin (1967/1971) or Siegfried Kracauer (1960); on the 'formalist' side, see, for example, the work of Berthold Brecht (summarized in Silberman, 2009) or debates outlined in Lovell (1980). For an intriguing attempt to reconcile these 'poles' of thinking, see Singer (1998).
3 The chapter will not directly deal with intriguing areas such as those discussed by Cristina Formenti (2014), who talks about animated *mockumentary* as a variant of what happens when the discourses of animation and documentary meet.
4 There will, of course, be varying reasons for the absence or nonuse of the live-action footage. Footage may exist but could not be used for whatever reason; there may be no footage for historical reasons; or there may be no footage because the phenomenon in question is impossible to film.
5 We might more accurately think of evocation in this context as a form of *enactment* rather than *reenactment* – the animation is not an attempt to *re*present some preexisting state of affairs (an encounter, event, interview, etc.) but rather an attempt to give form to something that is otherwise unrepresentable.
6 See Ward (2006) for a more detailed discussion of this specific film.
7 Noel Carroll (2003a) uses the term "film of presumptive assertion" instead of "documentary."
8 In a different context (discussing live action drama documentary) Steven Lipkin refers to 'warranting procedures,' where specific strategies will attest to the fact (or 'warrant') that what we are seeing did actually happen (key examples here are the use of actual locations, casting (some) real people, or use of official records like court transcripts).
9 Clearly, characters and scenarios represented in *animated* documentaries also do not exist in and of themselves until the *animation* is projected. But

there is a real-world basis for the events and characters – they are of 'the world' of actuality rather than 'a world' of fiction, and crucially viewers are (invariably) aware of this.
10 http://wordsideasandthings.blogspot.co.uk/2011/09/lingo-locutionary-illocutionary-and.html [accessed 12 December 2017].
11 Clearly, puppets exist in the real world, but their movement does not.
12 Or, alternatively, we might choose to *not believe* in them, but by so doing we would not be making any argument about the animation's ability to make truth claims; we would instead be concluding something very specific about the documentarist – namely, that they are incorrect or lying.
13 Smith's model is expressly critical of psychoanalytical approaches to understanding viewer engagement with filmic characters. In psychoanalysis, the term 'identification' has a very specific meaning – in many ways, Smith's breaking down of 'identification' into 'recognition,' 'alignment,' and 'allegiance' is indicative of his stance toward psychoanalysis.
14 On speaking with the director, he confirmed that the photograph is actually a dramatic device, a piece of poetic license on his part, and is not a reference to an actual photograph which he subsequently rotoscoped/animated.

References

Austin, John. L. *How to Do Things with Words*. Oxford: Clarendon Press, 1962.
Ayisi, Florence and Catalin Brylla. "The Politics of Representation and Audience Reception: Alternatives Visions of Africa." *Research in African Literatures – Visibility in African Cultures*, 44 (2), 2013: 125–141.
Bazin, André. *What Is Cinema?* (vols. 1 and 2). Berkeley: University of California Press, 1967/1971.
Bruzzi, Stella. *New Documentary: A Critical Introduction*. London/New York: Routledge, 2000.
Burkeman, Oliver. "How to Pick (and Stop) an Argument." *The Guardian*, February 16, 2016: https://theguardian.com/lifeandstyle/2016/feb/19/how-to-pick-and-stop-an-argument-oliver-burkeman (18.07.2016).
Canet, Fernando and Héctor Perez. "Character Engagement as Central to the Filmmaker–Subject Relationship: *En Construcción* (José Luis Guerin, 2001) as a Case Study." *Studies in Documentary Film*, 10(3), 2016: 215–232.
Carroll, Noel. "Fiction, Nonfiction, and the Film of Presumptive Assertion: Conceptual Analyses." In: Carroll, Noel (Ed.). *Engaging the Moving Image*. New Haven/London: Yale University Press, 2003a.
——— "Nonfiction Film and Postmodernist Skepticism." In: Carroll, Noel (Ed.). *Engaging the Moving Image*. New Haven/London: Yale University Press, 2003b.
Cook, Malcolm. "Book Review: Shadow of a Mouse: Performance, Belief, and World-Making in Animation by Donald Crafton." *animation: an interdisciplinary journal*, 8(3), 2013.
Crafton, Donald. *Shadow of a Mouse: Performance, Belief, and World-Making in Animation*. Berkeley: University of California Press, 2013.
Fore, Steve. "Reenacting Ryan: The Fantasmatic and the Animated Documentary." *animation: an interdisciplinary journal*, 6(3) 2011: 277–292.
Formenti, Cristina. "When Imaginary Cartoon Worlds Get the 'Documentary Look': Understanding Mockumentary Through Its Animated Variant."

102   *Paul Ward*

Alphaville: Journal of Film and Screen Media, 8, 2014: www.alphavillejournal. com/Issue8.html (12.01.2018).
Grierson, John. "The Documentary Producer." *Cinema Quarterly*, 2(1), 1933: 7–9.
Hill, Annette. "Documentary Modes of Engagement." In: Austen, Thomas and Wilma De Jong (Eds.). *Rethinking Documentary: New Perspectives, New Practices*. New York: Open University Press, 2008: 217–231.
Hochstetler, Garren. "Lingo: Locutionary, Illocutionary, and Perlocutionary Acts." *Words, Ideas and Things* [blog]. 2011: http://wordsideasand things.blogspot.co.uk/2011/09/lingo-locutionary-illocutionary-and.html (12.12.2017).
Honess Roe, Annabelle. "Uncanny Indexes: Rotoshopped Interviews as Documentary," *animation: an interdisciplinary journal*, 7(1), 2012.: 25–37.
—— *Animated Documentary*. New York: Palgrave Macmillan, 2013.
Huang, Yan. *The Oxford Dictionary of Pragmatics*. Oxford: Oxford University Press, 2012.
Kahana, Jonathan. "Introduction: What Now? Presenting Reenactment." *Framework*, 50(1&2), 2009: 46–60.
Kracauer, Siegfried. *Theory of Film: The Redemption of Physical Reality*. Princeton: Princeton University Press, 1997 [1960].
Lovell, Terry. *Pictures of Reality: Aesthetics, Politics and Pleasure*. London: BFI, 1980.
MacDougall, David. *Transcultural Cinema*. Princeton: Princeton University Press, 1998.
Mackinnon, Carla. "Autobiography and Authenticity in Stop-Motion Animation." In: Ruddell, Caroline and Paul Ward (Eds.). *The Crafty Animator*. Palgrave (forthcoming).
Nichols, Bill. "Documentary Reenactment and the Fantasmatic Subject." *Critical Inquiry*, 35(1), 2008.
Plantinga, Carl. *Moving Viewers: American Film and the Spectator's Experience*. Berkeley: University of California Press, 2009.
Prince, Stephen. *Digital Visual Effects in Cinema: The Seduction of Reality*. New Brunswick: Rutgers University Press, 2012.
Radford, Colin. "How Can We Be Moved by the Fate of Anna Karenina?" *Aristotelian Society Supplementary*, 49, 1975: 67–93.
Ruddell, Caroline. "'Don't Box Me In': Blurred Lines in *Waking Life* and *A Scanner Darkly*." *animation: an interdisciplinary journal*, 7(1), 2012.: 7–23.
Scheibler, Susan. "Constantly Performing the Documentary: The Seductive Promise of *Lightning over Water*." In: Renov, Michael (Ed.). *Theorizing Documentary*. New York/London: Routledge, 1993.
Silberman, Marc. "Brecht, Realism and the Media." In: Nagib, Lucia and Cecília Mello (Eds.). *Realism and the Audio-Visual Media*. New York: Palgrave Macmillan, 2009.
Singer, Irving. *Reality Transformed: Film as Meaning and Technique*. Cambridge: MIT Press, 1998.
Smith, Murray. *Engaging Characters: Fiction, Emotion, and the Cinema*. Oxford: Oxford University Press, 1995.
Ward, Paul. "'Rotoshop' in Context: Computer Rotoscoping and Animation Aesthetics." *animation journal*, 12, 2004: 32–52.

——— "Animated Interactions: Animation Aesthetics and the 'Interactive' Documentary." In: Buchan, Suzanne (Ed.) with David Surman and Paul Ward (Associate Eds.). *Animated 'Worlds'*. Eastleigh: John Libbey, 2006: 113–129.

——— "Animating with Facts: The Performative Process of Documentary Animation in *The Ten Mark* (2010)." *animation: an interdisciplinary journal*, 6(3), 2011.: 293–305.

——— "Animated Documentary, Recollection, 'Re-Enactment' and Temporality." In: Murray, Jonathan and Nea Ehrlich (Eds.). *Drawn From Life*. Edinburgh: Edinburgh University Press, 2018.

Warner, Chantelle. "Literary Pragmatics and Stylistics." In: Burke, Michael (Ed.). *The Routledge Handbook of Stylistics*. Abingdon/New York: Routledge, 2014.

Wells, Paul. "'Perfect Bridge over the Crocodiles': Tacit Contracts, Listen Thieves, and Emotional Labour in the Animated FAGO." In: Uhrig, Meike (Ed.). *Emotion in Animated Films*. London/New York: Routledge, 2019.

Films & TV Series

Andersartig [Different.] Directed by Dennis Stein-Schomburg. 2011; DE: Ocean Pictures Filmproduktion.

The Even More Fun Trip. Directed by Bob Sabiston. 2007; USA: Flat Black Films.

Grasshopper. Directed by Bob Sabiston. 2003; USA: Flat Black Films.

Model Childhood. Directed by Timothy Mercier. 2017.

Project Incognito. Directed by Bob Sabiston. 1997; USA: MTV.

Roadhead. Directed by Bob Sabiston. 1998; USA: Flat Black Films.

Ryan. Directed by Chris Landreth. 2004; CAN: Copperheart Entertainment, NFB, Seneca Collage/Canada Council for the Arts.

Snack and Drink. Directed by Bob Sabiston. 1999; USA: Flat Black Films.

Walking with Dinosaurs: UK 1999, BBC, created by Tim Haines.

Part IV
Diegesis and Formal Features

Worlds and Characters

6 Aesthetics and Psychology of Animated Films

Torben Grodal

Animated films and photographed films share the same platforms, cinema and TV, and appeal to the same senses, vision and hearing, and only indirectly to the other senses via synesthesia. However, the history of their aesthetic background is very different. The aesthetic default mode of photographed films has been to be copies of the exterior world in the Bazinian sense of being a photographic imprint of reality (Bazin 1967). In contrast, the aesthetic default mode of the aesthetics of animated films is based on ways in which the brain may process the visual world and imagine real or possible worlds. This mode is inherited from a long history of drawing and painting that often perform a radical abstraction of the physical world. This process of abstraction we know very well from children's early paintings where, for example, a human is portrayed in outline with a circle for the head, points for the eyes, a line for the mouth, and lines for the arms and feet.

Such drawings of a person are somewhat similar to a simplified version of Jack Skellington in *The Nightmare Before Christmas* (Burton 1993) or the sculptures of Giacometti. The simplicity of such drawings should not fool us into thinking that they are easy to make, that such a simple representation of a human being is made on the basis of how children see the world at birth. On the contrary, such drawings are the result of several years of cognitive processing of the complex input of the world in order to extract the essentials and of linking these to the motor skills of drawing. You may even call this process of being able to draw a human being by dots and lines showing eyes, mouth, and a circle for the outline of the face an extraction of 'platonic ideas' of the essence of the phenomenon 'human face' based on the ever-fluctuating visual inputs from the exterior world. It demands that the child reduces the millions and millions of inputs from the eyes into much simpler representations – templates and schemata – of figures.

Such templates and schemata are in principle 'nonconscious,' invisible brain structures that only with language get perceptual forms by sounds or letters ('man,' 'fish,' 'tree,' 'leg,' 'arm,' 'head'). Schemata are radical complexity reductions of, for example, the hundreds of variations of what a dog or a human being looks like, for instance, regarding the rich variation of texture, size, color, into prototypes. The neurologist Semir Zeki has (in 1999) described this as representing 'constancy.' This reduction implies that such prototypical reductions are easy to perceive and thus provide such drawings with what you might call *schematic salience* and *perceptual fluency* so that the figures – due to the ease of perception – pop out of space into the eyes of the beholders. The ease is supported by the way in which the drawings fully control the figure-ground relations. Further, prototypicality is linked to aesthetic beauty (cf. Langlois and Roggman 1990). The image of Snow White, for example, is prototypical; it has a strong complexity reduction, the skin being a smooth and nearly invisible background for eyes, eyebrows, and mouth.

Linked to complexity reduction by prototypicality is another central aesthetic mechanism that the neuropsychologists Ramachandran and Hirstein (1999) call peak shift mechanisms but that I might just call *exaggeration*. The basis for exaggeration is to transform a prototype of a given figure, such as a given person, by exaggerating those features that are distinctive for the given figure. Ramachandran and Hirstein have argued that caricatures of a person are easier to recognize than an uncaricatured, unexaggerated representation. Animated films rely extensively on exaggeration. For example, you may take a prototypical man and/or woman and then exaggerate those features that distinguish them from each other. In *The Incredibles* (Bird 2004), Mr. Incredible has a strongly exaggerated maleness with extreme broad shoulders and tiny feet so that his body resembles an inverted triangle (and an ultra-big chin), whereas his wife, Elastigirl, has an exaggerated hip-to-waist ratio and her smaller muscularity is shown by an exaggerated elasticity. Peak-shift exaggeration provides, as argued by (Ramachandran and Hirstein 1999), salience and perceptual fluency because the brain tags a given object or person with information about the significant deviant aspects of a given object from the prototype – like the prototype man and a deviation man or a deviation woman, or a man with an extra-large nose – to distinguish the object or person from other members of the group.

Exaggeration in Animated Body Language

The disposition for caricature is, so to speak, a built-in feature of the brain. Humans are extremely social animals, and therefore those brain areas that process one's face and body as well as those of other people take up a significant part of the brain. In psychology, there is a concept called the homunculus – the little man – that expresses how much processing space the different parts of the human body take up in the brain in the so-called somatosensory cortex. Figure 6.1 (left) is one of those illustrations that you may find on the net when searching for 'homunculus image' and represent the space allocated to the different body parts in the so-called somatosensory cortex that, as discussed later, is also linked

Figure 6.1 A drawing of homunculus (left) emphasizes the face and hands, just as Mickey Mouse (middle); in Mike Wazowski (right), the face has even cannibalized the body (©Disney/Pixar).

to areas for social intelligence in the temporoparietal cortex. Not all parts of the body are equally important for the brain: The face and especially the eyes, mouth, and tongue are enormously interesting, and so are the hands, because those parts of the body are vital for the expression of intentions and emotions and for the interaction with the environment. These parts of the body are therefore represented by relatively large areas of the brain. In contrast, the body and legs are represented in diminutive forms, nearly as a copy of a stick figure. The similarity to Mickey Mouse (middle) and other cartoon figures is clear except for Mickey's large feet: Head, eyes, and mouth are disproportionately large. In some versions of Mickey, the two eyes fill out nearly the entire upper face. The central body of Mickey is not that much bigger than the head; the hands are big, the arms and legs thin. Thus, the figure does not only have extreme neonate proportions (small children have much larger heads relative to the body than grown-ups) but the exaggerations and disproportions match the priorities of the brain and thus make Mickey and similar animated figures ultra-salient. However, in contrast to the homunculus (and Mr. Incredible), also Mickey's feet are large. An extreme case of face dominance is Mike Wazowski (right) from *Monsters, Inc.* (Docter and Silverman 2001) for whom the face has 'cannibalized' the body so that he is a face-body with thin arms and legs. Other animated figures may, however, have more 'realistic' proportions between head and body. Thus, Shrek has a very salient head with very expressive eyes and mouth, but he also has a bulky body to support an impression of physical power. Because of the normal exaggeration of the head compared to the body that underline animation and intentionality, an exaggeration of the body mass will become more significant and express a dominance by the 'non-animated' mass.

The 'homunculus' exaggerations in the brain are partly based on the importance of controlling these areas for a given individual, but for ultra-social animals like humans, the prominence of eyes, mouth, and hands are also – via mirror neurons that mirror the facial expressions and body movements of others (cf. Keysers 2011) – of vital importance for our perception of others. Eyes and mouth are so all-important in the basic understanding of humanness and agency that they may be projected even into artifact objects such as *Wall·E* or the cars in *Cars* (Lasseter and Ranft 2006).

The portrayal of body language in animated films is thus based on exaggeration and complexity reduction. Facial expressions (in combination with situational context) have first priority, focusing on the eyes and mouth and the surrounding muscles that are important for expressing emotions. Eyes are mostly enlarged, and their expressive qualities are emphasized by an excessive use of white sclera (that in real life is a human prerogative evolved through evolution to facilitate understanding of other people's eye direction and attention by contrasting the pupil/iris with its white surrounding (cf. Kobayashi and Kohshima 2001; Tomasello et al. 2007). White sclera is non-existent in animals other than humans, except of course, when drawn in animated films because here nearly all animals have white sclera for expressivity. Eyes may often make up a quite exaggerated part of the face and of the narrative space. The animated figure of Fear in *Inside Out* (Docter and del Carmen 2015) even has eyes that stand out of the tiny head.

Often animated films represent a super-agency space or super-attention space consisting of a multitude of agents with supersized eyes with a lot of white sclera to exaggerate space as animated and 'intentional.' Thus, when Snow White runs through the haunted forest, she is surrounded by eyes with wildly exaggerated white sclera, just as the animated dream sequence that Salvador Dali made for Hitchcock's *Spellbound* (Hitchcock 1945) starts out with a dark background perforated with gigantic sclera-surrounded eyes that in a nightmarish fashion observe the dream scenes. Miyazaki sometimes makes a nearly wall-to-wall tapestry of eyes of small insects to provide a feeling of being surrounded by diffuse intentionality. An even more surreal social space may be found in *Cars*. The front windows are represented as being a gigantic white sclera in which two relatively small dark dots for pupils are inserted, with most of the rest of the front of the cars being represented as mouths. Thus, a racecourse and the onlookers are transformed from being perceived as steel and glass to being fully a living being with most of the car's front being cannibalized by facial elements.

The Ultrasocial Animated World of Humans

As discussed by, for instance, Boyd and Richerson (1998) and Tomasello (2009), humans are ultra-social and their success partly depends on group/tribal living. An aspect of their ultra-sociality is the way in which the ultra-slow development of the human babies born 'too early' means that human infants for years have other humans – the caregivers – as their prime contact with the world, and therefore, social interaction is the main tool for survival and control. To establish contact with the body and especially the head and its facial expressions of mothers and other caregivers is in the beginning much more important than the physical world.

When the need for control of the physical world sets in by the need for grasping, crawling, walking, and so on, it is often concomitant with a reliance on 'transitional objects' such as dolls and pet animals that are conceived as 'animated' (cf. Winnicott 1971). The transitional objects serve as means of trying out social relations. The world of animated films is crowded with transitional objects. The physical world is often a nearly invisible background for the characters and their transitional objects; or rather, the transitional objects are the main characters as in the *Toy Story* films (Lasseter 1995; Lasseter, Brannon, and Unkrich 1999; Unkrich 2010).

Typical of many children's relation to their favorite transitional object is ambivalence: Sometimes they treat it as being animated, caring for it, but sometimes treating this transitional object as a physical object, mistreating and controlling it as if it were a physical thing. *Toy Story* plays with this ambivalence between emotional and physical control by letting the viewers identify with the toys and through them experience the loss of safety when the toys are sometimes treated as physical objects by the boy that owns them.

The widespread use of animals and toys in animated films for children has a double function. The animals and toys provide a 'natural' salience so that, for example, complicated psychological differences may be portrayed as differences between different kinds of animals (wolves versus pigs or cats versus mice, for instance). The animated films then perform salience cropping in the world of animals. Role differences among humans may be linked to simpler salient categorical differences between types of animals like the difference between Simba the noble lion and the clownish warthog Pumbaa in *The Lion King* (Allers and Minkoff 1994).

To select very salient, contrast-rich figures such as the central savanna animals – elephant, giraffe, lion, or warthog – facilitates the fluency of viewing. At the same time, the use of animals provides an emotional buffer zone in relation to the emotional problems described: Bambi's suffering from the loss of his mother may be easier to accept than if he had been a human. Social and racial conflicts may be easier to deal with emotionally if the agents are animals; thus, *Zootopia* (Howard and Moore 2016) might be interpreted as dealing with racial prejudice but portrayed in an animal world. The brutality of the fights between Tom and Jerry may not fully have the same scary effect as similar fights between two humans. Thus, the use of nonhuman agents provides vital symbolic tools for dealing with strong emotional problems, shielding the viewer from the full impact of these problems as when dealt with by means of humans, especially if portrayed with full photographic realism that may be difficult to control emotionally, especially for a younger audience.

Agency as a Superior Mental Model

Controlling the physical world and controlling the 'animated' world are very different. Central to the 'animated' approach to understanding and controlling the world around us is that in the animated world everything is controlled by animated agencies. Pascal Boyer (2001) and Justin Barrett (2004) have described how humans have built-in mechanisms in the brain, primed to look for agencies as the prime causes of actions, called hyperactive agency detection devices by Justin Barrett. The famous experimental cartoon by Heider and Simmel in 1944 (www.youtube.com/watch?v=VTNmLt7QX8E) showed how even crude cartoons of the movements of a dot and two triangles was experienced as possessing agency and intentionality. What we normally call superstition, like thinking that lightening is the angry effect of a god, is centrally based on this 'ultra-social' understanding of the world that contrasts a physical understanding. When branches suddenly move or doors open or close, we may have agency detection as our default mode: Some animated agency is suspected to be in control.

Michael Graziano (2013) has made a description of the brain mechanisms that are central to the hypersensitivity to agency, especially human agency. He has focused on areas in the temporal parts of the brain (temporoparietal junction and superior temporal sulcus) that (in combination with the prefrontal cortex) are central to social intelligence; these temporal brain areas have, for example, subdivisions for spotting the gaze of others, for spotting their facial expressions, or for spotting their hand activities. There are also subcenters that recognize human body movements; these centers may recognize people just from their body movements.

These areas are, according to Graziano, essential for our attention and intentionality and our experience of consciousness, not only in our self but also our perception of consciousness and intentionality in other people and living beings. When hyper-activated, we may, for instance, feel that we are objects of hidden gazes: for example, that somebody is looking at us behind our back, or dead people are watching us, or some gods are watching us. Thus, a constant effort to monitor gazes and their origin and purpose is vital for our experience of the world. The centers for social intelligence are located close to principal language areas, and thus we have a cluster of brain centers that smoothly process an animated world in which animals or things speak, have intentions, glances, and emotions.

On some dimensions, such a hyper-social world may be like a universal embrace, as when all the animals participate in Bambi's birth and surround Bambi and us with warm gazes or in the many parties and festivities in animated films. However, the animation also means that agents are lacking control over the physical world, as when the branches of the trees in *Snow White and the Seven Dwarfs* (Cottrell et al. 1937) have hands that try to catch her or when the wolf in *Little Red Riding Hood* uses his social skills to lure the girl.

In animated film, you are also often back in an animal or hunter-gatherer world in the sense that a dominant danger is to be eaten by some hostile agents. The ambivalence between the world of care and embrace and the world of fear of being eaten by a predator is, for example, beautifully orchestrated in a scene in Miyazaki's *My Neighbor Totoro* (1988). A little girl explores a wood and finds an enormous, living teddy-bear-like creature that is sleeping. She crawls on its stomach in a happy embrace, and the Totoro opens its mouth a little, making it uncertain for the viewer whether it is smiling or it will bite. In *Pinocchio* (Ferguson et al. 1940), the spirited world of care, represented by the guardian fairy, is opposed to the dented[sic!] whale that has eaten Pinocchio's father; *Finding Nemo* (Stanton and Unkrich 2003) also has continuous conflicts between caring smiles and biting mouths.

Interaction

The control of the world in animated fiction may be divided in three major categories:

1   *Social interaction* by means of communication using body language and verbal communication.
2   *Animal interaction* by which humans or animals experience physical conflicts that are carried out by means of what I (in Grodal 2010, 2011, 2012, 2017) have called HTTOFF scenarios: Hiding, Tracking, Trapping, Observing, Fighting, and Fleeing.
3   *Physical world interaction* by which your body interacts with the inanimate physical world, for instance, by cutting branches, making huts and caves, finding fruit and other forms of food, avoiding avalanches, and so forth.

The typical animated film has a combination of social and animal interaction. Central to a fairy tale-like social interaction is what is called social exchange that you may also call 'tit for tat': You do something for others and they – other agents or supernatural forces – do something in return. In order to signal that you are a good member of a community that will fulfill your part of the social obligation, you may perform what is called costly signaling (cf. Gintis et al. 2001). You perform altruistic and noble deeds that are costly to you so that you signal your honesty and commitment. Classic folktale research (Greimas 1966; Propp 1968) has described the narrative 'tit for tat' mechanisms in classical fairy tales. There are up to three trials that the hero or heroine has to perform in order to have their wishes fulfilled. Pinocchio's father cares intensely for his doll, Pinocchio, and wishes for and receives supernatural help from a fairy as a reward for his care, and Pinocchio has to do a good deed to signal by difficult and costly actions that he has become a good person and therefore worthy of being fully human.

Cinderella (Geronimi et al. 1950) performs social exchange by caring for animals and in exchange receives their help. She thus also qualifies for supernatural help from her good fairy godmother, who is sensitive to her unhappiness. Snow White's care for the dwarfs qualifies her for the help from the prince. In *Cars,* McQueen achieves success by learning humility and human bonding. In Miyazaki's *Spirited Away* (2001), Chihiro performs a series of duties of submission and care that enable her to free her parents from their transformation into pigs. Such stories presuppose a totally social framework for the universe based on moral principles with visible or invisible agents to implement the social contracts that even rule the physical world and control, for instance, the transformation of humans to pigs and back again. In such a world, mental activities such as wishing and praying have causal effects on a world that is more animated than physical.

Animated films, including fairy tale-inspired films, do, however, also use animal interaction based on HTTOFF scenarios. Snow White and Bambi, for instance, flee through woods and thus avoid being killed. *Shrek* (Adamson and Jenson 2001) has strong social–moral interactions between the main protagonists based on care and bonding, but it also makes extensive use of the whole arsenal of HTTOFF scenarios. Shrek fights, flees, tracks, and traps, but he also transforms interaction that is normally portrayed as violent animal interaction into social interaction. Thus, one of the central turning points in the story in the first *Shrek* film consists of transforming the classic fight between hero and dragon into a love affair between a gigantic, horrible-looking dragon and a donkey that is the precondition for the final rescue of the princess.

Animated films also make extensive use of some kind of physical interaction, often in connection with animal interaction or, as mentioned, in connection with tasks linked to social exchange. Snow White and Cinderella perform housewife duties, and Chihiro performs cleaning lady tasks that are part of the costly signaling. Perhaps the most famous animated scene ever – Bambi on ice – is a kind of physical interaction, and earlier in the film, we have a firsthand introduction to Bambi's baby problems of interacting with the world, from walking to orienting himself in space. However, the most salient and most numerous examples of physical interaction may be found in the classic cartoons that will be dealt with in the next paragraph.

The Physical World and Its Disruption in the Cartoon World

Pascal Boyer (2001) has described a cognitive system that he calls onto-logical categories that partition the world into certain general catego-ries that he thinks has partly innate support. The main categories are humans, animals, plants, artifacts (like dolls or toys), and physical ob-jects. He argues that religion and other forms of supernaturalism, on one hand, are based on the violation of such ontological categories (as dis-cussed here in relation to animated films). He, on the other hand, argues further that people that produce and enjoy such ontological violation do it against the background of a basic reliance on the ontological category. The fascination with talking animals happens against the background of a basic knowledge that animals do not talk. Thus, violations create interest that may be concomitant with arousal that may be evaluated as positive or negative. The provision of human skills and emotions to the animal world in animated films is often – as discussed – evaluated as positive and is, on a certain dimension, a complexity reduction: Every-thing can communicate. In *Cars,* we are not surrounded by hard phys-ical things; the steel of the cars is fleshlike and may bend and provide a soft look. However, we know from horror films that animation may create strong experiences of loss of control.

Violation of ontological templates and schemata may at the same time function as complexity increase as well as functioning as complexity reduction. In classic cartoons, the violation of the specifications of the physical world often portrays such ontological violations as empower-ment, and at the same time uses the violations in order to create arousal by their deviations from expectations. This buildup of arousal may serve a comic function. When hitting a wall, a person may become totally flat but then regain his or her three-dimensional shape after a while. Here one aspect of the physical world (that when you throw a ball of mud on the ground, the mud becomes flat) is projected onto another object in the physical world, in this case, a body. Although such a shape shift to flatness and back again is impossible, there is a certain fascination, a certain 'logic' in this mental playful projection of process schemata from one type of objects onto another type of objects.

Comic entertainment is, as described in Grodal 2014, based on a re-definition of arousal. Normally arousal functions as support for action and action tendencies such as avoiding danger, confronting enemies, ob-taining some wanted objects, experiencing shame and degradation, and so forth (see the PECMA model, Grodal 2009). But innate mechanisms originating in the mammalian play system allow for a redefinition of situations and their arousing effects as being 'not real' so that we get a pleasant self-regulating outlet in laughter. Violations of our expectations of the world, based on ontological categories, creates arousal that may generate an outlet in laughter, given a context that cues a definition of the violation as being 'not real.' Purzycki (2010) described how violations of the superior ontological templates of the world may often create a comic outlet.

Central to the salience of classic cartoons are such comic violations of ontological templates and schemata. In the early *Popeye the Sailor* (1960–1962) cartoons, Popeye may smash a big iron anchor that is instantly transformed into a multitude of small iron fishing hooks or he may smash a big picture of a fish that is transformed to many small sardine tin cans. Popeye runs around in a wood and hits the trees with his fists, and they are then transformed to timber that by themselves produce a cabin.

Often animals get machinelike features. *Steamboat Willie* (Iwerks and Disney 1928) plays with the violation of the two ontological categories: animals and artifacts. Here the process is not one of the animation of physical objects but, on the contrary, a 'physicalization' of animals: A cat is partly transformed into a barrel organ by turning around the tail, and the teeth of a cow are treated as a xylophone. The animals do not have any fixed size; they may change from fat to ultrathin and back. In *The Karnival Kid* (Disney and Iwerks 1929), objects and animals may be torn apart but then miraculously return to their original form. The hotdogs shift from being just sausages to being alive. They may remove their skin in the middle in order to dip their naked behind in mustard (that may create some arousing disgust) and then return to a more sausage-like shape.

Animated Metaphors

Typical violations may be divided in two categories (cf. Purzycki 2010). One is based on schemas, the other on higher order templates. We may have a schema of dogs based on experience so that when we see a rosy dog or a black rose, it may provide a minor violation of our schemas. However, if we meet a plant that can talk, an artifact such as a toy dog that can talk, or a person that has a body that behaves like a barrel of water, this is a violation of templates, of our superior models of the world that even if learned may be based on innate brain features. To create figures that mix different ontological categories is a very old activity; think, for example, of the old Egyptian gods, such as Hathor, who was sometimes provided with a cow's head for expressiveness.

Purzycki calls projections between templates for *transfers*, and such transfers may be used to create violations of ontological properties.

A typical violation based on transfer is in Disney's *Steamboat Willie*, where a cow moos and the body shrinks dramatically: To make sounds is to empty the body of air in the fashion of balls or balloons. Such transformations – transfers of qualities and properties – are based on the mental mechanisms that we know from metaphors. Basic aspects of language – as argued by, among others, George Lakoff (1987) and Mark Johnson (1987) – are built on metaphoric projections from one conceptual area to another: In the sentence 'He tried to balance his budget,' the source domain is the body that may have a preference for balance, and this source domain is projected onto the target domain, 'the budget.' In the example above of a cow mooing, the source domain is the radically shrinking balloon, and the target domain is the body of the cow when producing the sound of mooing. A commonly used metaphor is when a person is highly interested in something, the eyes pop out of the head: The approach of the eyes to the target is the source domain for an expression of deep interest.

Metaphors are rather difficult to make in live-action films (see Grodal 2015), but animated films have excellent tools for making metaphors because they are able to visualize the effects of the projections. When eyes visually pop out of the head to suggest interest or surprise, or a body shrinks by making sounds, we have a direct visualization of the projection process. When the Road Runner is provided with a car-like speed and also with a beep-beep sound, we are sensually confronted with a mixed identity based on metaphoric projections. The metaphoric projections are playful uses of the viewer's knowledge of physics and biology. A classic projection consists in letting bodies become flat when hitting a hard surface and then shift back again to their normal form. The metaphoric projection may also consist of tearing down the mind/matter barrier. In *Frozen* (Buck and Lee 2013), the mental 'frost' in Elsa's mind is projected as a physical force that exerts a powerful freezing impact on the environment.

Cartoons even play with the reality status differences between world and representation: In a scene from a Wile E. Coyote and the Road Runner cartoons, the Coyote paints a deviation of a road, so that the road ends at a solid rock, on which he paints a continuation of the road by means of a tunnel road. However, the Road Runner is able to drive through the painted tunnel road – but the Coyote is not. Therefore, even the ontological difference between a physical world and a world of representation may be violated. The comic violations of ontological templates are complexity increases – but facilitated by the complexity reductions in the portrayal of the visual elements where only the significant elements are shown. Animated films, especially the cartoon variation, are therefore training programs for those mental models of the world and its objects and forces that also provide the background for higher concept buildings based on metaphoric projections.

Ara Norenzayan et al. (2006) have argued, based on written fairy tales, that successful stories only attain a salience optimum when you have no more than two or three ontological violations. This is due to processing and memory constraints when you have more than three violations. Thus, *Little Red Riding Hood* has about three violations: a wolf that talks, a wolf that may dress as a grandmother, and a wolf that is able to eat a grandmother in such a fashion that the hunter is able to cut her out of the stomach alive. But the rest of the story presupposes a normal world with roads, woods, houses, beds, fountains, and so forth. However, animated films often have very many violations, maybe because the audiovisual medium supports the viewer's processing of violations better. Clearly, a transformation such as the one in which the evil stepmother in *Snow White* is transformed from a normal human form into a witch is directly visible. The viewer need not use much mental capacity to realize that now she is a witch with all that this implies, whereas in the oral form, it may demand more mental work to keep track of ontological violations.

Horrible Violations of Ontological Categories

Besides the comic violations of ontological categories, there are also the horrific violations. I have already mentioned above the fear elicited by the way in which Snow White is attacked by trees with hands that try to catch her. In *The Nightmare Before Christmas,* we find some other horrific violations based on dissolving the human–artifact distinction in a Frankenstein's monster kind of mode. Thus, the animated doll Sally has stitches that indicate total fractures sewn together, and, for example, sometimes her hand and arm are severed but still maintain the ability to grasp. This feature is well known from horror films and is a very powerful violation of what you might call the ontological template of body behavior, where the parts are dead unless related to the whole. In Burton's *Corpse Bride* (2005), the dead bride's skeleton hand is able to crawl on its own.

Somehow it is even more fear- and disgust-evoking to be confronted with such autonomous and possibly dangerous body parts than to be confronted with a full-bodied evil agent, perhaps because when you move to an autonomous, subagent level, normal intentionality also disappears. In horror films such as *Corpse Bride,* disgust is also linked to what you may call low-level intentionality creatures, such as worms and insects that may crawl in and out of bodies, just as the horrific, skeleton-like hands of the trees in *Snow White* represent a kind of diffuse autonomous intentionality. Thus, the full-bodied and fully intentional agents are 'wholesome,' are whole, and the destruction of wholeness is strongly negative. An aspect of this is the role of shadows in which aspects of a whole agent may be given autonomy. Animated films may therefore play with the part–whole relationship, whether it is through hands that attain autonomy, bones that are severed from their normal human flesh cover, or eyes or shadows that break loose and attain relative autonomy.

Conclusion

Animated films take place mostly out there, in the world. But they shape the world in accordance to our mental makeup. One basic feature is the ability to produce a world that on some dimension has a radical complexity reduction, facilitating the viewer's comprehension and focus and, at the same time, providing salience cropping by selecting contrasts (as in the use of savanna animals) and by exaggeration. The animation allows for producing an ultra-social and ultra-intentional space in which humans, animals, and even things or plants may share a common intentional space. Central to this creation of intentionality is that, in most animated films, everybody is provided with large eyes and plenty of white sclera and mostly speaks the same language. The social-intentional dominance matches the way in which social interaction is the dominant form of interaction for children. On one dimension, this ultra-sociality is a complexity reduction because you may interact with the world using basic social interaction patterns and may control the elicited emotions better because the fantasy world functions in parallel with 'transitional objects' such as dolls and animal toys. On the other hand, the animated world also allows for radical violations of the intuitive ontological perception of the world – a complexity increase that may create strong arousal that may fuel either comic reactions, as in cartoons, or horror reactions, as in the 'Halloween' animated horror fictions.

Even if you make animated films for grown-ups, they are more popular with young people. The young have minds in which the ontological rules of the world are under construction, supported by innate capabilities. They may therefore enjoy disruptions more than grownups whether the disruptions evoke laughter or horror.

References

Bazin, André. *What Is Cinema?* Berkeley: University of California Press, 1967.
Boyd, Robert and Peter Richerson. "The Evolution of Human Ultrasociality." In: Eibl-Eibesfeldt, Irenäus and Frank Kemp Salter (Eds.). *Indoctrinability, Ideology and Warfare*. New York: Berghahn Books, 1998: 71–93.
Boyer, Pascal. *Religion Explained*. London: William Heinemann, 2001.
Gintis, Herbert, Eric A. Smith, and Samuel Bowles. "Costly Signaling and Cooperation." *Journal of Theoretical Biology*, 213, 2001: 103–119.
Greimas, Julien A. *Structural Semantics: An Attempt at a Method*. Translated and edited by Daniele McDowell, Ronald Schleifer and Alan Velie. Lincoln: University of Nebraska Press, 1983 [1st Edition 1966].
Grodal, Torben. *Embodied Visions*. New York: Oxford University Press, 2009.
——— "High on Crime and Detection." *Projections*, 4(2), 2010: 64–85.

—— "Crime Fiction and Moral Emotions: How Context Lures the Moral Attitudes of Viewers and Readers." *Northern Lights*, 9, 2011: 143–157.

—— "Tapping Into Our Tribal Heritage: The Lord of the Rings and Brain Evolution." In: Christie, Ian (Ed.). *Audiences*. Amsterdam: Amsterdam University Press, 2012: 128–142.

—— "A General Theory of Comic Entertainment: Arousal, Appraisal, and the PECMA Flow." In: Nannicelli, Ted and Paul Taberham (Eds.). *Cognitive Media Theory*. New York: Routledge, 2014: 177–195.

—— "Film, Metaphor, and Qualia Salience." In: Fahlenbrach, Kathrin (Ed.). *Embodied Metaphors in Film, Television, and Video Games: Cognitive Approaches*. New York: Routledge, 2015: 101–114.

—— "Die Hard as an Emotion Symphony: How Reptilian Scenarios Meet Mammalian Emotions in the Flow of an Action Film." *Projections*, 11(2), 2017: 87–104.

Johnson, Mark. *The Body in the Mind: The Bodily Basis of Meaning, Imagination, and Reason*. Chicago: Chicago University Press, 1987.

Keysers, Christian. *The Empathic Brain: How the Discovery of Mirror Neurons Changes our Understanding of Human Nature*. New York: Social Brain Press, 2011.

Kobayashi, Hiromi and Shiro Kohshima. "Unique Morphology of the Human Eye and Its Adaptive Meaning: Comparative Studies on External Morphology of the Primate Eye." *Journal of Human Evolution*, 40, 2001: 419–435.

Lakoff, George. *Women, Fire, and Dangerous Things. What Categories Reveal about the Mind*. Chicago: Chicago University Press, 1987.

Langlois, Judith H. and Lori A. Roggman "Attractive Faces Are Only Average." *Psychology Science*, 1, 1990: 115–121. (doi:10.1111/j.1467–9280.1990.tb00079.x).

Norenzayan, Ara, Scott Atran, Jason Faulkner, and Mark Schaller. "Memory and Mystery: The Cultural Selection of Minimally Counterintuitive Narratives." *Cognitive Science*, 30, 2006: 531–553.

Propp, Vladimir. *Morphology of the Folktale*. Austin: University of Texas Press, 1968.

Purzycki, Benjamin G. "Cognitive Architecture, Humor and Counterintuitiveness: Retention and Recall of MCIs." *Journal of Cognition and Culture*, 10, 2010: 189–204.

Ramachandran, Vilaymur S. and William Hirstein. "The Science of Art." *Journal of Consciousness Studies*, 6, 1999: 15–51.Tomasello, Michael. *Why We Cooperate*. Cambridge, MA: Boston Review/MIT Press, 2009.

Tomasello, Michael, Brian Hare, Hagen Lehmann, and Josep Call. "Reliance on Head versus Eyes in the Gaze Following of Great Apes and Human Infants: The Cooperative Eye Hypothesis." *Journal of Human Evolution*, 52, 2007: 314–320.

Winnicott, Donald W. *Playing and Reality*. London: Tavistock, 1971. Zeki, Semir. *Inner Vision: An Exploration of Art and the Brain*. Oxford: Oxford University Press, 1999.

Films & TV Series

Bambi. Directed by David Hand et al. 1942; USA: Disney.

Cars. Directed by John Lasseter and Joe Ranft. 2006; USA: Disney/Pixar.

Cinderella. Directed by Clyde Geronimi, Wilfred Jackson, and Hamilton Luske. 1950; USA: Disney.

Corpse Bride. Directed by Tim Burton and Mike Johnson. 2005; USA: Warner Bros.

Finding Nemo. Directed by Andrew Stanton and Lee Unkrich. 2003; USA: Disney/Pixar.

Frozen. Directed by Chris Buck and Jennifer Lee. 2013; USA: Disney.

The Incredibles. Directed by Brad Bird. 2004; USA: Disney/Pixar.

Inside Out. Directed by Pete Docter and Ronnie del Carmen. 2015; USA: Disney/Pixar.

The Karnival Kid. Directed by Walt Disney and Ub Iwerks. 1929; USA: Disney.

The Lion King. Directed by Roger Allers and Rob Minkoff. 1994; USA: Disney.

Looney Tunes: USA 1930–1969 (original; 1987–present (revival)), Cartoon Network, Nickelodeon, ABC, created by Warner Brothers.

Monsters, Inc. Directed by Pete Docter, David Silverman. 2001; USA: Disney/Pixar.

My Neighbor Totoro. Directed by Hayao Miyazaki. 1988; JP: Tokuma/Studio Ghibli/Nibariki.

The Nightmare Before Christmas. Directed by Tim Burton. 1993; USA: Touchstone Pictures/Disney.

Pinocchio. Directed by Norman Ferguson, Thornton Hee, Wilfred Jackson, Jack Kinney, and Bill Roberts. 1940; USA: Disney.

Popeye the Sailor: USA 1960–1962, ABC, created by Elize C. Segar.

Shrek. Directed by Andrew Adamson and Vicky Jenson. 2001; USA: DreamWorks/Pacific Data Images.

Snow White and the Seven Dwarfs. Directed by William Cottrell, Wilfred Jackson, Larry Morey, Perce Pearce, and Ben Sharpsteen. 1937; USA: Disney.

Spellbound. Directed by Alfred Hitchcock. 1945; USA: Selznick International Pictures/Vanguard Films.

Spirited Away. Directed by Hayao Miyazaki. 2001; JP: Tokuma/Studio Ghibli/Nippon.

Steamboat Willie. Directed by Ub Iwerks and Walt Disney. 1928; USA: Disney.

Tom and Jerry: USA 1940–1969, CBS, created by William Hanna and Joseph Barbera.

Toy Story. Directed by John Lasseter. 1995; USA: Disney/Pixar.

Toy Story 2. Directed by John Lasseter, Ash Brannon, and Lee Unkrich. 1999; USA: Disney/Pixar.

Toy Story 3. Directed by Lee Unkrich. 2010; USA: Disney/Pixar.

WALL·E. Directed by Andrew Stanton. 2008; USA: Disney/Pixar.

Zootopia. Directed by Byron Howard and Rich Moore. 2016; USA: Disney/Pixar.

Narration and Sound

7 Creating (Artificial) Emotion in Animation Through Sound and Story

Nichola Dobson

Classic narrative structure has been a feature of animation since the early days of the form, from adaptation of fairy tales and fables, through replication of radio plays via television structures. Beyond the style and technique used in animation, there can be a combination of factors – sound, voice, performance, and color that can influence the level of emotional response.

Since the first computer-animated features, popularized by Pixar in the 1990s and *Toy Story* (Lasseter 1995), certain sectors of the animation industry have been striving to create photo realistic animation via computer but as discussed by Bode (2006) there is often a fall into the uncanny valley instead and the audience is left cold. The most engaging animation is one that brings in many of the elements listed here but creates a compelling narrative.

This chapter will examine several examples of contemporary cinematic and television animation, including the Pixar *Toy Story* trilogy (Lasseter 1995; Lasseter, Brannon, and Unkrich 1999; Unkrich 2010), the extent to which they conform to what we can call a classic, or Proppian narrative structure, and the success of the animation (in terms of audience engagement and review). The chapter will deconstruct the examples in terms of narrative structure, sound, and character to consider the capacity for the creation of emotion in the texts and the way in which the use of computer animation may help or hinder this. By also taking into account Paul Wells' seminal discussion of the 'specificity of animation' (1998) and its unique modes of narrative, we can argue that there are particularities that need to be considered.

Meaning of Narrative and Form in Animated Films

During its long history, animation has often been described in terms of the technology used to create it. In a paper delivered at the 1994 Society for Animation Studies conference, Phil Denslow looked to the dictionary to outline the ways in which animation worked, suggesting it was a "[...] motion picture made by photographing successive positions of inanimate objects [...] motion picture made from a series of drawings simulating motion [...]" (1997: 1). This reveals a lot about the way in which the animation was created but little else. Many scholars look to the oft-quoted description by Scottish-born animator Norman McLaren, "Animation is not the art of drawings-that-move, but rather the art of movements-that-are-drawn" (Solomon 1987: 11). Here McLaren is going beyond the mechanics of the technology used to create the moving images and speaks to the creative output, the 'art' of the animation. This covers a lot of forms of animation but is still suggestive rather than explicit, though tellingly they both mention movement as a key element.

Neither of these definitions goes far enough for other scholars, such as Cholodenko (1991, 2007) (and more recently Manovich 2001), who suggests that all cinema is animated and looks at the Latin "animus" as a key aspect of the image coming to life to become animated and moving rather than still photographs or drawings. This theoretical approach has been explored more in recent years among academics in the field, but arguably excludes industry or audience in the description. A more generalized view which has recently emerged is to simply suggest that animation is 'not live action'; however, as Manovich explores in his 2001 text *The Language of New Media*, this fails to take into account the further technological changes in moving image where live action is becoming increasingly animated in its production.

This lack of agreement on a concrete definition of animation has plagued animation scholars but less so the industry and audiences, who exist within a system of generic categorization in marketing and consumption. The contemporary animated landscape includes mainstream blockbuster features; television series of various genres; experimental films in short and long form, screened at festivals and increasingly distributed online; and pervasive advertising on all media platforms. This vast output suggests that definitions of what animation is are perhaps redundant, and the question may be, instead, 'what does animation do?'

Animation is being created in a variety of ways for a variety of reasons, and the increasing use of computer-generated animation (CG) in the mainstream, as Mihailova suggests, arguably created a "renaissance of animation as a popular form of entertainment" (2013: 146). This renaissance includes an increasing use of stop motion animation (albeit often augmented with CG technology) as well as the stylistic aesthetic of 2D drawn animation, using computer technology in the animation and postproduction stages to speed production. These different forms are used across a variety of genres that feature different narrative strategies animators can utilize, ranging from classic literary narratives to nonnarrative abstract films.

If we examine the narratives used, we can understand both the content and meaning of the film and, potentially, the animators' motivation. In doing so, however, we also need to consider the language of animation itself, which Wells argues is distinctly different from that used in the live-action film:

> [...] its very language represents the world in an intrinsically differ-ent way. The animated film creates a narrative space and visual en-vironment radically different to the live action version of the world [...] it is my contention that animation as a film language and film art is a more sophisticated and flexible medium than live action film, and thus offers a greater opportunity for film makers to be more imaginative and less conservative.
>
> (Wells 1998: 6)

Early animated short cartoons used print cartoons as source material. As such, they retained the sequential plotting of the heavily used sight gags and punch lines. These translated into the short comedic films that came to dominate the early animation market. The audiences' fa-miliarity with this narrative form aided the transition from print to moving image, and in the early silent films, included the dialogue in the speech bubble format. The narrative structure of the introduction of the protagonist, the setup of the gag, and the punch line/resolution continued with the development of the cartoon and continued through the introduction of synchronization of sound and into the "Golden Age" of Hollywood animation through the 1940s.[1] By using the speech bubble, the early animation is foregrounded with its artifice on display, but the purpose of these cartoons would be to maintain and reproduce the comedy accepted by both the animator and the audience. How-ever, the flexibility of the animation could be used to heighten the co-medic effect when the animated characters could be manipulated into forms/shapes/positions and situations unavailable to the live-action actor, such as those in the *Felix the Cat* series (Sullivan and Messmer 1919–1932 for the initial run), creating slapstick beyond the capacity of Charlie Chaplin.

The foregrounded artifice would continue to be common throughout animation history, and to further describe the language, Wells uses the example of the classic Warner Bros. short *Duck Amuck* (Jones 1953). This particular film plays with the boundaries of *mise-en-scène* and narrative and highlights the language of animation by placing the pro-tagonist in fantastic situations that change around him as well as by manipulating his physical being. Wells suggests,

> [...] Jones demonstrates the dimensions of the animated form and shows its capacity to support a number of meanings, particularly with regard to character construction, modes of narrative expec-tation and plausibility, and the conditions of comic events. It is a model which usefully reveals the range of possibilities within the

animated cartoon and, as such, the readily identifiable conventions of orthodox animation.

(Wells 1998: 42)

Chuck Jones uses the malleability of the animated form to create various settings for Daffy Duck, confusing the duck and the audience as to his whereabouts and consequent behavior. The soundtrack is used to accompany Daffy in his various locations throughout the film but, like Daffy, is one step behind the scenery, which is being changed around him; so, for example, his rendition of *Jingle Bells* as he moves through a winter landscape has to be changed to a Hawaiian melody when a tropical beach background is created. The hand of the 'animator' is seen, and the nature of the practice is revealed to the audience, highlighted in order to reinforce the comedic nature of the gag; the punch line is revealed to be Daffy's sometimes rival Bugs Bunny as the animator, with Bugs reciting the classic line "Ain't I a stinker?" The classic cartoon is often cited as an audience favorite and suggests that by showing the animation, the narrative and comedy effects are heightened as our expectations are played with. It could be argued, then, that the success of the film lies in the narrative of the comedy gag being concluded with an unexpected punch line driven by Jones' highlighting the animatedness of the short.

In addition to the comedy narrative (both familiar and unexpected), animators have utilized the narrative structure of literature through the popular live-action strategy of the adaptation as the source; with the fairy- and folktales from Walt Disney (and in recent years, Studio Ghibli), fables by Paul Terry and Van Beuren, and the literary classics from the Fleischer Brothers, it was easy to once again appropriate a familiar structure that the audience could be comfortable with. These narratives can be summarized using both Todorov's structuralist theories of narrative (1981) and the Proppian functions of characterization (1968). The setup and resolution of the stories as well as the main characters are translated into animated form. By utilizing familiar narrative structures and character groupings, the audience can be essentially removed from the animatedness of the films. In these films, the narrative is the key element, and the animation becomes the tool for storytelling, a technique or technology similar to the live-action filming process.

The use of familiar narrative allows the audience to be fully engaged with the film and the emotional journey of the characters. The Disney studio made great use of this in comedy, horror, and tragedy in most of their early features, and arguably they found their greatest and most consistent successes in adaptation. From their first feature-length film, *Snow White and the Seven Dwarfs* (Cottrell et al. 1937), to their record-breaking, studio-regenerating film *The Lion King* (Allers and Minkoff 1994), Disney maintained clear narrative structures and characters that could be engaged with by audiences of varying ages. As discussed later in the chapter, the Disney animators were tasked with creating very specific emotional responses from their audiences. The studio was at the forefront of technological development, which served them well, though when they strayed from this narrative strategy in the lavish, classical music-based film *Fantasia* (Armstrong et al. 1940), they were less successful, and the audience was largely unconvinced. This type of animation, which synchronized music and sound with image, had been produced by animators who were considered experimental artists such as Oskar Fischinger, Mary Ellen Bute, Norman McLaren, and Len Lye, but the mainstream cinema audience was not used to this from Disney; the studio had already established their brand identity. In later years, audiences who had been exposed to more experimental animation were more forgiving, and the home video market enabled the studio to release the film in different versions for the home and collectors' markets.

In addition to adapting classic literary narratives, animated films and television shows have been produced by looking up to previous live-action examples as templates. In television in particular, animation has become extremely successful in the animated sitcom, or 'anicom' (Dobson 2003). The anicom uses the language of animation to create an animated 'manifestation' or interpretation of the live-action television genre, but goes beyond the capabilities of the live. I have discussed this distinct genre elsewhere (2009, 2018) but it is worth noting that it follows the very clear sitcom narrative of equilibrium > incident/event > resolution/restoration of equilibrium. This has proven successful and enduring – *The Simpsons* is the longest running sitcom on US television, 1990–present (Groening) – while live-action sitcoms have failed. Animation is able to manipulate situations and characters in a unique way, with extremes such as violence and fantasy easily created where live action could not do so; likewise, in the case of long-running series, the aging of actors is not a consideration when their likeness is drawn. While it is true that the resolution of the status quo is easier to achieve if the previously endangered character can simply be redrawn or re-rendered, the language of animation also enables producers to address complex sociopolitical topics while often going unnoticed by the censor or network.

This is in part due to the very perception of animation as a 'cartoon,' a comedic or children's medium and thus not to be taken as seriously as live action. Here animation can be used to subvert the initial, apparent meaning of the film. An oft-cited example (and discussed in some depth in Wells 1998) of this is Jiri Trnka's *The Hand* (1965), a stop motion puppet animation; the animator created a short film about persecution by the state, with the characters of villain and hero clearly defined, but was still able to screen the film in said state without raising too much attention. In this case, animation used its history and status to include material that would perhaps be more difficult in live action. The perceived distance from realism allows animation to deviate from the standard narrative or to go beyond and expand existing, common narrative structures. Here, again, the unique language of animation creates what Wells refers to as "a system of images which interrogate social conditions, and resist the fiction of reported fact, and the selective representations of reality available through the state-controlled systems of mass communication." (1998: 88). Thus, the film can subvert common assumptions about animation (and politics) through animation.

In addition to existing classical narrative structures, animation can utilize specific narrative strategies to drive the narrative. Wells outlines a thorough list of these in *Understanding Animation* (1998) and includes animation specific techniques such as condensation, where cinematic cuts are used to move the action between "the *narrative premise* and the *relevant outcome*" (1998: 76); metamorphosis, which sees the image shift and change from one into another; and acting and performance – similar to that of live action (but can be problematic when 'names' are used) within the animation and sound. There are several others that further demonstrate the unique language of animation, but are best represented in Wells' work rather than in an attempt to replicate them here.

Meaning of Sound in Animation

This section will examine the use of sound, as it has several effects and uses within narrative. Sound can play a vital role in the narrative of animated films, from the earliest animated shorts – such as Disney's *Silly Symphonies* (beginning in 1929 with *The Skeleton Dance*) and Warner Bros.' popular *Merrie Melodies* and *Looney Tunes* from the 1930s and 1940s, where a particular piece of music was essentially illustrated by the animation – to musical features and *avant-garde* music videos. Several of these aspects of sound will be examined here, including soundtrack, diegetic and non-diegetic music, and the use of voice.

Soundtrack is one of the most noticeable uses of music in any film or television production, either live action or animated. The first animated films, like early cinema, were accompanied by music, often performed live, forming part of an act. Due to the lack of synchronization of sound, there would be no dialogue, only generally written text as part of, or intercut into, the animation. Here, the music was vital in providing narrative clues to the audience, who was slowly becoming accustomed to these practices. The speed of the music related to the suspense and drama of the onscreen action leading to some sort of conclusion or crescendo. As shorts became more commonly produced, studios were able to make use of their music libraries and thus the popular songs of the day were transformed and interpreted (usually in a comedic way) into animation.

An early example from Harman and Ising, *Sinkin' in the Bathtub* (1930), was a play on a popular song of the time and was very successful, spawning the Warner Bros. *Merrie Melodies* series. The use of popular music drew audiences, and animators were able to create narratives around the subject or, indeed, the existing narrative of the songs. This type of animated short fulfilled a very specific purpose on the bill (see Ward 2000 for further discussion) and to a certain extent is very straightforward with the question of what animation does. As part of a longer variety of material it would serve as an interlude; emotional engagement here would likely come in the form of the pleasure of familiar music and lively images.

As animators began to experiment with different techniques, many were influenced by music, which they attempted to 'animate.' The result, from filmmakers such as Oskar Fischinger and Norman McLaren, could be described as animated music, with rhythmic forms moving in time to the accompanying musical score. Though less of a conventional narrative strategy, it was an interesting way to develop the use of sound in animation and could arguably be seen as a precursor to the music video, which has developed the industry as well as the audience for animation in the last 30 years. This type of animated music was part of the effect Disney was looking for in the aforementioned *Fantasia* but as suggested earlier the audience did not engage with the outcome. While the film was less successful than other Disney films of the day, it did at least introduce the concept of animated music to mass audiences. All of these examples can again link the emotional response to the music, which accompanied the animation. The animation is not foregrounding its artifice here but rather is creating visual elements to compliment or challenge the music. In some cases, such as McLaren and Evelyn Lambart's *Begone Dull Care* (1949), the music creates the mood and tempo, which in turn evokes an emotional or as Power (2009: 114) would suggest, a sensory response.

Since the advent of sound synchronization in 1927, dialogue has become vital in the progression of the narrative and supports the performance of the characters. Scriptwriting in animation can be as vital to the process as it is in live action, with good dialogue important to the film. In the case of television animation, where the techniques of limited animation are employed to improve efficiency and reduce cost, the dialogue can distract the audience from the 'quality' of the animation. A good example of this is in the Hanna-Barbera anicom *The Flintstones* (1960), the first animated sitcom on television, which used the limited system heavily. Though the animation did not fully present the action on screen, the dialogue was of a very high quality and as such became more important to the success of the show. Indeed, despite often being criticized for the animation, the Hanna-Barbera studio was praised for good writing throughout most of their television shows over the years. This practice has continued in the genre, with verbal gags becoming more important than the slapstick sight gags made famous in the cartoons from studios such as MGM and Warner Bros.

The importance of voice has increased in recent years, with marketing of feature animation becoming a vital part of ensuring the success of a large budget production. The discussion of the star in animation is a larger debate than we have space for here, but in drawing attention to the live-action actor giving voice and thus life to the animated character, the audience again must acknowledge the artifice but suspend disbelief. This is the case regardless of the form of animation, though it tends to occur more in large-budget US releases with the large market and arguably continuing star system.

As well as character dialogue, there can be the use of voice-over narration or in-scene diegetic sound, which is coming from a defined source, such as radio, television, or an instrument. This is often used to set the context of the narrative, perhaps featuring a news report on a radio that tells the character, and the audience, what the situation is or is about to be. This then sets the scene for the incident, or loss of equilibrium, that must be resolved at the end of the film. The use of non-diegetic sounds such as voice-over or narration is a strategy is often seen in animated adaptations, particularly in folk- and fairy tales. Disney combined the introductory voice-over to set up the narrative with an image of a storybook in many of their films, as if to reinforce the literary source and alert the audience to the type of narrative they were about to see.

The voice-over by protagonist (or other character) is often used to heighten the dramatic effect of the film, with the narrative driven from their perspective. It allows the audience to engage with the story through their eyes but can often be unreliable. A recent, and excellent, example of this is from the television series *BoJack Horseman* (Bob-Waksberg 2014–present), which utilized the language of animation to great effect in season 4, episode 6. The protagonist is having an existential crisis, and through voice-over and different animation styles, his state of mind is revealed to the audience. I have deliberately not termed this show as anicom, despite its outward appearance as such, as it does not feature a resolution of equilibrium at the end of each episode and features as much drama as comedy. The series is very socio-politically aware and it presents an often dark approach to adult life in contemporary American culture. The emotional responses are very much elicited via the dialogue and narration, as the drawing style (though it also uses computer technology, it has a 2D aesthetic) is not expressive in a realistic way. Thus, a combination of sound in the voice-over and dialogue, as well as accompanying music and soundtrack, can be vital in eliciting the emotional response in an audience and as such should be considered when discussing the overall narrative strategies in animation (Wells 1998). The expressiveness of character is discussed further in the next section.

Practicing Emotion

In the seminal book *Illusion of Life* (1981), by Disney animators Ollie Johnston and Frank Thomas, each stage of animation is outlined with detailed explanations of motivations and illustrations of best practice. They dedicate a whole chapter to emotion, and this lengthy quote demonstrates the overall approach from the studio:

> In every art form it is the emotional content that makes the difference between mere technical skill and true art [...][the artist] can become proficient in their crafts, achieving dazzling mechanical perfection, but their work will be empty and meaningless unless the personal perceptions of the artist are communicated as well [...] many of the young men "could animate beautifully, but that isn't what makes you laugh and that isn't what makes the tears come."
>
> (Johnston and Thomas 1981: 473)

Their overall argument, then, is that much of the performance of the character must come from the animator. Indeed, both Paul Wells (1998) and Donald Crafton (2012) have also argued that much of the performance in animation comes from that imbued through the animator, either in the hands of the stop motion animator or via the drawing of the 2D animator (and arguably latterly with the 3D software). Animators give life to the characters, and thus their own feelings on the subject will ultimately come through.

   As Johnston and Thomas further explain, "The actor and the animator share many interests; they both use symbols to build a character in the spectator's mind. Certain gestures, attitudes, expressions, and timing have come to connote specific personalities and emotions [...]" (474). The actor and animator share the same criteria for performance and, as Johnston and Thomas suggest, by the audience's judgment of the same. As an audience, we are said to suspend disbelief to engage with narrative and, as such, can be drawn into the emotional connection that a good performance can present. This notion of performance in animation is developed further in the next section on computer-generated animation, but here I will concentrate on the mechanics of emotion in an analogue way.

   Giving the example of Snow White's death scene in the 1937 feature, Johnston and Thomas explained that the animators had to change the mood of the dwarfs from comical to sad; they did so by reducing their movement and expression, by editing to a quieter moment, and by coming straight into the emotion of their responses, in order to elicit the same from the audience and eliminate any confusion. This was reinforced in the soundtrack, with no dialogue beyond the sounds of the characters' sobbing and the sad melody in the background. This demonstrates that the animation can be limited to create moments of connection between the audience and character, which can also be developed in the pacing of the story itself and, in this case, reinforced by the accompanying music.

They end the chapter with a list of 'points to remember when animating emotions,' which include defining the emotional state of the character (this can be shown in gestures and action or with simple moves); being thoughtful of editing; considering what you want to show and how the audience should react; and using the timing well: "Don't be ponderous, but don't take it away from them just as they start to enjoy it." (507). Despite the age of the book and the now relatively outdated modes of creating the animation itself, *Illusion of Life* is still valuable for animators and historians to understand the basic premises of all the main areas of creating a good narrative that has emotional connections – though we must also take into account the strength of the narrative that they are animating. As this chapter will go on to discuss, the technology used to create the animation rarely renders the basic understanding of storytelling obsolete, even if the method is.

Textbooks for animation practitioners (and primarily students) can be valuable in the consideration of creating emotion. Just as the previously discussed *Illusion of Life* presented valuable insights into the methods of the Disney studio, which are still applicable, so too does *Acting for Animators* by Ed Hooks (2017). Hooks takes a relatively informal and conversational approach to recounting his experience teaching acting to animators and, like Johnston and Thomas before him, provides a vital resource for the animator to consider how to convey emotion in a character.

One of the key aspects of this text is its discussion of both traditional and computer generated examples and the analysis of how successful they are. Hooks refers to the pioneering psychologist Paul Ekman and his work on facial expressions and the emotions they convey (72) to suggest that there are seven "core emotions which are universally recognized: Happiness, Sadness, Anger, Fear, Disgust, Surprise, Contempt" (Ibid.). Hooks does suggest that these are not generic but have shared elements that audiences can recognize. As previously suggested, suspension of disbelief plays a part in Hook's suggestion of taking the audience on the narrative journey being presented: "once you give them the instructions, you are creating an implicit contract." (73). He goes on to provide examples of when this has worked and where it has not, suggesting that logic either needs to be clear or at least consciously explained away, so the audience trusts the story.

Hooks provides a detailed analysis of recent feature animation that breaks down specific moments of acting, all of which is to reinforce a key point made at the end of the book: "The most glaring deficiency among today's new animators is weak story-telling skills...If the goal is to improve performance in animation, however, we must also improve storytelling because the story being told is the justification for the characters in the first place" (189).

(Hyper)real Emotion?

The Disney studio was always driving technological innovation and keen to produce what Wells (1998) classed as 'hyperrealism,' but as the Computer Age progressed and animation production (in some instances) utilized digital technology, the 'strive for realism' became something of a goal in production terms. As discussed earlier, audiences already accept animation (and live action film) with willing suspension of disbelief, but from the 1990s onward, CG was being pushed to move animation into a place where it essentially replicated the real rather than represented it (Wells 1998). As Sobchack (2006) has suggested, Pixar's *Toy Story* (1996) and subsequent sequels were very successful at the box office and with audiences as one of the first fully CG-animated features. The film has a now well-known, engaging story of childhood toys made animate, with a fully fleshed out world of supporting characters and merchandise as well as a recognizable voice cast (reinforced via the toys that talk) and Oscar-nominated soundtrack. Its landmark status as a first is still a benchmark of the potential for success in CG, but it is often ignored in terms of the quality of its narrative; however, Sobchack lists it, among the other follow-up releases from the studio in the late 1990s and early 2000s, as being successful specifically because it doesn't attempt photo-real CG animation and its 'realism' is emotional (2006: 173).

This would reinforce Hooks, Johnston, and Thomas' assertion that emotional animation can come from the performance and narrative rather than necessarily the emotional expression on the hyperreal face. We also need to consider the soundtrack; in this case Randy Newman's musical score which evoked nostalgia for childhood as well as in the high quality voice performances from actors such as Tom Hanks, Tim Allen and Don Rickles which engaged the audience aurally. Though *Toy Story* has been variously discussed by other authors (see Montgomery 2011, Haswell 2015a, b), it is worth briefly analyzing the narrative here in terms of how it conforms to the classic Proppian format (1968), which is still utilized in variation. The overall synopsis is of a group of toys belonging to a young boy, Andy, and what happens when new toys join them: are they replaced in his affections, pushed aside, or thrown away? The film deals in notions of childhood nostalgia and, in the later films in the trilogy, explicit ideas of growing up and moving on (some internet discussions also suggest that the final film is about death). In terms of the eight characters of Propp's mythology, Woody the Sheriff is initially identified as the hero; Bo Peep, the Princess (and reward for Woody); Slinky Dog as dispatcher/helper; and Buzz and Sid as the villains. Throughout the film, the narrative plays with the notion of Woody as false hero to add to the drama, as well as his initial jealousy and conflict with Buzz, a new hero. At the midpoint of the film, the perspective of the other characters, through misunderstanding, sees Woody as the villain, and it is through his Proppian functions via his literal journey, battles, and return that he is restored to his heroic status once more. That the animation is created digitally is not really a consideration any more than the fact that Jiri Trnka's *The Hand* (1965) is stop motion puppetry, or that *Snow White* is made of drawings. The narrative engages the audience and creates the emotional response through the performances of the character and the voice actors.

However, what *Toy Story* did, as a pioneering technological breakthrough, was to pave the way for other CG features. Some took the same stylistic cues from Pixar, such as DreamWorks Animation's *Antz* (Darnell and Johnson 1998) and *Shrek* (Adamson and Jenson 2001) and Blue Sky Studio's *Ice Age* (Wedge and Saldanha 2002) franchise, and followed a similar 'cartoon' or aesthetic, albeit 3D, which audiences would be comfortable with. These fantastic places, be it the frozen north or a fairy-tale land, never required photorealism to enable the narrative, and as such, the computers here were utilized as tools of animation to help produce it and to speed up the production process, rather than using the end result (of what the computer graphics could do) as the driver of the narrative. In many ways, this is what led to the criticisms of other 'groundbreaking' CG-animated features, such as *Final Fantasy: Spirits Within* (Sakaguchi and Sakakibara 2001) and *The Polar Express* (Robert Zemeckis 2004), which were promoted on their amazing new feats of advanced computer graphics. Sobchack examined several reviews of the former and argued that, "[...] its failure attributed previously to its apparently confusing and *emotionally* unengaging narrative." (2006: 172) (my emphasis). By spending so much time discussing the artifice but trying to demonstrate its realism, Sobchack argues that audiences became distracted by the lead character's 'perfect rendered hair' and did not engage with the story.

In Aldred's (2006) thorough reading of Robert Zemeckis' *The Polar Express* (2004), she compares the film and its overall aesthetic and narrative to that of the video game rather than an animated film. Her whole thesis is on the nature of the spectacle of the film and how it invites an audience into an almost game-style 'immersive' experience via its sweeping cinematography and their presumed familiarity with gameplay narrative logic, cause and effect, rather than classic Proppian narrative (though many games do follow that as well, particularly in regard to character). This is a particularly interesting take, however, as it never tries to conflate the language of animation and what it does to what *Polar Express* is. Indeed, in her final notes, she quotes animator Gene Deitch, who said "The Polar Express, it seems to me, opens up the possibility of an entirely new category [...] what is clear to me is that it is NOT animation in its traditional and technical meaning." (2005 in Aldred 2006: 168). This is worth considering then as we discuss the notion of emotional animation and CG animation. How far do we consider the motion capture performance as emotionally expressive? The film is further complicated by utilizing Tom Hanks as motion-capture subject 'performing' multiple roles. While he was able to portray Woody the Sheriff in *Toy Story* with an impressive range of emotion through his voice, his performance in *Polar Express* is commonly described as uncanny. We could argue, then, that his motion-capture performance lacked an expressivity that the toy cowboy did not. The sound is important, but it needs to be combined with engaging animation rather than performative spectacle.

Power discusses the notion of 'expressiveness' in animation: "Traditionally, animation has been one of the most expressive of the visual arts, but in 3D animation, quantitative has trumped qualitative [...]" (2009: 109). This reinforces Sobchack's view that by calling attention to the realism in CG, it actually draws the audience out. I would argue (as many others have, including Wells 1998 and Ivins-Hulley 2008) that the very nature of animation, which reveals or displays its artifice, as we saw with the example of *Duck Amuck*, is not new, so why should this new technology struggle with the audience? Can it be about the notion of what animation can do, as opposed to live action? Or is it as Power suggests: "The issue in question here is whether or how an aesthetic culturally and technologically rooted at one end of the continuum can be taken for a creative stroll at the other end." (2009: 109). Again, though, the spectacle of cinema, as Gunning (1993) describes, is about engaging the audience with the technology, not necessarily about immersive narrative but filling the audience with wonder about how the effect was achieved.

Animators and live-action filmmakers have regularly been keen to reveal the magic behind the art with books and behind-the-scenes features, which became more popular due to the DVD/home market. Thus, if we are being invited to look behind the narrative, why, as Sobchack posits, was *Final Fantasy* such a failure? Is there a limit to how much spectacle we want? Do audiences want to enjoy the spectacle and marvel at the detailed movement in Sulley the monster's fur in Pixar's *Monsters, Inc.* (Docter and Silverman 2001), while at the same time be engaged in the emotional connection he makes with Boo or the heightened drama of the chase with Randall? Much of this engagement again comes via the voice performances from Billy Crystal, John Goodman, and Steve Buscemi. Perhaps we demand too much, and, as Sobchack suggests, "Unfortunately, then, our attention – and that of the filmmakers – is greatly misdirected from a focus on 'the illusion of life' to the 'dis-illusion of life' [...]" (180). However, can the animator's performance and strength of narrative actually circumvent the notion of spectacle as in the example above? In the case of *Toy Story 3* (2010), the series' final installment (at that time), the film was released in full 3D (as well as 2D), but the spectacle of the fully immersive visual did not match the incredible emotional response from the audience, which saw adults weep at the conclusion of the journey for the characters they had engaged with so much in the 14 years since the initial release. [2] That the story spoke of children growing up and leaving home, as well as parents saying goodbye to their offspring, was heightened in the dramatic as well as comedic scenes in which the toys had to deal with what was essentially the end of their journey together.

Power argues that to create convincing and expressive 3D CG animation, we can consider the notion of 'modality cues' that cover four elements within the creative output, in our case, animation. These are naturalistic, technological, abstract, and sensory orientation, and each one can have different levels within. Power asserts that many of the most popular CG-animated features (he includes *Toy Story, Shrek, Monster House* (Kenan 2006) and *Happy Feet* (Miller and Coleman 2006)) feature "high modality aspiring to naturalism" (113) in terms of motion capture, modeling and dialogue, but low-modality characterization (animals). He suggests, then, that if the other elements are high, then one element can be low, much in the same way as the notion of the oft-cited 'uncanny valley,'[3] which suggests that if the robot/CG character becomes too real, then it becomes uncanny and unsettling to the audience. The animator can then consider which elements to develop as high and which as low to create the right balance for the audience. This, however, presumes a very logical approach to the creative practice of animation, and Power goes on to point out that "It is a lot to ask of animators (or anyone else) that they should excel in visual and motion design, character design and storytelling, and then be capable programmers as well [...]" (125).

If the animator is driven by a particular feeling they wish to convey through the movement of animation – or the combination of movement and music, such as Norman McLaren's *Boogie Doodle* (1941) – or prefer to tell narrative stories about life through stick-figure characters with voice over, such as Don Hertzfeldt – see, in particular, *It's Such a Beautiful Day* (2012) and *World of Tomorrow* (2016) – then they are not striving for high modality naturalism, technological orientation, or, in Hertzfeldt's case, abstraction. In both cases, however, they do reach high levels of modality in sensory orientation in expressiveness, one via movement and music and one via evocative voice-over. Both of these examples once more prove that animation can be expressive and emotional, without CG hyperrealism or, indeed, Disneyesque hyperrealism, but that sound is a key driver in the narrative engagement and emotional response.

In recent years, several scholars have discussed the rise in motion capture and the performance of the actor vs. the avatar (see Bode (2006), Mihailova (2016)), all considering the extent to which we can claim the realism of the performance. The nature of art and arguably vocation has seen a wider industrial debate around the credit (and award) for the labor, previously invisible in a film, particularly as the boundaries between animation and live action blur with the use of CG effects. However, what ultimately remains vital to audience experience is the quality of the narrative. Anecdotal evidence from recent discussion with my students suggests that while they are impressed with the capabilities of CGI technology, they are more impressed when they are engaged with what they generally describe as a classic narrative of Proppian or Todorov structure.

We should perhaps again think about what animation does. It can replicate the real, present a fantasyland, create mental states, make spectacular feats seem possible and make an audience of adults cry. CGI can do these things, but with a purpose – they need a narrative to drive them, whether as an effect in a live-action film, a video game experience, or an animated film. Ultimately, CG must do what it is programmed to do, just as a stop motion puppet or drawn cel must do what the animator makes it do.

Performance, acting, and accurate motion-capture are not, then, the only markers of what can connect the audience emotionally to the animation. Sound and movement, the very basic elements of Wells' animation language, must also be considered when discussing emotional animation.

Notes

1 This narrative structure was discussed by Todorov in several of his works (1977, 1981).
2 There are numerous newspaper articles and reviews that can be found online where the reviewer admits to crying at the end of the film, despite the public nature of the cinema screening.
3 This has been cited in a variety of papers over the years, but all refer back to Masahiro Mori's work on robotics in 1970 (translated in 1978).

References

Aldred, Jessica. "All Aboard the Polar Express: A 'Playful' Change of Address in the Computer-Generated Blockbuster." *animation: an interdisciplinary journal*, 1(2), 2006: 153–172.

Bode, Lisa. "From Shadow Citizens to Teflon Stars: Reception of the Transfiguring Effects of New Moving Image Technologies." *animation: an interdisciplinary journal*, 1(2), 2006: 173–189.

Cholodenko, Alan (Ed.). *The Illusion of Life*. Sydney: Power Institute of Fine Arts, 1991.

——— *The Illusion of Life II: More Essays on Animation*. Sydney: Power Institute of Fine Arts, 2007.

Crafton, Donald. *Shadow of a Mouse, Performance, Belief and World Making in Animation*. Los Angeles: University of California Press, 2012.

Denslow, Phil. "What Is Animation and Who Needs to Know." In: Pilling, Jayne (Ed.). *A Reader in Animation Studies*. Sydney: John Libbey, 1997: 1–4.

Dobson, Nichola. "Nitpicking the Simpsons: Critique and Continuity in Constructed Realities" *animation journal*, 11, 2003: 84–93.

———— Historical Dictionary of Animation and Cartoons. Lanham: Scarecrow Press, 2009.

———— "TV Animation and Genre." In: Dobson, Nicola, Annabelle Honess Roe, Amy Ratelle, and Caroline Ruddell (Eds.). *The Animation Studies Handbook*. London/New York: Bloomsbury Press, 2018.: 181–189.

Gunning, Tom. "'Now You See It, Now You Don't': The Temporality of the Cinema of Attractions." *The Velvet Light Trap*, 2, 1993: 71–84.

Haswell, Helen. "'Business. Business. Business. Numbers. Is This Working?' Art vs. Commerce in the Post-Disney Pixar Studio." *Animation Studies 2.0*, 2015(a).

———— "To Infinity and Back Again: Hand-drawn Aesthetic and Affection for the Past in Pixar's Pioneering Animation." *Alphaville Journal of Film and Screen Media*, January 2015(b).

Hooks, Ed. *Acting for Animators*. [4th Edition]. New York: Routledge, 2017.

Ivins-Hulley, Laura "The Ontology of Performance in Stop Animation." *Animation Studies*, 3, 2008: 60–66.

Manovich, Lev. *The Language of New Media*. Cambridge: MIT Press, 2001.

Montgomery, Colleen. "Woody's Roundup and Wall-E's Wunderkammer: Technophilia and Nostalgia in Pixar Animation."" *Animation Studies*, 6, 2011.

Mittell, Jason. Genre and Television: From Cop Shows to Cartoons in American Culture. New York: Routledge, 2004.

Mihailova, Mihaela. "The Mastery Machine: Digital Animation and Fantasies of Control." *animation: an interdisciplinary journal*, 8(2), 2013: 131–148.

———— "Collaboration without Representation: Labor Issues in Motion and Performance Capture." *animation: an interdisciplinary journal*, 1(1), 2016: 40–58.

Propp, Vladimir. *Morphology of the Folk Tale*. [2nd Revised Edition]. Austin: University of Texas, 1968.

Power, Patrick. "Character Animation and the Embodied Mind-Brain." *animation: an interdisciplinary journal*, 3(1), 2008: 25–48.

————"Animated Expressions: Expressive Style in 3D Computer Graphic Narrative Animation." *animation: an interdisciplinary journal*, 4(2), 2009: 107–129.

Sobchack, Vivian. "Final Fantasies: Computer Graphic Animation and the (Dis) Illusion of Life." In: Buchan, Suzanne (Ed.). *Animated Worlds*. Eastleigh: John Libbey, 2006: 173–185.

Solomon, Charles (Ed.). *The Art of the Animated Image: An Anthology*. Los Angeles: American Film Institute, 1987.

Thomas, Frank and Ollie Johnston. *Disney Animation: The Illusion of Life.* [1st Edition.] New York: Abbeville Press, 1981.

———— *Introduction to Poetics*. Harvester: Brighton, 1981.

Todorov, Tzvetan. *The Poetics of Prose*. Blackwell: Oxford, 1977.

Ward, Paul. "Defining 'Animation': The Animated Film and the Emergence of the Film Bill." *scope: an online journal of film studies*, December 2000.

————"Some Thoughts on Practice-Theory Relationships in Animation Studies." *animation: an interdisciplinary journal* 1(2): 2006: 229–81.

Wells, Paul. *Understanding Animation*. London: Routledge, 1998.

———— *Animation: Genre and Authorship*. London: Wallflower Press, 2002.

Films & TV series

Antz. Directed by Eric Darnell and Tim Johnson. 1998; USA: DreamWorks/
Pacific Data Images.

Begone Dull Care. Directed by McLaren and Evelyn Lambart. 1949; CAN:
National Film Board.

BoJack Horseman: USA 2014–present, Netflix, created by Raphael
Bob-Waksberg.

Boogie Doodle. Directed by McLaren. 1941; CAN: National Film Board.

Duck Amuck. Directed by Chuck Jones. 1953; USA: Warner Brothers.

Fantasia. Directed by Samuel Armstrong et al. 1940; USA: Disney

Felix the Cat series: USA 1919–1932 (initial run), created by Pat Sullivan and
Otto Messmer.

Final Fantasy: Spirits Within. Directed by Hironobu Sakaguchi and Motonori
Sakakibara. 2001; USA/JP: Chris Lee Productions/Square Company.

The Flintstones: USA 1960–1966; ABC, created by William Hanna and Joseph
Barbera.

Happy Feet. Directed by George Miller and Warren Coleman. 2006; USA/AUS:
Warner Brothers/Village Roadshow Pictures/Kennedy Miller Productions/
Animal Logic Film.

The Hand. Directed by Jiri Trnka. 1965; CZ: Ustredni Pujcovna Filmu/
Loutkovy Film Praha/Studio Kresleného a Loutkového Filmu.

Ice Age. Directed by Chris Wedge and Carlos Saldanha. 2002; USA: Twentieth
Century Fox/Blue Sky Studio.

It's Such a Beautiful Day. Directed by Don Hertzfeldt. 2012; USA: Bitter Films.

The Lion King. Directed by Roger Allers and Rob Minkoff. 1994; USA: Disney.

Looney Tunes: USA 1930–1969 (original); 1987–present (revival), Cartoon
Network, Nickelodeon, ABC, created by Warner Brothers.

Merrie Melodies.1931–1969 (original); 1988–1991 (revival), created by Warner
Brothers.

Monsters, Inc. Directed by Pete Docter and David Silverman. 2001; USA:
Disney/Pixar.

Monster House. Directed by Gil Kenan. 2006; USA: Columbia Pictures/
Relativity/Media/ImageMovers.

The Polar Express. Directed by Robert Zemeckis. 2004; USA: Castle Rock
Entertainment/Shangri-La Entertainment/Playtone/ImageMovers.

Shrek. Directed by Andrew Adamson and Vicky Jenson. 2001; USA:
DreamWorks/Pacific Data Images.

Silly Symphonies: USA 1929–1939. Created by Walt Disney.

The Simpsons. USA 1989–present, FOX, created by Matt Groening.

Snow White and the Seven Dwarfs. Directed by William Cottrell, Wilfred
Jackson, Larry Morey, Perce Pearce, and Ben Sharpsteen. 1937; USA: Disney.

Toy Story. Directed by John Lasseter. 1995; USA: Disney/Pixar.

Toy Story 2. Directed by John Lasseter, Ash Brannon, and Lee Unkrich. 1999;
USA: Disney/Pixar.

Toy Story 3. Directed by Lee Unkrich. 2010; USA: Disney/Pixar.

World of Tomorrow. Directed by Don Hertzfeldt. 2016; USA: Bitter Films.

Surface, Movement, and Color

8 Light, Color, and (E)Motion

Animated Materiality and Surfaces in *Moana*

Kirsten Moana Thompson

Giuliana Bruno has spoken of film, architecture, and clothing as linked aesthetic surfaces in that all three have the ability to "house the motion of emotion" or make mood. For Bruno, the motion of an emotion can be "drafted onto the surface, in the shape of a line or in the haptic thickness of pigment." (2016: 5, 18). As a 3D-animated film that also features some 2D sequences, *Moana* (Musker and Clements 2016) demonstrates specific capacities to create magical worlds through computer-generated imagery, and in particular, the animated surfaces of water, sky, and light that play a central role in the story. This chapter attends to the relationship of material surface, e(motion) and color in Disney's feature film *Moana*, which has received some popular attention as the 'first' Disney film to feature a Polynesian princess. First, it situates *Moana* within a longer, yet largely unexamined aesthetic history of midcentury modernism and 'tiki kitsch,' in which the Pacific (*te Moana* in Hawaiian and Maori) has played an influential role in Disney architecture, theme park design, and animated cartoons. I then turn to the film's treatment of several specific material surfaces: Maui's tattoos, and the scintillating hard gold surface of Jemaine Clement's glam crab Tamatoa, in order to consider the ways in which they help shape animated (e)motion, as aesthetic strategies with their roots in traditional 2D cel animation. For Jean Epstein, whose notion of photogénie suggested an architectural understanding of light, "the design of the world is materialized in light in palpable ways, as light saturates a space, the universe of things becomes animated" (cited in Bruno 2016: 134). Following Giuliana Bruno's claim that new forms of 'connectivity and relationality' are enabled by the contemporary moving image as an illuminated and permeable surface, I want to explore the ways in which *Moana* foregrounds material surfaces as the 'universe of things,' in which emotions are animated (Bruno 2016: 125).

Moana forms part of a shift in Disney's representational practices in the last twenty-five years from the dominant versions of white femininity with which it has long been associated to a more globally diverse series of stories with American and non-Western protagonists of color, marked first by *Aladdin* (Clements and Musker 1992) and *Mulan* (Bancroft and

Cook 1998) through *Lilo and Stitch* (DeBlois and Sanders 2002) and *The Princess and the Frog* (Clements and Musker 2009) to, most recently, *Coco* (Unkrich and Molina 2017), although each of these films have also been heavily contested sites for debate and critique for their representational practices. Opening at US$56,631,400, *Moana* has been a strong earner for the Disney company, earning over $643 million worldwide and garnering two Academy award nominations.[1] Although it has not reached the domestic box office success of the US $400 million smash hit *Frozen*, it is Disney's fourth biggest non-Pixar hit (Mendelson 2017). Also known as *Oceania* in Italy and *Vaiana* in Spain and several other European countries, the film's title was changed to avoid confusion with an Italian porn star (Saunders 2016). *Moana* marks new territories in linguistic marketing, with releases or redubbing underway in three new languages with *te reo* Māori, Hawaiian, and Tahitian. By releasing *Moana* in the indigenous languages of three Pacific nations (New Zealand, Hawaii, and Tahiti), Disney has promoted the film as a form of support for what it has called 'endangered' languages, which, when combined with its marketing of *Moana* as an educational lesson on the Pacific, offers the imprimatur of cultural and linguistic authenticity while monetizing that very indigeneity under the Disney brand (Anon 2017a; see also Kroulek 2017).[2]

Moana's narrative engages with a precolonial moment about two thousand years ago called 'The Long Pause,' or a disputed period of time in which Pacific voyaging halted for unknown reasons after the initial settlement of Western Polynesia, before settlement then resumed in the eastern Pacific by around 300 CE (Kirch 2017: 232). The film's narrative offers a fictional response to this period of stasis through the now codified conventions of the Disney formula: the bold feminist heroine breaking the conventions of her isolationist father and community and venturing out beyond the reef to initiate the return of voyaging. The script went through multiple incarnations, from American directors Clements and Musker's initial focus on Maui, to New Zealander Taika Waititi's version, in which Moana was the rebel in a family of six older brothers, to the changes of Aaron and Jordan Kandall, who introduced Tamatoa the crab, the Kakamora and the central relationship of Maui and Moana, to the final version by Jared Bush. Most script iterations were structured through Disney (and Hollywood's) continuing focus on Joseph Campbell's twelve-part structure of the Hero's Journey (Anon 2014; V, Billy 2016).

Disney emphasized its desire to be culturally sensitive, taking several research trips to the Pacific – to Fiji, Samoa and Tonga, and then to Hawaii and New Zealand – and also formed an Oceanic Trust consultancy made up of Pacific anthropologists, linguists and other scholars and cultural authorities who made certain key design changes on costumes and characters. As Producer Osnat Shurer observed, "we placed a huge emphasis on authenticity," noting also that "we're making a Disney animated film full of fantasy and imagination, not a documentary. But we tried to honor the people and be respectful of the Pacific cultures that inspired the movie" (Julius and Malone 2016: 13). Nonetheless, criticism about the representational politics of *Moana* have been extensive, largely focusing on questions of ethnographic and cultural fidelity (cited in Anon 2017b: 27) and challenging the film's narrative and aesthetic hybridization of the linguistic, cultural and topological diversity of Pacific nations and peoples. Some critics have pointed to the ways in which Disney has simplified key Pacific mythological deities, by turning Pele into a lava witch or making the trickster Maui into a more buffoon-like character (Ngata 2016). Others, like M. Healani Sonoda-Pale, have pointed to the ways in which Disney's film is a form of settler colonialism in its commodification of Pacific cultures, pointing to the irony of Disney's Hawaiian resort's location as near the impoverished community of Nanakuli, one of the largest indigenous Hawaiian communities, where 62% live below the poverty line (Sonoda-Pale 2016). Tina Ngata has pointed to the paradox of Disney's merchandising of collectable *Moana* toys, whose plastic content only further contribute to the great garbage gyres found in the Pacific ocean. Additionally, Vincente M. Diaz claims that *Moana* is a "21st Century reanimation of romanticized primitivism" through a setting in the precolonial past that emphasizes "tropical beauty and island paradise, exotic culture, the mystical and the sacred." (Diaz 2016). Many of these critiques about Disney as an arm of settler neocolonialism are arguments that were first made by Ariel Dorfman and Armand Mattelart in 1983 and are well taken,[3] but what Diaz and other critics give insufficient attention to are the affectively powerful ways in which Disney's aesthetics shape the spectatorial response of its viewers, which Pacific scholar Teresia Teiawa also acknowledged in a series of observations on Disney written shortly before her death:

> My job as an academic is not to police indigenous artists or creatives or tell them who they can and cannot sell their talents to. I would never tell my students that they should not see Disney's *Moana*. Other people may call for boycotts but it is my duty to offer a) different perspectives on the film's cultural as well as material impact and b) point towards indigenous Pacific intellectual/artistic/activist sources of inspiration that can provide alternative structures of feeling--and thinking--to what's easily available through mass entertainment and consumer culture.
>
> (Teiawa 2016)[4]

In contrast to Teiawa though, this chapter's goal is to explore in greater depth some of these 'structures of feeling' and to understand the ways in which two-dimensional and three-dimensional surfaces within American animated films like *Moana* play powerful roles in structuring emotional identification with the Disney hero and its narrative formula. The first part of my argument suggests that the emotive power of Disney's animation is rooted in longer aesthetic histories, which borrow from a vernacular American modernism that has a particular cartoonal variant in American visual culture. The Disney studio has had a long history of representing the Pacific that dates back to its earliest theme park designs and that capitalized on the popularity of what I call a 'tiki aesthetic' that first emerged in the 1920s in California. This tiki aesthetic was shaped by certain Polynesian and Melanesian graphic and architectural design features combined with a simplified Western graphic neo-primitivist modernism, and later intensified under the effects of the American military presence in the Pacific region during World War II. Along with the emergence and popularity of Hawaiian music, the first formations of an American-generated hybrid blend of Pacific and Californian aesthetics now known as tiki culture emerged, and which have been mapped by popular historians like Sven Kirsten (2003; 2014). As Kirsten's history tells us, key sites that shaped and channeled the popularity of Hawaiian music, and more generally, the representation of the Pacific, included international world fairs and expos, particularly that of the 1915 Panama–Pacific International Exposition in San Francisco (2014: 50). By the 1940s, the war in the Pacific intensified the tiki aesthetic, playing a paradoxical role in postwar Pacific tourism, with wartime construction of wharves, roads, and airfields creating the basic infrastructure for postwar international tourism while also stimulating or reviving the indigenous production of artisanal handcrafts for sale to American soldiers and sailors (Mallon 2012). In 1947, James Michener's Pulitzer Prize-winning novel *Tales of the South Pacific*[5] came out in the same year that Thor Heyerdahl's balsa raft was garnering headlines in its voyage across the Pacific from Peru to Tahiti. Rodgers and Hammerstein's smash Broadway musical *South Pacific* (1949) only intensified the American cultural popularity of this tiki aesthetic, while Don the Beachcomber and Trader Vic's bars and restaurants expanded architectural franchises they had begun in the twenties and thirties. Inspired by Melanesian A-frame architecture and Polynesian and Melanesian tapa cloth and carvings, restaurants, bowling alleys, hotels, and bars adopted tiki aesthetics, which by the 1950s were increasingly ubiquitous forms in the United States.

Disney and Tiki Aesthetics

To further capitalize on the financial and cultural popularity of this *imaginary* Pacific, in 1963 the Disney studio built the Enchanted Tiki Room as the first showcase for its animatronic technology. With interior and exterior designs by Rolly Crump, it still operates today (Titizian 2013) (see Figure 8.1).

Figure 8.1 Enchanted Tiki Room, Walt Disney Themepark [Public domain], via Wikimedia Commons.

The Tiki Room's animatronic parrots and colorful fountain staged a traditional Western chromophilic association of color and exoticism in which anthropomorphized macaws and colored water displays were choreographed in a stage show whose technological novelty was long an enormous attraction at the theme park.[6] A year after the Enchanted Tiki Room first opened, Disney designer and noted colorist Mary Blair, whose work shaped the look of Disney features like *Alice in Wonderland* and *Peter Pan* (Geronimi, Jackson, and Luske 1951, 1953) with her flat color blocks and childlike designs, was hired to create individual drawings and figures for the studio exhibit *It's a Small World* for the 1964 NY World's Fair. This exhibition was later opened at Disneyland, with sections devoted to New Zealand, Australia, and the Pacific, and was based on designs sketched by Blair.[7] She also designed murals for the Contemporary Resort, which opened in the same year, 1971, as Disney's Polynesian Village Resort. These tiki aesthetic forms have received some nostalgic revival in American popular culture recently, from Hawaiian episodes on *Mad Men* to Squidward's "Enchanted Tiki Dreams" episode of *SpongeBob SquarePants,* which spawned a popular song. These moments of televisual nostalgia have joined major tiki art collection expos since the 1990s and the commercial popularity of retro artists like Californian artist Shag, whose work adopts the flat, bold colors and simplified linear outlines of a mid-century graphic modernism.[8] For the 50th anniversary of the Enchanted Tiki Room, Disney upgraded their exhibit with some changes to its sound design and length, and Shag was hired to create his own artwork homages to the Enchanted Tiki Room, which went on sale at Disney stores. This was followed by a new comic book series, *Enchanted Tiki Room*, in 2016.[9] The relationship between the Los Angeles film and animation industries and the design industry in Tiki pop continues with John Lasseter's collection of custom made Hawaiian shirts, which went on display at Disney Expo D23 in 2015 (Lasseter, the head of animation at Disney/Pixar, has had a custom shirt made for each Disney feature film he has helmed since 1999 – see Fox 2015).

But it's not just theme park architectural design and studio merchandising that were influenced by the cultural popularity of tiki aesthetics. In the 1950s, a new style in animation was pioneered by a group of Disney artists who had been fired after the 1941 strike and who then formed their own studio, UPA (United Production of America). Influenced by mid-century graphic modernist styles in advertising and design, UPA's new form of limited animation featured a self-reflexive engagement with the graphic line, angular rather than curvilinear characters, stylized movement, minimalist backgrounds, and planes of flat color to create mood or stand in for lighting or spatial effects, in innovative experimental cartoons like *Gerald McBoing Boing* (Cannon 1951) or *Rooty Toot Toot* (Hubley 1951).[10] While tiki design certainly had its genealogical roots in the neo-primitivist fascinations of European modern art in the 1920s, what has not been considered has been the ways in which this tiki art became fused with the simplified forms of mid-century animated aesthetics, sharing the leitmotifs of stark black outlines, bold flat colors, and recurring graphic design units like the A-frame, the triangle, the diamond, and the oval. As Lisa Keene, the Visual Development artist for *Moana* has observed "No matter what culture we come from, we visually interpret emotion in a similar way through color and shape language." (Julius and Malone 2016: 72). While her notion of the universality of color and shape language is certainly arguable, what I want to suggest here is the ways in which the surfaces of *Moana* interact with more self-evidently emotive devices like music, color, and characterization to shape the viewer's passage through the narrative.

Animated Surfaces in Moana: Maui

Moana deploys a number of mixed aesthetic modes, of traditional flat surfaces like tapa cloth[11] that alternate with more rounded, three-dimensional forms and immersive spaces or that combine flat and three-dimensional characters and objects. Early concept art, such as the Eyvind Earle-like turquoise and purple of Lalotai's ancestral world by James Finch, or the hot pink, black, and light blue color scenes of Tamatoa's underworld realm in Lalotai imagined by Kevin Nelson, featured tiki-like totems, as did the stylized character design of the coconut armor-wearing Kakamora characters, created by Leighton Hickman (Julius and Malone 2016: 110–111 (Finch); 114 (Hickman); 122 and 136 (Nelson)). Although the film was Musker and Clements' first foray into 3D animation, a choice which was driven by the technical demands of creating a visually plausible ocean, 2D was used to create Maui's tattoos, which appear in tapa- or *siapo*-cloth-like designs as a prologue to the film, as well as anthropomorphized 'animation within the animation' sequences throughout the film. Recycling a convention of drawings 'coming to life' has been part of animation's history since its beginnings, but *Moana*'s directors Musker and Clements also recycled this idea from their earlier film *Hercules* (1997), which featured simplified, flat black silhouette figures painted on vases and which spring into movement. Disney's *Moana* tells the backstory of Maui's epic legends using a device dubbed 'Mini Maui' by the animators where the tattoos on his arms, chest, and back come to life and move around (see Figure 8.2).

According to Disney, the circular design of these tattoos was inspired by Marquesan and Tahitian traditions, in contrast to the Samoan design of the villagers' tattoos (Julius and Malone 2016: 96; 99). As Maui sings his song "You're Welcome," we see allusions to some of his most famous feats as a demigod, with each tattoo on his body animating in turn; we see Maui lassoing the sun to create daytime, stealing fire from the underworld, pulling islands from the sea, harnessing the wind, creating the coconut tree by beheading the eel, and defeating an eight-eyed fruit-bat. (Maui's shameful origin story of his mother's abandonment is also shown but located under his hair on his back, where it is least visible and only later acknowledged by him in the narrative – see Figure 8.3).

Inspired by visual development artist Sue Nichols' initial idea and story artist Jeff Ranjo's boards, Maui's song tells us that the "tapestry here on my skin is a map of the victories I win," as the sequence alternates between 3D, computer-generated 'large Maui' and 2D drawings of 'Mini Maui' and various other elements. Shaking out a tapa cloth, Maui

Figure 8.2 Maui captures the sun to give us longer daylight hours. Mini Maui, detail. Framegrab (©Disney).

Figure 8.3 View of Maui's back tattoos (©Disney).

and Moana suddenly enter into a self-reflexively graphic universe, where they become characters placed against a tapa background and within and between tapa foreground cutouts of coconuts, flying fish, and fruit. The pulse of the song's beat as Maui taps out the rhythm on a coconut reminds us again of his mythic connections to the origin of the coconut in the Samoan legend Sina and the Eel,[12] and as we cut to a wider shot, we see a smiling monster, inside of which dances an eel, each dancing to the beat of Maui's song, along with an enthusiastic dancing crowd (which turns out to be another detail from the tattoo on the center of Maui's back – see Figure 8.3).

The representation of the demi god was decried by critics for implying that Maui was obese rather than large and powerful. Jenny Salesa, a member of New Zealand's parliament publically aligned herself with the Facebook post of a prominent Samoan former rugby player Eliota

Fuimaono-Sapolu, in which he wrote that Maui "looked like, after he fished up the Islands, he deep fried 'em and ate 'em." (see Jones 2016; see also Ito 2016). Indeed, this inflated shape was chosen by the animators, claiming that they wanted to represent Maui's *mana* (which can mean, prestige, status or authority) through his size and long hair, after an initial design of Maui as bald was rejected by the Oceanic Trust. According to Disney, the 'larger canvas' of Maui's body, from the planes of his chest and back to his rounded bicep and triangular pectal muscles, "posed a major technical challenge to supervising animators Mack Kablan and Eric Goldberg," as described in a New York Times interview that also noted, "The movement of human skin is much tougher to render in computer animation than clothing; since Maui is one of the most underdressed Disney characters in recent memory, Mr. Kablan's team had its work cut out for it." According to Kablan, "We looked at football players, pro wrestlers and 'world's strongest men'" as part of their research (Ito 2016). New software had to be written in order to figure out how skin slides believably over muscle. One of the unconventional aspects of Maui's design, in addition to the balloon-like texture of the torso and arms, was that Maui's design did not follow human proportions; rather, it was modeled on a square shape, with legs half the normal length: Marlon West, the head of visual effects noted that most Disney characters are fully clothed "but in *Moana*, we have characters like Maui with a lot of skin showing. That was a new test for both character and tech animation."[13] Indeed, there is an odd visual quality to Maui's character design, which appears balloon- or rubber hose-like in form and plastic in surface texture, lacking the more detailed shading and color gradations of human skin. Indeed, Maui's squared (dis)proportions, when coupled with his balloony scale and plastic-like surface, seems to suggest that Maui is already toylike, an aesthetic transformation of the character's body that is in keeping with an understanding of his corporeal surface as screen. This failed design was probably dictated by the narrative device of Mini Maui's tattoos coming to life and interacting with the larger Maui and seems borne out by director John Musker's acknowledgement that "[Maui] is a walking billboard of his great deeds, which is a great storytelling device for us." (Schwartz 2016).

Yet it is interesting that Musker shows an awareness of brown skin as reified surface, as Disney seemed blind to it in their franchising. The company's advertisement of a Maui Halloween skin costume for sale for $44 to $50 promised "Your little one will set off on adventures in this Maui costume featuring the demigod's signature tattoos, rope necklace and island-style skirt. Plus, padded arms and legs for mighty stature!" Widely attacked on social media as a twenty-first-century version of brownface ("Wear another culture's skin!") the skinsuit was criticized as Buffalo Bill-like and eventually withdrawn (Ngata 2016). However, hoodies and sweatshirts for adults that feature Maui's tattooed skin designs are still for sale.[14] As writer and Pacific scholar Albert Wendt has noted "In many Pacific cultures, body decoration and adornment is considered clothing. We have to be careful about those terms though because much of what has been considered 'decoration' or 'adornment' by outsiders is to do with identity (individual/*aiga* (family)/group), status, age, religious beliefs, relationships to other art forms and the community, and not to do with prettying yourself." (Wendt 1996). To wear a tatau or tattoo (black ink) is to be considered 'clothed,' not naked, and socially equipped and marked as having gone through the endurance ritual of the *pe'a* or *malu* (Samoan male and female traditional tattoos) that mark one as an adult and that publically inscribe one's personal, familial, and communal affiliations.

Disney's approach to the tattoo is to separate it from its bodily surface and cultural context and brand it as a detachable design surface. Indeed, the Disney artists repeatedly referred to tapestry and lace as their specific Western design referents for Maui and the villager tattoos.[15]Additionally, at the D23 expo in 2015, a biennial expo for Disney cosplay enthusiasts, collectors, and fans, visitors could photograph themselves against a background that featured Tinkerbell's wings designed with traditional Samoan male (*pe'a*) tattoo elements. Disney's approach to cultural design echoes missteps by other corporations, such as Fiji Airlines' controversial attempt to copyright 15 traditional Fijian *iTaukei* design elements in 2013 (Vaka'uta: 28). Artist Shigeyuki Kihara's 2011 art installation *Culture for Sale* has taken up this issue by turning an eye to the "inherent inequalities of parallel institutions in the nineteenth century colonial context" that also sought to monetize traditional cultural dress and performance, such as the German travelling Völkerschau, where Samoan men, women and children were toured across German cities, exhibited as part of a human ethnographic zoo, and described as "little chocolate-covered marzipan dolls" in a series of shows over two decades before World War II.[16] While Fatimah Rony has written of how cinema took over the exhibitory function of such tours and world fairs as the taxidermic impulse (1996: 101), what this nineteenth-century journalist's description of Samoans as 'marzipan dolls' points to is a remediation and displacement of cultural difference onto a kind of miniaturized, toylike surface, one which Melissa McCarthy's recent satiric performance as White House Press Secretary Sean Spicer also invokes through another toy. In her Emmy Award-winning Saturday Night Live skit, McCarthy's Spicer calls attention to the xenophobic immigration policies of the Trump administration with the aid of a Moana doll, by critiquing the racial profiling of brown skin surface, using a promotional toy from a film which itself foregrounded the racialized and embodied nature of surfaces.[17] (See Figure 8.4.)

Figure 8.4 Melissa McCarthy: "Uh-oh, It's Moana.!......Boom! Guantanamo Bay" Framegrab. *Saturday Night Live* (©NBCUniversal).

Animated Surfaces in Moana: Tamatoa

Along with an attention to miniature objects and surfaces like tattooed skin and tapa designs that playfully entertain the viewer's eye as they metamorphose, another key surface that is self-reflexively foregrounded in *Moana* is the shiny, gold-encrusted surfaces of the glam rock collector crab known as Tamatoa (voiced by Jemaine Clement). Like a robber pirate, his shell is made up of thousands of scintillating surfaces gathered from the ocean, from organic shells and mother of pearl to the flotsam of human wreckage (shipwrecked boat skeletons are also part of the assemblage of Tamatoa's shell). In Tamatoa's universe, both Maui and Moana are tiny figures in the underworld of Lalotai. They find themselves within an inverted shell that is his lair, where they "look like seafood" to the giant crab. As Tamatoa toys with his food, the staging magnifies Tamatoa's size through a low angle in which we are invited to optically identify with Moana's point of view and look up into Tamatoa's face. Behind him, we can periodically glimpse flares of light that signal the opening of the giant shell in which Tamatoa lives and in which Maui and Moana find themselves. Quick camera cuts alternate between Moana's subjective and imperiled point of view and objective shots in which the camera moves in rhythm with Tamatoa's performance as he dances in a clockwise motion. The space around Moana and Tamatoa is filled with dozens of rotating golden lights, presumably reflected by Tamatoa's shell, which acts as a kind of disco ball in the inverted shell, and the effect of this illuminated background is a hallucinatory one for the viewer, spectacularizing Tamatoa as performer and immersing the viewer in an underwater auditorium. This is Tamatoa's moment and he is enjoying every minute of it: With more than a little braggadocio, he sings in his song "Shiny," "Watch me dazzle like a diamond in the rough/Strut my stuff/my stuff is so Shiny." The transporting effects of the clockwise camera movement and Tamatoa's own performance, coupled with the illuminatory transformation of the underwater world into a nightclub, is only intensified when the scene shifts suddenly into black light, spatially disorienting us with a shift into an ultraviolet world of blacks, deep blues, hot pinks, and neon greens. Now Tamatoa's golden shell is like the night sky: a glittering constellation. Overhead shots of Tamatoa spinning around against an illuminated shell that now appears like the deepest reaches of the galaxy, demonstrates again how *Moana's mise-en-scène* inverts and transforms space.

While Tamatoa is distracted with his own fabulousness, Maui tries to intervene and rescue Moana, yet he fails to transform into the giant hawk that Mini Maui helpfully suggests, and instead cycles through a comical sequence of embarrassing failures, from a tiny fish to a shark, the reindeer Sven from *Frozen*, and a pig, before returning to his normal form. This gives Tamatoa the occasion to mock Maui again, giving particular attention to Maui's diminutive scale: "Well, well, well, Little Maui's having trouble with his look/You little semi-demi-mini-god/Ouch! What a terrible performance." This inversion of the normal order of scale between humans and crab is another example of the ways in which *Moana's* surfaces duplicate, mirror, or invert parallel universes – between Maui and his tattoos, between the mythic and the ordinary, between the living and the ancestors, between sea and sky, and ultimately between Earth and the universe.

Although Maui's plastic and toylike surface differs visibly from Tamatoa's shiny, hard, and reflective gold shell, both 'characters' are paralleled in that they are vainglorious narcissists whose bodies reflect their literal remediation and reconstruction of themselves. Their mobile, graphic, or sculptural autobiographies are a different form of taxidermy. After all, it takes one to know one, as Tamatoa sings to Maui: "For just like you, I made myself a work of art." We recall that the word taxidermy is derived from the Greek words 'taxis' and 'derma,' with 'taxis' meaning 'to move' or to arrange and 'derma' meaning 'skin' (the dermis); thus the word 'taxidermy' translates to an 'arrangement of skin.' Here, color functions in combination with sculptural surface to spectacularize and self-promote. Tamatoa's song, written by Lin-Manuel Miranda as a glam rock homage to David Bowie, emphasizes his taxidermic self-invention: He sings "Well Tamatoa wasn't always this glam/I was a drab little crab once," his bling based on his desire to be "shiny, like a wealthy woman's neck." With its reimagining of the ocean depths as a glam-rock disco of ultraviolet light and golden disco balls, the ocean becomes a cosmopolitan site, with Tamatoa inviting in those "dumb, dumb dumb fish, they chase anything that glitters (beginners)."

Moana, Maui, and Tamatoa are cosmopolites: not static or preservative in Rony's sense but, rather, figures of mobility, metamorphosis, and exchange, distinctively animated and emotionally transporting. This distinction between the characters of stasis and those of exchange are inscribed in the film through color key distinctions, between the muted browns associated with the villagers of the island of Motunui and the more colorful clothing of the voyagers. Producer Osnat Shurer noted of visual development artist Neysa Bové's costume designs: "The voyagers would find ti or palm leaves and quickly put them together, maybe shredding them at the bottom to add a bit of beauty. And they brought in a lot of color from the vegetation around them" (Julius and Malone 2016: 43). By contrast, Neysa Bové observed that "The Motunui villagers lose their color. They've established themselves. The plants they use are dried, and when things dry, they become brown. The materials are still beautiful, but it shows they've spent a bit more time on each thing because they have the time to make it." (Julius and Malone 2016: 43).

Giuliana Bruno has argued for a new understanding of the contemporary screen that shifts away from a window or frame to the screen as a site of mediation and projection in which surface luminosity and textural hapticity are foregrounded by the materiality of the image. She points to the spectacular role of light in recent contemporary art, like Cuban artist Carlos Garaicoa's *On How the Earth Wishes to Resemble the Sky* (2005), where the screen acts "as if it were a canvas, a material in which holes have been made, through which a shining light is made to shimmer" (Bruno 2016: 6).[18] Like Garaicoa, Yayoi Kusama's Infinity Rooms series also use the reflection and magnification of light through mirrors and water to emphasize the transcendent role that light plays.[19] Yet the reflective and projective techniques of contemporary artists like Kusama and Garaicoa are devices that animation has long been engaged in showing us.

I want to join Jean Epstein and Giuliana Bruno's notions of the architectonic notion of light to the Samoan notion of *Va*. *Va* is a philosophical and spiritual concept that refers to the space between, not as emptiness, but as connectedness, as relationality; in Albert Wendt's words, it is "the space that is context." (Wendt 1996). This 'space between' can be read through the visual figure of bioluminescent light. As the biochemical emission of light by living organisms (OED), bioluminescence collapses the boundaries between light and color, between the organism and the natural environment in which its light is contextualized. But *Moana*'s bioluminescent green, purple and blue colors also signal animated magical powers and realms, from Tamatoa's location in the underworld Lalotai, to Maui's magical transformations marked by his glowing tattoos and fishhook filigreed with scrimshaw, to the presence of Moana's voyaging ancestors, including her grandmother Tala as a stingray spirit. As Hannah Goodwin's recent work on cinema and cosmology reminds us, the night sky is akin to a movie theater. Like cinema, the night sky involves a temporal delay, between the time the light from a distant star is emitted, until the moment that we actually see it, a time that is determined by the fixed speed of light and separated by the millions of miles over which it must travel. The night sky and cinema share two fundamental ontological similarities: "as repositories of light from the past and as surfaces for the projection of human desires, aspirations, dislocations and uncertainties," (Goodwin unpublished: 2) cinema makes us voyagers, bringing the indexical light from the past into our present. In speaking of *Nostalgia for the Light*, we might well imagine Goodwin is speaking of the ending of *Moana,* "The night sky in this film becomes a space where the dead can be imagined, both immaterially and materially, even if their earthly traces are not recuperable." (Goodwin unpublished: 13).

By imagining the bowl of the night sky and the reflective surface of the black ocean at night as a kind of giant immersive movie theater, these surfaces are simultaneously, a constellational map of Moana's voyage across the Pacific, a site of reunification with the stingray spirit of her grandmother Tala, and a shared and reanimated space for the ancestors who came before her, and who together with Moana sing "We Know the Way" as they voyage again with her:

> Aue, aue, we are explorers reading every sign
> We tell the stories of our elders
> In the never ending chain[20]

Whether as colored light tattooing the night sky or the body, they mark the way for Moana across the ocean and the sky, which, at night and in the day, frequently have no boundaries between them. For, as Epeli Hau'ofa reminded us in *Our Sea of Islands* (Epeli Hau'ofa 1999), the Pacific is a vast continuum of water and islands, connected by voyaging. For Moana, and even the vainglorious Maui and Tamatoa, are animated figures of metamorphoses, mobility, and exchange, their corporeal or personal reinventions calling emotional witness to, and insisting upon a fundamental cosmopolitan understanding of the Pacific.

Notes

1 Moana had a domestic gross of 248,757,044 and international gross of 394,574,067; it has earned a total of US $643,331,111 in theatrical release: www.boxofficemojo.com/movies/?id=disney1116.htm (12.2.2017).
2 In a 40-page booklet for American elementary grades 2–6, Disney's *Educator's Guide* has sections that focus on (1) storytelling and mythology, with an emphasis on the heroic structure of Joseph Campbell's *The Hero With a Thousand Faces*; (2) navigational wayfinding, including constellations and the ocean's currents; and (3) conservation of the Pacific, with a specific case study focusing on different species of sea turtles. It also offers a series of student activities and puzzles.
3 *How to Read Donald Duck: Imperialist Ideology in the Disney Comic.* The Netherlands: International General, 1983.
4 I dedicate this article to Teresia Teiawa.

5 For a related story in the Samoan context that also connected to the popularity of James Michener's work see my article "The Construction of a
  Myth: Bloody Mary, Aggie Grey and the Optics of Tourism." *Journal of NZ
  and Pacific Studies,* 2(1), 2014: 5–19.
6 For more on the association of color and primitivism, see John Gage. *Color
  and Culture: Practice and Meaning from Antiquity to Abstraction.* Los
  Angeles: University of California Press, 1999; and David Batchelor. *Chromophobia.* Islingtoṅ: Reaktion, 2000.
7 See in particular the sketches Blair designed for New Guinea and Hawaii
  featured in *Magic Color, Flair: The World of Mary Blair* exhibit, March
  13–Sep. 7, 2014, Walt Disney Museum, San Francisco, and exhibition cat-
  alog, John Canemaker: *Magic, Color, Flair: The World of Mary Blair.* San
  Francisco: Walt Disney Family Foundation Press, 2014.
8 See Episode 1 & 2, Season 6, *Mad Men,* Director Scott Hornbacher, Show-
  runner, Matthew Weiner. Aired April 7, 2013; see also "Enchanted Tiki
  Dreams" *Spongebob Squarepants* (1999-present), Episode 145b, Season 7,
  aired June 29, 2010; for the revival in tiki aesthetics see Sven Kirsten "The
  Tiki Revival" in *Tiki Pop,* 367–383; retro Californian artist Shag has created artwork for Disney, see http://www.shag.com; for examples of tiki expos, see http://tikioasis.com/ and http://www.tikikon.com/ (12.2.2017).
9 Michelle Harker. "Walt Disney's Enchanted Tiki Room 50th Anniversary
  Event at the Disneyland Resort" February 28, 2013 Disney Parks Blog:
  https://disneyparks.disney.go.com/blog/galleries/2013/02/walt-disneys-
  enchanted-tiki-room-50th-anniversary-event-at-the-disneyland-resort/
  (12.2.2017). For the comic book series, see Steven Miller. "First Look: Enchanted Tiki Room Comic Series from Disney Kingdoms" Sept. 5 2016,
  https://disneyparks.disney.go.com/blog/2016/09/first-look-enchanted-tiki-
  room-comic-series-from-disney-kingdoms/ (12.5. 2017).
10 For more on the aesthetics of mid-century modernism and animation, see
  Maureen Furniss. "Full and Limited Animation." In: Furniss, Maureen. *Art
  in Motion: Animation Aesthetics,* rev. ed. London: John Libbey, 2007: 133–
  150; Amidi, Amid. *Cartoon Modern: Style and Design in Fifties Animation.*
  Chronicle: San Francisco, 2006.
11 Tapa, a term derived from the Cook Islands and Tahiti and often used to
  describe a material created by softening and beating the bark of the mul-
  berry tree and then dyeing it with red and brown colors, is also called *siapo*
  (Samoa), *kapa* (Hawaii) and *hiapo* (Tonga).
12 A version of the Sina and the Eel tale can be found in C. Steubel and Brother
  Herman, *Tala o le Vavau: The Myths, Legends and Customs of Old Samoa.*
  Auckland: Polynesian Press, 1976.
13 Maui was initially designed as bald (with designs by Ryan Lang) but hair
  was added in after speaking with the consultants from Tahiti, who talked of
  Maui's mana (Julius and Malone 2016: 86).
14 See, for example, Amazon's selection at: www.amazon.com/AOVCLKID-
  Sweatshirt-Children-Cartoon-3-4Y/dp/B075CHPLF7/ref=sr_1_1?ie=UTF8
  &qid=1512852883&sr=8-1&keywords=maui+hoodie (12.1.17).
15 Lisa Keene, visual development artist, described traditional women's tattoos
  (*malu* in Samoa) as "very feminine, delicate, and lacy, almost like they're
  wearing lacy stockings" (Julius and Malone 2016: 51).
16 On Fiji Airlines, see Cresantia Koya Vaka'uta, "The Pacific's Cultural
  Genocide," *República.* 6 (October) 2013: 28–31, 28. See "Culture for Sale"
  Tautai: Guiding Pacific Arts, http://www.tautai.org/culture-sale-forum/
  (1.5.2016); *Vossische Zeitung,* 19 Sept, 1895, cited in Thoda-Arora, Hilke.

"Around the World for Fifty Pence: The Phenomenon of the Ethnic Shows" *From Samoa With Love? Samoan Travellers in Germany 1895–1911 Retracing the Footsteps*. Museum Fünf Kontinente: München, 2014: 79–93.

17 Melissa McCarthy sketch, "Daily White House Press Briefing with Press Secretary Sean Spicer" *Saturday Night Live* Cold Open, Feb 17, 2017: www.youtube.com/watch?v=fbhz3XcNzGU (12.8.17).

18 See also Carlos Garaicoa: http://www.carlosgaraicoa.com/castleford/index.html (5.5.16).

19 See Yayoi Kusama: http://yayoi-kusama.jp/e/biography/index.html (4.6.16).

20 Music and Lyrics by Lin-Manuel Miranda and Opetaia Foa'i.

References

Amidi, Amid. *Cartoon Modern: Style and Design in Fifties Animation*. San Francisco: San Francisco Chronicle, 2006.

Anon, "Taika Waititi Behind Disney Script *Moana*." *The New Zealand Herald*, October 21, 2014: http://nzherald.co.nz/entertainment/news/article.cfm?c_id=1501119&objectid=11345855 (10.08.2015).

—— "Casting Underway for Hawaiian language Version of *Moana*" *Khon*, 2, November 2, 2017a: http://khon2.com/2017/11/02/casting-underway-for-hawaiian-language-version-of-moana/ (11.13.2017).

—— "Disney Depiction of Obese Polynesian God in Film *Moana* Sparks Anger." *The Guardian*, June 27, 2017b: https://theguardian.com/world/2016/jun/27/disney-depiction-of-obese-polynesian-god-in-film-moana-sparks-anger (07.05.2016).

Batchelor, David. *Chromophobia*. Islington: Reaktion, 2000.

Bruno, Giuliana. *Surface: Matters of Aesthetics, Materiality, and Media*. Chicago: University of Chicago, 2016.

Canemaker, John: *Magic, Color, Flair: The World of Mary Blair*. San Francisco: Walt Disney Family Foundation Press, 2014.

Diaz, Vicente M. "Don't Swallow (or be Swallowed by) Disney's 'Culturally Authenticated *Moana*'." *Indian Country Today*, November 13, 2016.

Dorfman, Ariel and Armand Mattelart. *How to Read Donald Duck: Imperialist Ideology in the Disney Comic*. The Netherlands: International General, 1983.

Fox, Steve. "Disney Expo 2015: John Lasseter Hawaiian Shirts on Display for Fans to See Fun Pixar Twists" D23, August 16, 2015: http://insidethemagic.net/2015/08/d23-expo-2015-john-lasseter-hawaiian-shirts-on-display-for-fans-to-see-fun-pixar-twists/ (12.06.2017).

Furniss, Maureen. "Full and Limited Animation." In: Furniss, Maureen (Ed.). *Art in Motion: Animation Aesthetics*. London: John Libbey, 2007: 133–150.

Gage, John. *Color and Culture: Practice and Meaning from Antiquity to Abstraction*. Los Angeles: University of California Press, 1999.

Garaicoa, Carlos. *Artist Website*: www.carlosgaraicoa.com/castleford/index.html (05.05.16).

Goodwin, Hannah. "Cosmic Archives: From Film Theory to *Nostalgia for the Light*" an excerpt from her larger book project *Modern Astronomy: Cinematic Cosmologies, 1896–1962* (unpublished manuscript).

Harker, Michelle. "Walt Disney's Enchanted Tiki Room 50th Anniversary Event at the Disneyland Resort" February 28, Disney Parks Blog, 2013: https://disneyparks.disney.go.com/blog/galleries/2013/02/walt-disneys-enchanted-tiki-room-50th-anniversary-event-at-the-disneyland-resort/ (12.02.2017).

Hau'ofa, Epeli. "Our Sea of Islands." In: Hereniko, Vilsoni and Rob Wilson (Eds.). *Inside Out: Literature, Cultural Politics and Identity in the New Pacific*. Oxford: Rowman & Littlefield, 1999: 27–38.

Ito, Robert. "How (and Why) Maui Got So Big in *Moana*." New York Times, November 15, 2016: https://nytimes.com/2016/11/20/movies/moana-and-how-maui-got-so-big.html?action=click&contentCollection=Movies&module=RelatedCoverage&region=EndOfArticle&pgtype=article&_r=1%20Nicholas%20Jones (12.01.2016).

Jones, Robert. "Labour MP Jenny Salesa says Disney Portrayal of Maui in *Moana* Movie Sends Wrong Message." *New Zealand Herald*, June 23, 2016: http://nzherald.co.nz/nz/news/article.cfm?c_id=1&objectid=11662159 (12.02.17).

Julius, Jessica and Maggie Malone. *The Art of Disney: Moana*. Preface by John Lasseter. San Francisco: Chronicle, 2016.

Kihara, Shigeyuki, "Culture for Sale" *Tautai: Guiding Pacific Arts:* http://tautai.org/culture-sale-forum/ (01.05.2016).

Kirch, Patrick Vinton. *On the Road of the Winds: An Archaeological History of the Pacific Islands Before European Contact*. Los Angeles: University of California Press, 2017.

Kirsten, Sven A. *The Book of Tiki: The Cult of Polynesian Pop in Fifties America*. Köln: Taschen, 2003.

——— *Tiki Pop: America Imagines its Own Polynesian Paradise*. Musée du Quai Branly. Köln: Taschen, 2014.

Kroulek, Alison. "The Languages of Moana." *K International: The Language Blog*, October 2. 2017: http://.k-international.com/blog/the-languages-of-moana/ (12.02.2017).

Kusama, Yayoi. *Artist Website*: http://yayoi-kusama.jp/e/biography/index.html (04.06.2016).

Mallon, Sean. "War and Visual Culture, 1939–1945." In: Brunt, Peter, Nicholas Thomas and Sean Mallon et al. (Eds.). *Art in Oceania: A New History*. London: Thames and Hudson, 2012: 326–347.

Mendelson, Scott. "Disney's *Moana* is no *Frozen* But it's Still a Big Hit." *Forbes.com*, January 9, 2017: https://forbes.com/sites/scottmendelson/2017/01/09/box-office-disneys-moana-is-no-frozen-but-its-still-a-big-hit/#1ffb1a1c7341 (11.13.2017).

Moana. Box Office Mojo http://www.boxofficemojo.com/movies/?id=disney1116.htm. (12.02.2017).

Miller, Steven, "*First Look: Enchanted Tiki Room Comic Series from Disney Kingdoms*." September 5, 2016: https://disneyparks.disney.go.com/blog/2016/09/first-look-enchanted-tiki-room-comic-series-from-disney-kingdoms/ (11.13.2017).

Ngata, Tina. "Maui Skin Suit isn't the End of Moana Trouble." *Honolulu Civil Beat*, September 27, 2016: http://www.civilbeat.org/2016/09/maui-skin-suit-isnt-the-end-of-moana-trouble/ (12.2.2016).

Rony, Fatimah Tobing. *The Third Eye: Race, Cinema and the Ethnographic Spectacle*. Durham: Duke University Press, 1996.

Saunders, Tristram Fane. "Disney Renamed its New Film *Moana* to Avoid Confusion with Porn Star." *The Telegraph*, November 16, 2016: www.telegraph.co.uk/films/2016/11/16/disney-renamed-its-new-film-moana-to-avoid-confusion-with-porn-s/ (03. 2. 2017).

Schwartz, Terri. "8 Reasons to Get Excited for Disney's *Moana*." *IGN*, September 7, 2016: http://ign.com/articles/2016/09/07/8-reasons-to-get-excited-for-disneys-moana (04.04.2017).

Sonoda-Pale, M. Healani. "Disney's Commodification of Hawaiians." *Honolulu Civil Beat*, October 7, 2016: http://civilbeat.org/2016/10/disneys-commodification-of-hawaiians/ (12.01.2016).

Steubel, C. and Bro. Herman (adapted from the collections). *Tala o le Vavau: The Myths, Legends and Customs of Old Samoa*. Auckland: Polynesian Press, 1976.

Teiawa, Teresia. "I Was Once Seduced by Disney. But No Longer." *E-Tangata*, October 9, 2016: https://e-tangata.co.nz/news/teresia-teaiwa-i-was-once-seduced-by-disney/issues (12.02.2017).

Titizian, Joseph *"Disneyland, The Classics: Walt Disney's Enchanted Tiki Room*!" Walt Disney Museum. June 28, 2013: https://waltdisney.org/blog/disneyland-classics-walt-disneys-enchanted-tiki-room (12.02.2017).

Thoda-Arora, Hilke. "Around the World for Fifty Pence: The Phenomenon of the Ethnic Shows." *From Samoa With Love?: Samoan Travellers in Germany 1895–1911 Retracing the Footsteps*. Museum Fünf Kontinente: München, 2014: 79–93.

Thompson, Kirsten Moana. The Construction of a Myth: Bloody Mary, Aggie Grey and the Optics of Tourism." *Journal of NZ and Pacific Studies*, 2(1), 2014: 5–19.

V, Billy. "Hawaii Brothers Write for Disney's *Moana*" *Hawaii News Now*. November 18, 2016: http://hawaiinewsnow.com/story/33746886/interview-aaron-and-jordan-kandell-hawaii-boys-in-hollywood (12. 2. 2016).

Vaka'uta, Cresantia Koya. "The Pacific's Cultural Genocide" *República*, 6, 2013: 28–31.

Wendt, Albert. "Tatauing the Post-Colonial Body." [Originally published in *Span*: 42–43] 1996: 15–29: http://nzepc.auckland.ac.nz/authors/wendt/tatauing.asp (12.08.17).

Films & TV Series

Aladdin. Directed by Ron Clements and John Musker. 1992; USA: Disney.

Alice in Wonderland. Directed by Clyde Geronimi, Wilfred Jackson, and Hamilton Luske. 1951; USA: Disney.

Coco. Directed by Lee Unkrich and Adrian Molina. 2017; USA: Disney/Pixar.

Gerald McBoing Boing. Directed by Robert Cannon. 1951; USA: UPA.

Hercules. Directed by John Musker and Ron Clements. 1997; USA: Disney.

Lilo and Stitch. Directed by Dean DeBlois and Chris Sanders. 2002; USA: Disney.

Mad Men: USA 2007–2015, AMC, created by Matthew Weiner.

Moana. Directed by John Musker and Ron Clements. 2016; USA: Disney.

Mulan. Directed by Tony Bancroft ans Barry Cook. 1998; USA: Disney.

Peter Pan. Directed by Clyde Geronimi, Wilfred Jackson, and Hamilton Luske. 1953; USA: Disney.

The Princess and the Frog. Directed by Ron Clements and John Musker. 2009; USA: Disney.

Rooty Toot. Directed by John Hubley. 1951; USA: UPA.

SpongeBob SquarePants: USA 1999–present, Nickelodeon, created by Stephen Hillenburg. "Enchanted Tiki Dreams" Episode 145b, Season 7, aired June 29, 2010.

Camera and Editing

9 Shot Scale and Viewers' Responses to Characters in Animated Films

Katalin E. Bálint and Brendan Rooney

Introduction

Dudok de Wit, in his Academy Award-winning animated film *Father and Daughter* (2000), presents a highly emotional story about a daughter's constant grieving of and deep longing for her father, whom she lost at a young age. Remarkable in this animated film is that the director chose not to show any facial detail of the characters. The mood is implied via simple colors of sepia, brown, and grey, repetitive music, and body language. As there are no close-ups on the face, the viewers are invited to fill in the emotional gaps for themselves and arrive at an emotional understanding of the character's mind without receiving ready-made information. Dudok's artistic decision to not show the face goes against the current trends in filmmaking (just think of the exaggerated facial expressions of *Inside Out,* discussed in this book) but also calls for a practical investigation: *What is the role of close-ups in animated narratives in viewers' understanding of characters? Do viewers of computer-animated narratives need close-ups for the understanding of characters' emotion? If yes, how many close-ups are enough (or too much) to activate understanding? At which point in the narrative is it the most effective to show the close-up to activate responses in viewers?*

Addressing these questions, the present chapter focuses on a key feature of visualization, namely shot scale, a formal feature of the moving image through which animation designers can regulate the apparent distance and size of objects on screen (Zettl 2013). Close-up is the type of shot scale suitable for showing the details on screen. When reviewing the role of close-up, this chapter draws primarily on a number of empirical studies conducted in media psychology and communication studies. These interdisciplinary fields apply empirical–experimental methods of the social sciences for studying psychological responses to mediated messages. Experimental methods are rarely used in film and animation studies, although they can provide scholars with important insights. One of the main advantages of experimental methods is that they can detect causal mechanisms between a selected visual feature and a specific response in viewers. This kind of knowledge is of great value for the advancement of animation studies.

Theoretical Framework

Computer-animated films are ideal objects for scientific investigations of emotional expressions. On the one hand, recent technological advancements in computer software, algorithms, and capacity made computer-animated narratives an extremely powerful media for expressing and eliciting emotions. On the other hand, the technique of computer animation is an ideal combination of total freedom and absolute precision. It offers an endless number of creative ways for displaying emotional experiences onscreen and makes highly systematic experimental investigation also possible. Visualization, the way and techniques through which content is visually presented, is considered a key element in this strong emotional effect (Wells 2013). For example, in visual stories, the scene can be staged to allow all characters to be seen at the same time or to focus on just one character. Colors and lighting can be used to draw attention to some elements of the scene, and music can communicate mood or other emotional information. Other techniques, such as crosscutting (successively switching between two elements), are a particularly effective way to prompt viewers to predict what will happen next (Magliano et al. 1996). These decisions on visual design have consequences for viewers' responses to the story. Despite the importance of visualization in film narratives, a systematic, evidence-based body of research on the role of formal–visual features in viewers' responses is still missing.

In order to understand the effect of close-ups on viewers' responses to animated narratives, first we present a model of the process of narrative comprehension. Then we review findings related to shot scale and, afterwards, present our own work on animated narratives – a series of experiments conducted with a special focus on issues related to close-ups, such as shot scale distribution, close-up frequency, and narrative sequential order of close-ups, and their effects on social cognition.

Although the significance of formal features in the emotional power of storytelling has been acknowledged by film studies for a long time, the empirical studies of visualization have been lacking a comprehensive framework that integrates formal features, narrative processing, and viewers' responses. Despite the important developments in the understanding of various kinds of emotional and cognitive responses in viewers of visual narratives, empirical findings on the role of formal features are scattered across different disciplines. In the following, we briefly introduce three theories that could serve as important building blocks of such a framework for the studies of emotion in visual narratives when sufficient empirical evidence is at hand.

The event-indexing model stresses the role of mental models in narrative comprehension (Zwaan et al. 1995). When people read or watch a story, they automatically construct a dynamic and constantly updating 'mental model' of the narrative. The mental model is a representation that includes the temporal, spatial, causal, and intentional information presented in the story events (Zwaan et al. 1995). The event-indexing model has been effectively applied to visual narratives (Magliano et al. 2001; Busselle and Bilandzic 2008; Cutting and Iricinschi 2015). For example, Busselle and Bilandzic (2008) claim that the ease and smoothness with which a story can be represented in such a model influences the level of narrative engagement viewers experience with the story. In this account, narrative engagement occurs via mental modeling. Based on previous findings it can be assumed that formal features have a crucial role in facilitating viewers' recognition of event boundaries, which makes mental modeling more effective (Brunick et al. 2013).

The landscape view theory of text comprehension emphasizes the dynamic nature of mental models (Van Den Broek 1996). Readers' allocate fluctuating amounts of attention to concepts as the story unfolds during reading (Van Den Broek 1996). Importantly, this theory claims that the attentional fluctuation is governed by formal characteristics of the text; for example, those concepts that are mentioned frequently will get more attention (i.e., activation) than others. By this account, the emerging memory of a story reflects the 'landscape of activation'; that is, content that attracted more attention during reading will be more available in a free recall after reading. Findings from other disciplines also suggest that visual features have a strong potential to determine which content attracts more attention and, in turn, will shape the emotional and cognitive experience of the story.

A particularly influential theory on the role of formal features in communication sciences is the Limited Capacity Model of Motivated Mediated Message Processing (LC4MP, Lang 2000). According to this, viewers only have a limited cognitive capacity that they can allocate to the processing of different parts of the mediated message. Viewers allocate attentional resources to process information, and the more they use on one aspect, the less they have available to process another at the same time. The allocation of 'extra' cognitive resources to some element of the message raises the probability that that element becomes part of the mental representation. Through underlying motivational systems, the allocation of attentional resources shapes the valence and the intensity of the emotional response to the message.

The LC4MP states that viewers can decide which part of the message they wish to process; however, non-content features have a strong potential to evoke automatic allocation of cognitive resources to message processing. Hence, varying the type and number of structural features in a message influences the extent of motivational activation and the way the message is processed. A growing body of empirical studies has supported this idea (Lang 2000; Morgan et al. 2003; Detenber and Lang 2010). For example, audiovisual formal features of films can synchronize viewers' attention (Mital et al. 2011) as well as brain activity

(Hasson et al. 2008); that is, when people watch the same professionally composed film scene they look at similar parts of the image for similar amount of time (Smith and Henderson 2008). This synchronicity has been dubbed by some researchers as the *"Tyranny of Film"* (Loschky et al. 2015) and suggests that creative designers can regulate the depth and source of information processing (Smith 2013).

But how do they do it? In this chapter, we propose that one of the most powerful ways that storytellers can regulate cognition and emotion is through the formal features they use to tell the story. In the following, we will focus on the way in which shot scale can be used as a powerful tool in animation to shape viewer engagement.

Shot Scale and Close-Ups

Shot scale, defined as the apparent spatial distance of the camera from the main subject of the shot as well as the relative proportion of the figure of the character and the background (e.g., close-up, medium shot, long shot) (Salt 1992; Bowen and Thompson 2013), is one of the most salient stylistic feature of audiovisual messages (Kovács 2014). When describing shot scale, shots are generally considered to fall within one of the categories of long shot, medium shot, or close-up shot. Long shots typically portray the character from a distance where they occupy a small area of the scene and are surrounded by a larger space or environment. The medium shot depicts the human figure from what seems to be about 3–5 feet away, so usually they can be seen from the waist up. The close-up shot typically shows the character's face (or some element of the story) in detail, usually from the upper shoulder and including their entire head and face (Bowen and Thompson 2013). From these descriptions, it is clear that varying shot scale is an effective tool to arrange film content according to its saliency (Carroll and Seeley 2013), and regulate the relative size and visibility of the image on the screen.

Shot scale influences cognitive and affective processing of the image. Larger images increase automatic allocation of cognitive capacity (Lang et al. 2006), most importantly attention (Reeves et al. 1999; Franconeri and Simons 2003), and in return, they are recalled better (Mutz 2007). Other studies showed that larger images increase the intensity of viewers' reactions (Lombard 1995; Reeves and Nass 1996). Shot scale operates through similar perceptual mechanisms to viewing distance. Viewing at a shorter distance from the screen increases complex attention-related narrative responses, such as immersion (Baranowski and Hecht 2014) and presence (Lombard et al. 1997, 2000; Hou et al. 2012).

Shot scale is also an effective tool to influence the intensity of affective responding. Specifically, closer shots increase the intensity of emotions (De Cesarei and Codispoti 2006, 2008), physiological arousal (Codispoti and De Cesarei 2007; Mühlberger et al. 2008; De Cesarei and Codispoti

2010), and self-reported arousal in viewers (Codispoti and De Cesarei 2007; Canini et al. 2011). It seems that closer shots increase the intensity of emotional responses in general.

One of the most theorized shot scales in film and media studies is the close-up shot. The close-up is a shot with a smaller scale, showing the object of the shot from a short distance in a relatively large size (Zettl 2013). The central importance of shot scale, and close-ups specifically, especially those presenting human faces, has been recognized already in early film theory, linking close-ups with attention (Münsterberg 2013), emotion (Balázs and Carter 2013), and interpretation of context by the famous Kuleshov effect, recently replicated by Calbi et al. (2017). Contemporary film scholars agree also that when presenting faces and facial expressions, close-ups can effectively communicate the emotional experience of the character and powerfully elicit cognitive and affective responding in viewers (Carroll 1993; Plantinga 1999; Tan 2005). Close-up shots can have powerful effects on viewers because they make the emotional expression of characters visually accessible (Plantinga 1999). Empirical studies have provided some explanation of the underlying mechanisms. For example, studies have found that close-ups make person and emotion recognition faster (Loftus and Harley 2005; Cutting and Armstrong 2016) and more accurate (Lampinen et al. 2014). This suggests that viewers can probably arrive at an emotional understanding of characters much quicker when they are presented in close-ups.

The emotional power of close-up shots is reflected in van Kleef's (2009) Emotions as Social Information (EASI) model. This theory proposes both inferential and affective reactions as the mechanism that connects emotional expression and the observers' response. Specific emotional expressions such as disgust or misery communicate social information that is key to narrative engagement (Parkinson 1999, 2001; Hareli and Hess 2010). Research within this framework has demonstrated how emotional expressions affect viewers' judgments about the characters (Hareli and Hess 2010), on viewer attributions (van Doorn et al. 2015), and viewer inferences about character intentions (van Kleef et al. 2004; de Melo et al. 2014).

Close-Ups and Theory-of-Mind

Close-ups make the emotional expression of the character more visible, and in doing so, they can facilitate an important psychological process in viewers called 'theory-of-mind'. Theory-of-mind is a social cognition process that refers to the awareness and understanding of mental states in others, both real (Premack and Woodruff 1978; Baron-Cohen 2001) and mediated others (Black and Barnes 2015). Theory-of-mind, sometimes referred to as cognitive empathy, is different from the affective component of social cognition, called embodied simulation, which is the involuntary process in which one physiologically resonates with affective bodily states of the observed person (Decety and Jackson 2004; Gallese 2007; Lieberman 2007). Previous findings suggest that theory-of-mind and embodied simulation processes are connected to disparate neural systems (Zaki and Ochsner 2012) and function independently when people read or watch stories (Dziobek et al. 2008; Wallentin et al. 2013). It is assumed that cognitive and affective empathy are triggered by different cues (Raz et al. 2014). For example, cognitive empathy is more sensitive to external situational information, whereas affective empathy is to signals coming from the own body of the individual, for example, to the level of arousal or distress (Lieberman 2007; Raz and Hendler 2014).

Once activated, theory-of-mind is closely associated with empathic care; the more people understand the perspective of another person, the more willing they are to help that person. One study suggests that shot scale can facilitate this connection: Cao (2013) presented public service announcements to viewers in a medium shot or a close-up shot version and found that viewers – especially female viewers – of the close-up shot version were more willing to donate for the cause presented in the PSA. It is most probable that close-ups exert their effect on empathic care via activating theory-of-mind responses towards characters and intensifying emotional reactions to the image. While Cao's research used live-action videos, research findings in this area have been derived from work using a range of different narrative media with various formal features.

In the past few years, there has been an increased interest in how fictional narratives can improve theory-of-mind responses in readers and viewers. A growing body of evidence indicates a close association between the processing of visual dramas (e.g., Black and Barnes 2015) and printed literary narratives (see Mumper and Gerrig 2017) and theory-of-mind responding. It seems that exposure to literary narratives and film dramas can improve theory-of-mind ability. Despite the social relevance of this statement, there is a very limited understanding of the underlying narrative mechanism – in other words, we do not know yet what the important media-specific features are that make one visual narrative more effective than others. One of the main assumptions of our research project is that those formal features that regulate the visibility of socially relevant cues may be crucial in the theory-of-mind enhancing effect of movies. In the rest of this chapter, we review the findings of a series of experiments on the effect of various aspects of close-ups on theory-of-mind responding in viewers of animated films.

Experiment 1: Average Shot Scale Distribution and Theory-of-Mind

In the first experiment (Bálint et al. 2016), we showed four animated short films to viewers: *Father and Daughter* (de Wit 2001), *Invention of Love* (Shuskhov 2010), *Lavatory – Lovestory* (Bronzit 2007), and *Lettin' Go* (Whitaker 2008). We selected these movies because they represented different levels of average shot scale distribution. If we observed differences between the films, we wanted to be confident that it was related to shot scale rather than any other major differences between the films. This is difficult to achieve but it is an important consideration for our first study. For this reason, we selected films that were similar on many other features. Specifically, each of the chosen films featured a self-contained fictional narrative with a linear narrative structure. They were each relatively short 2D animations. We also selected films that had continuous music along the story without lyrics, and without any verbal information (e.g., dialogue, voice-over narration, textual inserts). This allowed for removing any problems with differences of voice or intonation of speech. In addition to the formal and visual features, the selected films also shared thematic and content features. Each one showed only two anthropomorphic protagonists (a female focal character and a male character) and each centered around a theme of separation from, and reunion with, a beloved person. This theme requires a viewer to use theory-of-mind in order to fully appreciate the content of the film.

Confirming our main hypothesis, the average shot scale distribution of the movie influenced theory-of-mind responding in viewers. More specifically, the story of the films with closer shots were retold with a higher frequency of mental state references. This result suggests that apparent spatial distance can influence the extent to which the viewers' mental models of the narrative included the characters' mental states. In other words, seeing the story with a closer visual-spatial proximity to the characters (more close-ups) brings the mind and consciousness of the characters into the foreground of the narrative experience (Bruner 1986). The findings also make an important contribution to our understanding of theory-of-mind by suggesting that it is more than just a stable trait-like capacity of the viewer; rather, it can be evoked and fostered by features of the narrative. By designing visual narratives, directors are regulating the extent to which audiences ascribe mental states to characters beyond the viewers' usual tendency to do so. This is in line with previous findings (Bálint et al. 2014; Meins et al. 2014).

One of the main limitations of the aforementioned experiment is that we used four different movies for manipulating shot scale. Despite our efforts to include very similar movies, we could not totally exclude the possibility that the differences in theory-of-mind response were caused by some other feature of the films. To address this problem, we conducted a series of experiments showing the manipulated versions of the same animated film to viewers. These aim to hold everything about the film constant, except the one thing we are interested in: shot scale.

Experiment 2: Close-Up and Facial Expression

For our research purposes, we selected Dudok de Wit's animated film entitled *Father and Daughter*, discussed at the opening of this chapter. The same movie has been already used in research of emotional responses (Suckfüll 2010). The film tells the life story of a woman who lost her father at a young age, showing ten sequences from ten different life stages of the female protagonist. In the first sequence, she is a little girl, riding a bicycle with her father. They stop at a tree at a lake; the father walks down to a boat on the water, and after hugging his daughter, the father rows away with the boat. The little girl stays there, watching the man row away. In the next eight sequences, the same female protagonist (in eight consecutive stages of her life) comes back to the same spot and looks at the lake. In the last sequence, she is a very old woman; she comes alone, stops at the same tree, and looks at the water. She walks into the dried-up lake and, in an imaginary scene, unites with her long-lost father again.

The most important visual characteristics of this animation are that it is a two-dimensional, hand-drawn film created in a simplistic style with a very limited color palette and simple, clean lines. It is accompanied by instrumental music (the waltz melody of "Waves of the Danube") that creates a special atmosphere in the film. It was important for our purposes that the film tells its story in a linear narrative, so viewers did not have to make an effort to understand the general causal structure of the story. Another reason why we chose this animated film was that it contains no dialogue or lyrics; therefore the most important source for viewers' emotional understanding of the character was the visuals.

The animated film has a clear visual structure. Each sequence consists of a point-of-view shot presenting the female protagonist as she looks at the water where she has seen her father for the last time. Conventionally, point-of-view shots comprise a gaze shot (depicting a person who is looking at something) and an object shot (depicting the object of the looking) (Branigan 1984). In the original version of the film, the gaze shots are long shots; that is, the protagonist is far away and her face is not visible.

In order to investigate the effect of close-ups on viewers' responses in a true experimental setting, we manipulated this animation. Our aim was not to test any kind of artistic qualities; rather, we aimed to dissect 'mechanisms' in the visualization of the animation. In the manipulated versions of the film, we replaced the long shot of the gaze shot by a close-up with either a sad or a neutral facial expression in one of the sequences (see Figure 9.1). In order to keep the style of the film intact, we worked with professional animation designers, who created and edited these reposition shots into the film in a way that they were a perfect fit to the style of the original artwork. The length of the gaze shots (two seconds each), as well as the length of the versions, were kept constant.

In this second experiment (Rooney and Bálint 2018), we used three versions of the first two sequences of Father and Daughter: (a) the original version with long shots; (b) the manipulated version with two close-ups presenting sad facial expressions; and (c) the manipulated version with two close-ups presenting neutral facial expressions. Participants watched one of the three versions and were asked to describe the story of the film and their own experiences with the movie. Just as in the previous experiment, we examined the mental state references in these story descriptions. Our findings demonstrated that shot scale and facial expression did affect theory-of-mind responses. Specifically, we observed that the close-ups of sad faces produced a significantly higher frequency of mental state references than other conditions, and that the use of a neutral close-up produced no more mental state references than the long-shot version. This suggests that the increase in mental state references was not driven by merely presenting the character's face larger in the frame (i.e., at a smaller spatial distance from the viewer); rather, it is the social and emotional information carried by the face.

We also examined the nature of the mental state that viewers referred to in their story descriptions. We found that close-ups primarily increased references to the characters' affective mental states, rather than their cognition or intention. In line with our previous results, these findings indicate that depiction of the character can direct attentional focus towards their mental states, making them more accessible to the viewer and thus increasing viewers' tendency to use those mental states in a representation of the narrative.

In addition to others' mental states, theory-of-mind includes understanding and attribution of mental states to the self. In this study, our findings also demonstrated that our manipulation of character depiction affected how much the participants referred to their own mental states. Specifically, showing the character close up with a sad facial expression was associated with more references to participants' own mental states than other conditions. This was followed by the neutral close-up condition; the long-shot condition was associated with the least reference to one's own mental states. Altogether, the findings of this study show that the way the character's face is depicted in a shot is a powerful tool for eliciting theory-of-mind, that is, for prompting viewers to represent the mental states of characters and self as part of their mental models.

Experiment 3 and 4: Close-Up Frequency

In the third experiment (Bálint et al. forthcoming), we used the entire *Father and Daughter* animation to examine the effect of close-up frequency on theory-of-mind responding in viewers. We created different

Figure 9.1 Two levels of facial expression intensity: neutral facial expression (left), sad facial expression (right).

versions of the film varying the number of close-ups inserted into the movie. Next to the original version (zero close-ups), we had versions with one, two, three, four, five, and ten close-ups with either neutral or sad facial expressions. Participants watched one version of the movie and were asked to freely describe the story of the film, the perspective of the protagonist, and their own feelings. In these free responses, theory-of-mind responding was measured by a quantitative content analytic method, where independent coders assessed the frequency and complexity of cognitive and affective mental state reasoning and attribution of intention. The results showed that close-up frequency had an effect on affective mental state references. Interestingly, we did not observe a linear relationship between the frequency of close-ups and theory-of-mind responding. Instead, the relationship appeared to have an inverse U-shape. That is, viewers' theory-of-mind responding did increase in a linear fashion until the insertion of three close-ups; beyond that, the frequency of theory-of-mind responding decreased. This suggests that there may be an optimal distribution of shot scale for prompting theory-of-mind responses, and designers need to consider the increased cognitive load close-ups may put on the recipients, which may decrease the capacity for social cognition.

In a related experiment (Bálint et al. 2017), we extended the investigation of close-up frequency to several responses in viewers, including 'approach motivation' (measured by electrophysiological correlates and explained further in the following text), narrative engagement, enjoyment and emotional impact. We also administered viewers' general trait empathy in order to test if individual differences moderate viewers' responses. This study employed three versions of the film *Father and Daughter*, containing zero, five, or 10 close-up shots of the protagonist. Other parts of the movies were identical across conditions. After filling out an empathy questionnaire, 102 participants watched one of the three movies at random in an individual setting while their brainwaves were recorded. After watching the movie, participants' emotions, narrative engagement, and enjoyment were assessed. This study used a technique exploring EEG frontal asymmetry, which serves as an indicator of approach motivation, that is, how appealing or engaged the participant is by the stimulus. In this study, frontal asymmetry averages were calculated for the two-second intervals during the close-up shots, and the previous two seconds (to serve as a baseline). Preliminary results revealed a complex interaction between shot scale and trait empathy on audiences' responses to the narrative. We found that a higher frequency of close-ups increased narrative engagement, emotional impact, and enjoyment. Importantly, these main effects were more pronounced in the case of viewers with high levels of trait empathy. The participants who were more empathic (higher levels of trait empathy), enjoyed all the versions of the movies more than others. However, inserting 10 close-up shots also made the movie more enjoyable for those with lower empathy. More empathetic participants experienced a larger variability in approach motivation as a function of close-up shots, which suggests that they are more responsive to shot scale changes on screen. These findings indicate that the right use of shot scale can be an effective tool to increase emotional intensity, approach motivation, and enjoyment in viewers with varying levels of empathy.

Experiment 5: Narrative Sequential Order of Close-Ups and Theory-of-Mind

In these aforementioned studies, we explored the way in which the presence and number of close-ups might elicit theory-of-mind response in viewers. The findings thus far have demonstrated that close-ups can elicit theory-of-mind, but also that there is some nuance to the effect, namely, that there may be an optimal ratio of shot scale, and that individual differences in viewers also play a role. In the fifth experiment, we were interested to explore how the point in the film at which the close-up appears may have an effect. In the previous studies, we were careful to control for the serial order of the close-ups, but we did not investigate its effect. Narrative sequential order effect can be defined as the point in time (e.g., beginning, middle, ending) when a close-up (i.e., the face of the character) appears in a visual narrative. Based on prior findings, it can be assumed that narrative sequential order of a close-up shot in a narrative influences theory of mind responding in viewers.

Exploring the narrative sequential order of close-ups is important as it speaks to the role of context in the interpretation of close-ups. Recently, a series of experiments have empirically demonstrated a phenomenon known in film theory as the Kuleshov effect (Barratt et al. 2016; Calbi et al. 2017). This occurs when a close-up shot is interpreted differently depending on the content of the preceding shot. For example, an ambiguous facial expression presented in a close-up may be interpreted differently if the shot immediately before it was the appearance of a love interest smiling and waving (positive) or the appearance of a love interest in a coffin (negative). The findings from these studies demonstrate that viewers automatically contextualize the information from the facial expression with the preceding information (see Wieser and Brosch 2012). Consequently, the information preceding the close-up in the narrative can determine the semantic context of the close-up.

For our fifth experiment, we created ten different versions of the animated film *Father and Daughter*. We inserted one close-up, either with a sad or neutral facial expression, into five different sequences of the film, that is, into the first, fourth, sixth, eighth, and tenth (last) sequences. Participants watched one version of the film, and afterward they were asked to write down the story from the perspective of the female protagonist. In line with our hypothesis, we found that the narrative sequential order of close-ups did indeed influence theory-of-mind responding in viewers. Inserting a close-up shot into one of the first or last two sequences of the animation produced a significantly higher level of theory-of-mind response compared to other conditions. Interestingly, the use of neutral and sad facial expressions did not influence these results. This finding suggests that it is not only the presence or absence of a close-up shot that drives processing of animation narratives but rather the narrative context by which the close-up is surrounded. This study demonstrated that the decision about when to present a character's face in a narrative has important consequences on viewers' story processing of an animated film.

Conclusion

To gain a deeper understanding of the role of close-ups in expressing characters' emotional and cognitive states in animated narratives, this chapter presents experiments conducted with Dudok de Wit's Academy Award-winning animated film *Father and Daughter*. Together, our findings demonstrate that the content, the frequency, the narrative sequential position of the close-up and individual differences in empathy can all contribute to how effective a close-up can be in expressing emotional and cognitive states of animated characters. More specifically, we found that close-ups activate viewers' willingness to understand the protagonist's mental states; however, this willingness decreases when close-ups are overused. Inserting only one or two close-ups in a short animated narrative can result in the strongest effect. The findings indicate that close-ups of the animated character's face toward the end of the narrative can elicit theory-of-mind responding more effectively. These results are of great importance for offering animation designers targeted practice to manipulate (up or down) the extent to which the characters' mental states are salient components within the viewers' mental model.

Together, our findings suggest that the function of close-ups of animated characters operate through three essential features: they show (1) a large sized image of (2) a face that belongs to (3) a character in a story. Studies have shown that large image size increases activation, motivational relevance, and allocated cognitive resources in viewers. In case of close-ups on characters, these resources are directed toward the processing of a highly relevant source of information, the human(like) face (as opposed to, for example, the close-up of a gun). When viewers are presented with a face, they can quickly identify the character as well as the type of facial expression (whether the character is sad or angry, for example). Therefore, the rest of their capacity can be allocated to narrative processing. This latter point brings us to the third aspect of close-ups. All pieces of information that viewers extract while looking at the character face, are important building blocks of mental modeling. It means that viewers do not simply comprehend the emotional reaction of the character, but that they also integrate this information into their mental model of the narrative. In other words, viewers need to think about the function of the emotional reaction in the causal chain of the story. They may wonder what made the characters feel this specific way and how this emotion may explain other actions of the character. When viewers see facial expressions onscreen, they become more aware of how the character judges, understands, and responds to the fictional situation. This raises the probability that the characters' mental states become part of the viewers' mental representation of the story and facilitates viewers' own understanding of the narrative. Closer shots can effectively activate this whole process. However, we have also shown that the prediction is not simple and linear; the overuse of close-ups in a short animated film can hinder viewers' emotional understanding.

The empirical approach used to explore how formal features relate to character engagement is important for building upon the tacit expertise of creative designers and identifying the psychological, perceptual, and neural mechanisms that link these qualities. Previous research has argued that certain narrative forms such as literary fiction and award-winning drama are associated with higher levels of theory-of-mind. Our research suggests that the way in which these stories are presented may be the active component in prompting social cognition and character engagement. Future research may even establish the importance of formal features over other possible mechanisms such as the outcome of the story or the cultural appetite for the genre.

Further to this, employing close-ups effectively in animated narratives offers the opportunity to embed catalysts for positive change within the story. Consider, for example, an animated narrative that can prompt empathy in viewers for particular characters with minority backgrounds or disabilities or one created to be accessible to those with social cognition deficits or related vulnerabilities. Socially accessible animated narratives could be designed for viewers with autism and or social cognition defi-cits, who may have been alienated by the subtle, more sophisticated ways that traditional audiovisual narratives might present social interactions. Technological developments may even facilitate animated narratives with interactive formal features that could be adjusted to suit the needs of the viewer. We suggest that findings from studies like ours that ex-plore such social cognition can contribute to a society that fosters such empathy in all its citizens.

Acknowledgment

The authors thank David Quinn and Kayleigh Scullion for collaborating on the film materials and Lauren Christophers and Janine Blessing for data coding.

References

Balázs, Béla and Erica Carter. *Bela Balazs: Early Film Theory: Visible Man and the Spirit of Film.* Film Europa. New York: Berghahn Books, 2013.

Bálint, Katalin E., Janine Blessing, and Brendan Rooney. *Formal Features and Social Cognition: How Do Close-up Frequency Drive Theory of Mind in Viewers of Animated Films?* (Forthcoming, Manuscript submitted).

Bálint, Katalin E., Thomas Klausch, and Tibor Pólya. "Watching Closely: Shot Scale Influences Theory-of-Mind Response in Visual Narratives." *Journal of Media Psychology*, 2016: 1–10. doi:10.1027/1864-1105/a000189.

Bálint, Katalin E., Tamás Nagy, Brendan Rooney, Ágoston Török, Márton Czető, Dániel Pálma, Dávid Ottlik, and Ádám Divák. "Bring It Closer: The Effect of Shot Scale on Approach Motivation, Narrative Engagement, and En-joyment in Film Viewers." *Paper Presented at 10th Conference of the Media Psychology Division.* Koblenz, Germany, 2017.

Baranowski, Andreas M. and Heiko Hecht. "The Big Picture: Effects of Surround on Immersion and Size Perception." *Perception,* 43(10), 2014: 1061–1070. doi:10.1068/p7663.

Baron-Cohen, Simon. *Mindblindness: An Essay on Autism and Theory of Mind.* Cambridge/London: MIT Press, 2001. http://books.google.com/books?id=MDbcNu9zYZAC.

Barratt, Daniel, Anna Cabak Rédei, Ase Innes-Ker, and Joost van de Weijer. "Does the Kuleshov Effect Really Exist? Revisiting a Classic Film Experiment on Facial Expressions and Emotional Contexts." *Perception,* 45(8), 2016: 847–874. doi:10.1177/0301006616638595.

Black, Jessica and Jennifer L. Barnes. "Fiction and Social Cognition: The Ef-fect of Viewing Award-Winning Television Dramas on Theory of Mind." *Psychology of Aesthetics, Creativity, and the Arts*, 9(4), 2015. doi:10.1037/aca0000031.

Bowen, Christopher J. and Roy Thompson. *Grammar of the Shot.* New York/London: Focal Press, 2013: https://books.google.nl/books?id=Rl7IyLPt5ucC.

Branigan, Edward. *Point of View in the Cinema: A Theory of Narration and Subjectivity in Classical Film.* Berlin: Mouton de Gruyter, 1984.

Bruner, Jerome S. *Actual Minds, Possible Worlds*. Cambridge: Harvard University Press, 1986: http://books.google.nl/books?id=YNuBf6W2rt0C.

Brunick, Kaitlin L., James Cutting, and Jordan DeLong. "Low-Level Features of Film: What They Are and Why We Would Be Lost Without Them." In: Shimamura, Arthur P. (Ed.). *Psychocinematics: Exploring Cognition at the Movies*. Oxford/New York: Oxford University Press, 2013: 133–148. doi:10.1093/acprof:oso/9780199862139.003.0007.

Busselle, Rick and Helena Bilandzic. "Fictionality and Perceived Realism in Experiencing Stories: A Model of Narrative Comprehension and Engagement." *Communication Theory*, 18(2), 2008: 255–280. doi:10.1111/j.1468-2885. 2008.00322.x.

Calbi, Marta, Katrin Heimann, Daniel Barratt, Francesca Siri, Maria A. Umiltà, and Vittorio Gallese. "How Context Influences Our Perception of Emotional Faces: A Behavioral Study on the Kuleshov Effect." *Frontiers in Psychology*, 8, 2017: 1684. doi:10.3389/fpsyg.2017.01684.

Canini, Luca, Sergio Benini, and Riccardo Leonardi. "Affective Analysis on Patterns of Shot Types in Movies." *Image and Signal Processing and Analysis (ISPA) Conference Publications*, 2011: 253–258.

Cao, Xiaoxia. "The Effects of Facial Close-ups and Viewers' Sex on Empathy and Intentions to Help People in Need." *Mass Communication and Society*, 16(2), 2013: 161–178.

Carroll, Noël. "Toward a Theory of Point-of-View Editing: Communication, Emotion, and the Movies." *Poetics Today*, 14(1), 1993: 123–141. www.jstor. org/stable/1773144.

Carroll, Noël and William P. Seeley. "Cognitivism, Psychology, and Neuroscience: Movies as Attentional Engines." In: Shimamura, Arthur P. (Ed.). *Psychocinematics: Exploring Cognition at the Movies*. Oxford/New York: Oxford University Press, 2013: 53–75.

Codispoti, Maurizio and Andrea De Cesarei. "Arousal and Attention: Picture Size and Emotional Reactions." *Psychophysiology*, 44(5), 2007: 680–686. doi:10.1111/j.1469-8986.2007.00545.x.

Cutting, James E. and Kacie L. Armstrong. "Facial Expression, Size, and Clutter: Inferences from Movie Structure to Emotion Judgments and Back." *Attention, Perception, and Psychophysics*, 78(3), 2016: 891–901. doi:10.3758/ s13414-015-1003-5.

Cutting, James and Catalina Iricinschi. "Re-Presentations of Space in Hollywood Movies: An Event-Indexing Analysis." *Cognitive Science*, 39(2), 2015: 434–456. doi:10.1111/cogs.12151.

De Cesarei, Andrea and Maurizio Codispoti. "When Does Size Not Matter? Effects of Stimulus Size on Affective Modulation." *Psychophysiology*, 43(2), 2006: 207–215.

——— "Fuzzy Picture Processing: Effects of Size Reduction and Blurring on Emotional Processing." *Emotion*, 8(3), 2008: 352–363. doi:10.1037/1528-3542.8.3.352.

——— "Effects of Picture Size reduction and Blurring on Emotional Engagement." *PloS One*, 5(10), 2010: e13399.

Decety, Jean and Philip L. Jackson. "The Functional Architecture of Human Empathy." *Behavioral and Cognitive Neuroscience Reviews*, 3(2), 2004: 71–100. http://bcn.sagepub.com/content/3/2/71.abstract.

Detenber, Benjamin H. and Annie Lang. "The Influence of Form and Presentation Attributes of Media On Emotion." In: Doveling, Katrin, Christian von Scheve, and Elly A. Konijn (Eds.). *The Routledge Handbook of Emotions and Mass Media.* New York: Routledge, 2010: 275.

Doorn, Evert A. van, Gerben A. van Kleef, and Joop van der Pligt. "Deriving Meaning from Others' Emotions: Attribution, Appraisal, and the Use of Emotions as Social Information." *Frontiers in Psychology*, 6. Frontiers Media SA, 2015: 1077. doi:10.3389/fpsyg.2015.01077.

Dziobek, Isabel, Kimberley Rogers, Stefan Fleck, Markus Bahnemann, Hauke R. Heekeren, Oliver T. Wolf, and Antonio Convit. "Dissociation of Cognitive and Emotional Empathy in Adults with Asperger Syndrome Using the Multifaceted Empathy Test (MET)." *Journal of Autism and Developmental Disorders*, 38(3), 2008: 464–473. doi:10.1007/s10803-007-0486-x.

Franconeri, Steven L. and Daniel J. Simons. "Moving and Looming Stimuli Capture Attention." *Perception and Psychophysics*, 65(7), 2003: 999–1010.

Gallese, Vittorio. "Before and Below 'Theory of Mind': Embodied Simulation and the Neural Correlates of Social Cognition." *Philosophical Transactions of the Royal Society B: Biological Sciences*, 362(1480), 2007: 659–669. doi:10.1098/rstb.2006.2002.

Hareli, Shlomo and Ursula Hess. "What Emotional Reactions Can Tell Us about the Nature of Others: An Appraisal Perspective on Person Perception." *Cognition and Emotion*, 24(1), 2010: 128–140. doi:10.1080/02699930802613828.

Hasson, Uri, Ohad Landesman, Barbara Knappmeyer, Ignacio Vallines, Nava Rubin, and David J. Heeger. "Neurocinematics: The Neuroscience of Film." *Projections*, 2(1), 2008: 1–26. doi:10.3167/proj.2008.020102.

Hou, Jinghui, Yujung Nam, Wei Peng, and Kwan Min Lee. "Effects of Screen Size, Viewing Angle, and Players' Immersion Tendencies on Game Experience." *Computers in Human Behavior*, 28(2), 2012: 617–623. doi:10.1016/j.chb.2011.11.007.

Kleef, Gerben A. van. "How Emotions Regulate Social Life: The Emotions as Social Information (EASI) Model." *Current Directions in Psychological Science*, 18(3). SAGE Publications, 2009: 184–188. doi:10.1111/j.1467-8721.2009.01633.x.

Kleef, Gerben A. van, Carsten K. W. De Dreu, and Antony S. R. Manstead. "The Interpersonal Effects of Anger and Happiness in Negotiations." *Journal of Personality and Social Psychology*, 86(1), 2004: 57–76. doi:10.1037/0022-3514.86.1.57.

Kovács, András Bálint. "Shot Scale Distribution: An Authorial Fingerprint or a Cognitive Pattern?" *Projections*, 8(2), 2014: 50–70.

Lampinen, James Michael, William Blake Erickson, Kara N. Moore, and Aaron Hittson. "Effects of Distance on Face Recognition: Implications for Eyewitness Identification." *Psychonomic Bulletin and Review*, 21(6), 2014: 1489–1494. doi:10.3758/s13423-014-0641-2.

Lang, Annie. "The Limited Capacity Model of Mediated Message Processing." *Journal of Communication*, 50(1), 2000: 46–70. doi:10.1111/j.1460-2466.2000.tb02833.x.

Lang, Annie, Samuel D. Bradley, Byungho Park, Mija Shin, and Yongkuk Chung. "Parsing the Resource Pie: Using Strts to Measure Attention to Mediated Messages." *Media Psychology*, 8(4), 2006: 369–394.

Lieberman, Matthew D. "Social Cognitive Neuroscience: A Review of Core Processes." *Annual Review of Psychology*, 58, 2007: 259–289.

Loftus, Geoffrey R. and Erin M. Harley. "Why Is It Easier to Identify Someone Close Than Far Away?" *Psychonomic Bulletin and Review*, 12(1), 2005: 43–65. doi:10.3758/BF03196348.

Lombard, Matthew. "Direct Responses to People on the Screen: Television and Personal Space." *Communication Research*, 22(3), 1995: 288–324. doi:10.1177/009365095022003002.

Lombard, Matthew, Theresa B. Ditton, Maria Elizabeth Grabe, and Robert D. Reich. "The Role of Screen Size in Viewer Responses to Television Fare." *Communication Reports*, 10(1), 1997: 95–106.

Lombard, Matthew, Robert D. Reich, Maria E. Grabe, Cheryl C. Bracken, and Theresa B. Ditton. "Presence and Television." *Human Communication Research*, 26(1), 2000: 75–98.

Loschky, Lester, C., Adam M. Larson, Joseph P. Magliano, and Tim J. Smith. "What Would Jaws Do? The Tyranny of Film and the Relationship between Gaze and Higher-Level Narrative Film Comprehension." *PloS one*, 10(11), 2015: e0142474.

Magliano, Joseph P., Katinka Dijkstra, and Rolf A. Zwaan. "Generating Predictive Inferences While Viewing a Movie." *Discourse Processes*, 22(3), 1996: 199–224.

Magliano, Joseph P., Jason Miller, and Rolf A. Zwaan. "Indexing Space and Time in Film Understanding." *Applied Cognitive Psychology*, 15(5), 2001: 533–545. doi:10.1002/acp.724.

Meins, Elizabeth, Charles Fernyhough, and Jayne Harris-Waller. "Is Mind-Mindedness Trait-Like or a Quality of Close Relationships? Evidence From Descriptions of Significant Others, Famous People, and Works of Art." *Cognition*, 130(3), 2014: 417–427.

Melo, Celso M. de, Peter J. Carnevale, Stephen J. Read, and Jonathan Gratch. "Reading People's Minds from Emotion Expressions in Interdependent Decision Making." *Journal of Personality and Social Psychology*, 106(1), 2014: 73–88. doi:10.1037/a0034251.

Mital, Parag K., Tim J. Smith, Robin L. Hill, and John M. Henderson. "Clustering of Gaze during Dynamic Scene Viewing is Predicted by Motion." *Cognitive Computation*, 3(1), 2011: 5–24. doi:10.1007/s12559-010-9074-z.

Morgan, Susan E., Philip Palmgreen, Michael T. Stephenson, Rick H. Hoyle, and Elizabeth P. Lorch. "Associations between Message Features and Subjective Evaluations of the Sensation Value of Antidrug Public Service Announcements." *Journal of Communication*, 53(3), 2003: 512–526. doi:10.1111/j.1460-2466.2003.tb02605.x.

Mühlberger, Andreas, Roland Neumann, Matthias J. Wieser, and Paul Pauli. "The Impact of Changes in Spatial Distance on Emotional Responses." *Emotion*, 8(2), 2008: 192.

Mumper, Micah L. and Richard J. Gerrig. "Leisure Reading and Social Cognition: A Meta-Analysis." *Psychology of Aesthetics, Creativity, and the Arts*, 11(1), 2017: 109–120. doi:10.1037/aca0000089.

Münsterberg, Hugo. *Hugo Munsterberg on Film: The Photoplay: A Psychological Study and Other Writings*. New York: Routledge, 2013.

Mutz, Diana C. "Effects of 'In-Your-Face' Television Discourse on Perceptions of a Legitimate Opposition." *American Political Science Review*, 101(04), 2007: 621–635.

Parkinson, Brian. "Relations and Dissociations between Appraisal and Emotion Ratings of Reasonable and Unreasonable Anger and Guilt." *Cognition and Emotion*, 13(4), 1999: 347–385. doi:10.1080/026999399379221.

——— "Putting Appraisal in Context." In: Scherer, Klaus R., Angela Schorr, and Tom Johnstone (Eds.). *Appraisal Processes in Emotion: Theory, Methods, Research*, New York, NY: Oxford University Press, 2001: 173–186.

Plantinga, Carl R. "The Scene of Empathy and the Human Face on Film." In: Plantinga, Carl R. and Greg M. Smith (Eds.). *Passionate Views: Film, Cognition, and Emotion*. Baltimore: Johns Hopkins University Press, 1999: 239–55.

Premack, David and Guy Woodruff. "Does the Chimpanzee Have a Theory-of-Mind?" *Behavioral and Brain Sciences*, 1(04), 1978: 515–26.

Raz, Gal and Talma Hendler. "Forking Cinematic Paths to the Self: Neurocinematically Informed Model of Empathy in Motion Pictures." *Projections*, 8(2), 2014: 89–114.

Raz, Gal, Yael Jacob, Tal Gonen, Yonatan Winetraub, Tamar Flash, Eyal Soreq, and Talma Hendler. "Cry for Her or Cry with Her: Context-Dependent Dissociation of Two Modes of Cinematic Empathy Reflected in Network Cohesion Dynamics." *Social Cognitive and Affective Neuroscience*, 9(1), 2014: 30–38.

Reeves, Byron, Annie Lang, Eun Young Kim, and Deborah Tatar. "The Effects of Screen Size and Message Content on Attention and Arousal." *Media Psychology*, 1(1), 1999: 49–67.

Reeves, Byron and Clifford Nass. *How People Treat Computers, Television, and New Media like Real People and Places*. CSLI Publications and Cambridge University Press, 1996.

Rooney, Brendan and Katalin Bálint. "Watching More Closely: Shot Scale Affects Film Viewers' Theory-Of-Mind Tendency but Not Ability." *Frontiers*. Accepted for publication in *Frontiers in Psychology*, 8, 2018: 2349. doi:10.3389/fpsyg.2017.02349.

Salt, Barry. *Film Style and Technology: History and Analysis*. London: Starword, 1992.

Smith, Tim J. "Watching You Watch Movies: Using Eye Tracking to Inform Cognitive Film Theory." In: Shimamura, Arthur P. (Ed.). *Psychocinematics: Exploring Cognition at the Movies*. Oxford/New York: Oxford University Press, 2013:165–192.

Smith, Tim J. and John M. Henderson. "Edit Blindness: The Relationship between Attention and Global Change Blindness in Dynamic Scenes." *Journal of Eye Movement Research*, 2(2), 2008: 1–17.

Suckfüll, Monika. "Films That Move Us: Moments of Narrative Impact in an Animated Short Film." *Projections*, 4(2), 2010: 41–63.

Tan, Ed S. "Three Views of Facial Expression and Its Understanding in the Cinema." In: Anderson, Joseph D. and Barbara Fisher Anderson (Eds.). *Moving Image Theory: Ecological Considerations*, Carbondale: Southern Illinois University Press, 2005: 107–127.

Van Den Broek, Paul. "Models of Understanding Text. A 'Landscape' View of Reading: Fluctuating Patterns of Activation and the Construction of a Stable Memory Representation." In: Britton Bruce. K. and Arthur C. Graesser (Eds.). *Models of Understanding Text*. Mahwah: Erlbaum, 1996: 165–187.

Wallentin, Mikkel, Arndis Simonsen, and Andreas Højlund Nielsen. "Action Speaks Louder than Words: Empathy Mainly Modulates Emotions from Theory of Mind-Laden Parts of a Story." *Scientific Study of Literature*, 3(1), 2013: 137–153. doi:10.1075/ssol.3.1.11wal.

Wells, Paul. *Understanding Animation*. New York: Routledge, 2013.

Wieser, Matthias J. and Tobias Brosch. "Faces in Context: A Review and Systematization of Contextual Influences on Affective Face Processing." *Frontiers in Psychology*, 3, 2012: 471. doi:10.3389/fpsyg.2012.00471.

Zaki, Jamil and Kevin Ochsner. "The Neuroscience of Empathy: Progress, Pitfalls and Promise." *Nature Neuroscience*, 15(5), 2012: 675–80. doi:10.1038/nn.3085.

Zettl, Herbert. *Sight, Sound, Motion: Applied Media Aesthetics*. Cengage Learning, 2013.

Zwaan, Rolf A., Mark C. Langston, and Arthur C. Graesser. "The Construction of Situation Models in Narrative Comprehension: An Event-Indexing Model." *Psychological Science*, 6(5), 1995: 292–297.

Films

Father and Daughter. Directed by Michael Dudok de Wit. 2000; UK/BEL/NLD: CinéTé Filmproductie, Cloudrunner.

Invention of Love. Directed by Andrey Shuskhov. 2010; RUS: HHG Film Company.

Lavatory – Lovestory. Directed by Konstantin Bronzit. 2007; RUS: Melnitsa Animation Studio.

Lettin' Go. Directed by Malika Whitaker. 2008; FRA.

Part V
Young Audiences

10 How Infants Perceive Animated Films

Sermin Ildirar Kirbas and Tim J. Smith

Introduction

Due to their reduced mobility and linguistic immaturity, infants are good watchers spending a lot of time sitting and watching the actions, reactions, and emotions of other people. In this way, they learn how to interpret and predict others' behaviors and relate this to their own behavior. Prior to the twentieth century, the source of such exposure was entirely limited to observing real people performing real actions in the infant's immediate surroundings or dramatizations of human behaviors in a play. However, after the Lumière brothers premiered their moving images to the public in 1895, the physical proximity constraints on watching human behaviors disappeared and audiences of all ages could be exposed to an infinite repertoire of human behaviors projected on to the two-dimensional (2D) surface of the movie screen. Initially, infant exposure to moving images would have been infrequent but as television brought the images into our homes and then mobile technologies brought them into our hands the opportunity for learning from screens became pervasive. Using data collected during the early 1990s, Certain and Kahn (2002) reported that 17% of 0- to 1-year-olds and 48% of 1- to 2-year-olds watch television. More recently, researchers have reported that by 3 months of age, about 40% of children regularly watched television, DVDs, or videos. By 24 months, this proportion rose to 90%. The median age at which regular media exposure was introduced was 9 months. Among those who watched, the average viewing time per day rose from 1 hour per day for children younger than 12 months to more than 1.5 hours per day by 24 months (Zimmerman et al. 2007). Prior to the advent of infant-directed media, children under 2 years paid little attention to television, beginning regular TV viewing at about 30 months. With the introduction of *Teletubbies* in 1991 and *Baby Einstein* in 1996, however, modern programs and videos now target babies who have not even spoken their first words or taken their first steps. The revenue of *Baby Einstein* grew from $1 million in 1998 to $200 million in 2005 (Bronson and Merryman 2006). BabyTV, which is one of the television channels targeting infants and toddlers, was launched in 2003 and became distributed in over 100 countries in 2013. Unlike adult-directed TV, most of the infant-directed TV content is animated. The precise motivation for the prominence of animation in kid's TV is not fully known but one potential key component may be that animated films give an animator absolute control over the visual content of each shot in a way that might be financially impossible in live-action. Such control allows the animator to shape the flow of visual storytelling across 'shots.' The colors, light, movement, dialogue, and music can be tailored to direct immature gaze to semantic features. Characters who are at the same age as their viewers (which would not be easy in live action) can be designed in their entirety and their actions and emotions scripted to create age- and educationally appropriate stories. And most importantly, fascination, humor, and entertainment can be foregrounded above a strict adherence to reality, so that the young viewers enjoy the experience and come back for more.

However, this great potential for infant-directed TV to captivate young audiences through the power of animation fuels a major controversy. On the one hand, producers market their programs as being educationally or developmentally beneficial (Christakis and Garrison 2005); on the other hand, the American Academy of Paediatrics recommends that children younger than 18 months of age should not be exposed to electronic screens (unless for the purpose of video chat; AAP 2016). The AAP is concerned that media exposure may contribute to language delays and potential attention problems in young children, citing a correlational study by Zimmerman, Christakis, and Meltzoff (2007). However, another study reanalyzing the Zimmerman et al. (2007) data set did not find a strong connection between exposure to media and language development in young children (Ferguson and Donnellan 2014). With debates continuing to rage as to whether or not screen exposure is negative, what babies understand from what they watch and what factors play a role in this understanding are fundamental questions trying to be answered by conducting experiments on babies.

In this chapter, we will summarize the empirical studies on how babies perceive visual scenes and how these skills inform our understanding of film and TV perception. We will cover the perceptual and cognitive skills the babies need to have or develop in order to make sense of their visual environments and moving images. We will also discuss how infants perceive the similarity between a 2D image and the real three-dimensional (3D) entity; what the difficulties they face in understanding the representational nature of 2D images are; if they can learn from videos; what strategies contemporary kids' program makers use to help their little viewers make sense of the content; and how these strategies are related to the early days of cinema. Discussion of the perception of live-action content will be interspersed with animation, as infant-directed TV is unique in the flexible way in which the images are created, traditionally promoting animation above live-action (the inverse of adult-directed TV) and also intermixing a cornucopia of other techniques, including cel animation, cutouts, CGI, stop motion, collage, and puppetry. But to begin with, we will briefly discuss the unique challenges of running studies on perception with infants and the methods used to overcome such challenges.

Testing Babies

Babies are very hard to conduct experiments on. They can't understand instructions or press buttons, they get bored, they cry, they get hungry, thirsty, cry again, and they fall asleep. On the other hand, their looking is a major gateway to their minds before language develops, since their visual abilities are quite sophisticated: A baby pays attention and looks at anything that is new and interesting, which is the root of preferential looking tasks frequently used in developmental studies. *Preferential looking* tasks present two stimuli to a baby, and the length of time the infant looks at each is measured. The longest amount of time can be inferred to be indicative of the stimuli that the baby finds the most interesting. *Habituation* is a technique developed from the ideas of preferential looking. In such experiments, babies are shown a stimulus until they are bored of it and look at it no longer. This habituated stimulus is presented alongside a test stimulus. The preferential looking technique is then applied. If the baby now looks at the novel stimulus more than the habituated one, it is concluded that it can understand the difference between them. *Violation of expectation*, which is another method used to illustrate different aspects of infant cognition, means pretty much what it says: When babies' expectation is violated, then they look longer at the stimuli.

For decades, researchers have studied infant looking by relying on human observers who were coding the duration and direction of looking. Since the beginning of 2000s, there has been an explosion of research using *eye tracking* with infants (Smith and Saez De Urabain 2017). Eye tracking records the movements of the eye (typically using high-speed infrared cameras and pupil image tracking) relative to a calibrated field of view (usually a screen) allowing researchers to see exactly where the participant's center of gaze was directed and to infer from this which parts of a visual scene were preferentially processed. Researchers have examined infants' memory processes, perceptual learning, understanding of joint attention, face processing, and many other topics by using eye-tracking procedures. Eye-tracking procedures have been successfully implemented in infants as young as 3 months. Since eye trackers provide detailed information about infants' point-of-gaze from moment to moment, it is possible to ask how infants' distribution of looking over the area of stimulus or over time varies by age or stimulus type, which is great for studying perception of moving images by very young children. As well as devising innovative techniques for quantifying infant behavior, developmental scientists have also needed to find ways to make their experimental stimuli as intrinsically motivating so that babies continue watching. Interestingly, from the perspective of this book, a lot of the techniques they learned to employ have been directly borrowed from kid's TV, and specifically, animation. The use of bold color schemes, caricatures, simple audiovisual events (e.g., "Boing!"), puppets for live-action studies, and short/simple video sequences have all been used as proxies for studying how cognition develops in real-world scenes. As such, the studies we will review below often endeavor to further our understanding of real-world cognition through the use of animation and can therefore also provide insight into the perceptual foundations required for film cognition.

2D or Not 2D: Can Babies Learn from Screens?

The first potential barrier between film content and infant comprehension is the 2D nature of the stimulus. The absence of full 3D depth cues in the image, as well as other optical and physical aberrations, such as impossible object sizes or framing (e.g., an extreme, upside-down long shot showing tiny people hanging from the top of the screen) may cause problems for infant comprehension of the content. You may also consider these problems exacerbated by the prominent use of 2D animation in kids' TV, in which depth and perspective are often absent or creatively flaunted. However, studies have shown that infants are able to perceive the similarity between a 2D image and the real 3D entity that is depicted. For example, 2- to 5-month-old infants respond to the video image of another person with smiles and increased activity, much as they would to the actual person (Muir et al. 1996). By 6 months, infants can recognize video images of their parents and associate them with a familiar label like 'Mama' and 'Papa' (Tincoff and Jusczyk 1999). Other research shows that infants are capable of discriminating video images of people and objects from their real counterparts. Four- to six-month-old infants smile more at a real person than at a live video view of that person, even though the person is equally responsive to the baby in both cases (Hains and Muir 1996). Infants can also acquire new information from screen media. For example, 12- to 18-month-olds play with toys that they see on television more than they do with novel toys (McCall et al. 1977); 14-month-olds can duplicate actions depicted on television, even when they are presented by a stranger using an unfamiliar object and even when there is a 24-hour delay between watching the action and having access to the real 3D object (Meltzoff 1988); 18-month-olds – but not 14-month-olds – show a visual preference for a novel toy after a televised model engages infants in joint reference during familiarization with another toy (Cleveland and Striano 2008). Infants can also predict televised models' actions as they do with real people. Twelve-month-olds – but not 6-month-olds – look at the target of the action in a video before the agent's hand arrives in the goal area (Falck-Ytter et al. 2006). Such action prediction doesn't require the infant to map those actions onto their own motor repertoire (a common previously held assumption; see de Klerk et al. 2016 for discussion). The actions do not even have to be performed by a human to be predicted: infants that are 6.5 months old can attribute a goal to an inanimate box (Csibra 2008), which is an important finding regarding perception of animated films.

While responses to 2D screen content may resemble ones to natural 3D content in babies, there is considerable evidence that they struggle with understanding the representational nature of 2D images. Despite the fact that young infants can recognize onscreen objects, even 3-year-olds still make errors in this regard, believing, for instance, that photographs taken in advance will change if the represented scene changes (Donnelly et al. 2013). Similarly, 3-year-olds assume that popcorn would spill out of a televised popcorn bowl if the television were turned upside down (Flavell et al. 1990). As these results show, the development of representational insight follows a similar course for video as for still images; while 9-month-old infants try to grasp objects on the screen, between 15 and 19 months of age they will instead begin to point at the screen (Pierroutsakos and Troseth 2003). In time, toddlers progress from perceiving a 'picture as object' to a 'picture as representation.' When they perceive the videos as object, before 18 months of age, they probably do not understand what kind of an object a video is. This may be why research focusing on learning from video has also found that toddlers have trouble using information appearing on a TV screen to learn new words (Krcmar et al. 2007), solve problems (Troseth and DeLoache 1998), and imitate new skills (Hayne et al. 2003), but find these tasks easier if they get the information in person, which is referred to as the *'video deficit'* effect (Anderson and Pempek 2005). Toddlers require twice as much exposure to learn from video than from a real-life event (Barr et al. 2007; Strouse and Troseth 2008). Until at least 30 months of age, toddlers more often imitate target behaviors demonstrated by an in-person model than by that same model on video (Barr and Hayne 1999; Hayne et al. 2003). Research using many tasks (e.g., imitation, word learning, self-recognition) suggests that the video deficit is most pronounced around 15–24 months of age (when they realize that video differs from reality, and that is why it is not trustworthy) and then declines until about 36 months (see Anderson and Hanson 2010; Barr 2010; DeLoache et al. 2010; Troseth 2010). The video deficit in performance of more difficult tasks may even persist beyond 36 months (Roseberry et al. 2009; Dickerson et al. 2013). In a more recent study (Kirkorian et al. 2016), recorded two-year-olds' eye movements while they were watching an experimenter hiding a sticker behind a different shape on a felt board. Then children were given the felt board and asked to find the sticker. For half of the participants, the hiding events were in person; for the other half, the hiding events appeared on screen via closed-circuit video. Compared to those watching in-person events, children watching video spent more time looking at the target location overall, yet they had relatively poor search performance. Children who watched in-person hiding events had high success rates even if they paid relatively little visual attention to the correct location. Their findings also confirmed the video deficit hypothesis.

What are the Minimum Cognitive Skills Necessary for Babies to Perceive Movies?

To be able to make sense of any audiovisual medium, whether cinematographic representations or real-world scenes or animations, infants need (i) the sensory abilities to competently see and hear the content, (ii) to develop some perceptual and cognitive skills to organize and interpret the sensory information in order to represent and understand the events represented, and finally (iii) to learn to decode some cinematic techniques that do not have a real life counterpart. In other words, they need to gain film literacy.

Regarding sensory skills, we know that infants do not arrive with all of their senses fully formed. Although *hearing* is the most mature sense at birth, the quietest sound a newborn responds to is about four times louder than the quietest sound an adult respond to. Moreover, adults usually hear in a narrow band of sound, while babies seem to be listening broadband or to all frequencies simultaneously. *Vision*, on the other hand, is the least mature of all the senses at birth, since the fetus has very little to look at. Newborns are extremely nearsighted. Their lenses are immature. The smallest stripes to which newborns respond are about 40 times larger than what can be resolved by adults with normal vision (Brown and Yamamoto 1986). There is at least a fivefold improvement in visual acuity – sharpness of vision – by 6 months of age, increasing slightly more than one octave every 3 months. Visual acuity further improves by about half an octave at each of 12, 24, and 36 months. However, even at 36 months, mean acuity is still 0.75 octaves less than that of adults (Courage and Adams 1990). Visual acuity was found to be fully mature between the ages of five and the mid-teenage years, while contrast sensitivity was found to mature fully between the ages of 8–19, which is later than previously thought (Leat et al. 2009).

Another question regarding infant vision is what they look at. Newborns actively scan their surroundings, even in a completely darkened room, which may be an initial, primitive basis for looking behavior (Haith 1980). Newborns can follow moving objects with a series of saccades. The ability to smoothly track moving objects develops rapidly over the first few months. Nevertheless, infants prefer to look at moving objects instead of nonmoving objects. It is easier for them to track horizontally moving objects than vertically moving objects. They also prefer to look at patterned stimuli instead of plain, non-patterned stimuli. More relevantly to our topic, infants prefer to look at faces and face-like configurations over almost anything else (Johnson et al. 1991; Farroni et al. 2005) where they can receive attentional and emotional cues (Phillips et al. 2002), which we will discuss in detail in the next section.

A challenging part of visual perception is that the same object can look very different from different distances. We need to see an object as its real size, despite its distance from us, to perceive stability. This feature of perception is called *size constancy*, and as studies using the preferential-looking method reveal, it presents at birth (Granrud 1987; Slater et al. 1990). This, however, does not mean that babies can transfer this ability to moving images. Even adults who have no prior exposure to moving images fail to understand that an object depicted across shots of varying sizes is actually the same object. An anecdote about first-time adult viewers in Africa suggested that naïve viewers thought that the mosquitoes shown in close-up shots were giant mosquitoes and since they did not have such big mosquitos in their villages, they did not need to worry about malaria (Forsdale and Forsdale 1966). This anecdote shows that a viewer needs to have the notion of camera and know that it can approach or move away from objects or scenes to be able to perceive the size of the depicted object constantly. Similar misinterpretations can be observed in children. Before the age of two-years, author Sermin Ildirar's daughter thought that a dog depicted in a closer shot was the mother of the dog presented in a previous long shot in her picture book. So this visual skill needs to be supported by literacy of the conventions of each medium, and infants needs to decode this symbolic system used to present content.

Another perceptual skill we need to have in order to make sense of our visual environment is *perceptual completion*. In the real world and in films, many visible objects are partly occluded by other objects; in films, we usually see a part of an object, but adults do not have difficulty in perceiving them as complete. They do this by registering missing portion of the object and using available information from the visible segments, including their shape, position, orientation, motion, relative distance, luminance, color, and texture. Research on the development of perceptual completion uses the object unity paradigm, developed initially by Kellman and Spelke (1983). After habituation to a moving rod with its center occluded by a box, 4-month-old infants look longer at a non-occluded presentation of a broken rod than at a complete rod, which indicates that this is not what they expect. In contrast, newborns consistently prefer the complete rod test display, implying that the broken rod is familiar relative to the habituation display (Slater et al. 1990, 1994, 1996). Viewers need this perceptual skill to make sense of shot sizes other than long and very long shots. Although an early film theorist, Yhcam, recommended directors to avoid using medium-long shots as well as frequent close-ups to make their films understandable, and argued against the American shot size (medium-long, 'knee' film shot), saying that such shots show people on the screen as though they were disabled, the majority of filmmakers in film history did not listen to him, and contemporary adult viewers in Western countries seem to have no problem with making sense of such shot sizes (Abel 1912). Film-illiterate adults, however, interpreted the medium shot size (showing only the upper part of the depicted person) as showing the person sitting (although this was not the case – see Ildirar and Ewing 2018).

Mental rotation is another perceptual skill we need to have to make sense of both the real world and films. Studies reveal that 2-month-old infants appeared to perceive the 3D shape of rotating objects (Johnson et al. 2003). Other studies found that 4-month-old infants form dynamic mental representations that allow them to both track the movement of a 2D object rotating in the frontal plane and anticipate the object's ultimate orientation (Rochat and Hespos 1996; Hespos and Rochat 1997). We also know that infants who manually explore the test object before testing (Moehring and Frick 2013) and infants who are able to crawl (Schwarzer et al. 2013) are both more successful in performing the mental rotation task than infants of the same age. Boys are also better than girls at mental rotation (Moore and Johnson 2008). The ability to rotate mentally (measured in terms of a decline in response time) peaks in young adulthood and declines thereafter. This ability is essential to make sense of different camera angles edited together. In a study with film-illiterate adults (Ildirar and Schwan 2015), we asked participants how many animals they saw in the film clips, each showing an animal from two different camera angles edited together. The majority of first-time adult viewers thought that there were two different animals, while all of the experienced viewers of the same age, from the same culture, and with the same education level thought there was only one animal, shown from different perspectives. Here the problem was not an inability of mental rotation but the lack of the knowledge about the filmmaking process: the possibility of recording the same scene from different camera angles and editing them together.

Perceiving Continuity Across Cuts

To make sense of moving images, after gaining required perceptual and cognitive abilities one also needs to perceive the continuity between film shots. In the early days of cinema, most films depicted simple, real-world scenes or staged narratives filmed in a single run (a shot) from a static camera. Such *tableaux* often creatively intermixed live action with animation to create fantastical effects in these single images, as seen, for example, in the sudden transformations of Georges Méliès' stop motion shorts or the hand-painted color tinting and stop motion animation of his *Le Voyage Dans la Lune* (1902). Shortly thereafter, filmmakers combined multiple shots to create more compelling visual narratives, and the number of the shots they use has increased dramatically over the history of film (see Cutting and Candan 2015 for numbers). The children's programs also got their share: For instance, the editing pace of *Sesame Street* increased from four cuts per minute in 1977 to eight cuts per minute in 2003 (Koolstra et al. 2004). What real-world cognitive abilities do infants need to develop before they can perceive continuity across cuts?

Matched-Exit/Entrance

One of the most primitive types of cut depicts a character moving out of the shot and their motion continuing in the next shot. These *matched-exit/entrances* emerged in the earliest edited films as a direct loan from the method of leaving a scene via the wings of a theatre and gave filmmakers a method of joining together two or more *tableaux* (Smith 2006). This technique is prominent in any live-action film depicting human motion and is also very common in cel animation (see Wile E. Coyote' never-ending chases of the Road Runner in the classic *Looney Tunes* cartoons). Perceiving the character as continuing to exist during their absence from view directly exploits the basic perceptual ability of *object permanence*: perception of objects as persisting in time and space even with interruptions in perceptual contact. By four months after birth, infants provide evidence of occlusion perception in displays that depict fully occluded objects (Johnson et al. 2003). Newborn infants, in contrast, have been shown consistently to perceive similar partial occlusion displays solely in terms of their visible surfaces, failing to perceive object permanence (Slater et al. 1990, 1994, 1996). At 6 months of age, object permanency skill matures. Infants begin to have expectations of the direction of object movement during occlusion (Kochukhova and Gredebäck 2007). At 7–9 months of age they start to track an object with smooth pursuit prior to occlusion, crosses the occluder with a saccade and continues smooth tracking once it becomes visible again (Leigh and Zee 1999).

Object permanence is also related to an individual's working memory capacity. Infants can accurately update their representation of a hidden two-object array when one object is subtracted from it (Moher and Feigenson 2013). Six-month-old infants are only able to recall the shape of the easier-to-recall object, while -month-olds can recall the shape of both objects (but not their colors, Kibbe and Leslie 2013). This raises the question, however, of whether film cuts function as occluders or, again, as a filmic code that prevents the perception of continuity by film illiterates before learning about the notion of editing in films. A recent study (Kirkorian and Anderson 2017) compared eye movements of 12-month-olds, 4-year-olds, and adults to see if they would anticipate the reappearance of objects in successive animated shots depicting simple cartoon characters interacting. In the stimuli, the characters or objects were moving laterally or vertically on the screen, disappearing from one edge of the screen at the end of one shot and then reemerging from the opposite side of the screen in the next shot. The logic behind the study was that if viewers comprehended these transitions and perceived the video as occurring within continuous space, viewers would anticipate object and character movement across cuts by shifting their gaze to the side of the screen opposite where the object or character was last seen (Dmytryk 1986). Thus, the researchers tested the effectiveness of one of the classic editing techniques, believed by filmmakers to encourage effortless integration across film cuts by all viewers, but the researchers found that anticipation across cuts did not happen as much in children compared to adults. Kirkorian and Anderson (2017) suggest that children might not be able to anticipate the actions when they are presented in edited moving images. Twelve-month-old infants did not anticipate the object's reappearance across a cut (instead infant eye movements were reactive to the new shot content), and 4-year-olds responded to transitions more slowly and tended to fixate the center of the screen. Kirkorian and Anderson (2017) conclude that infants cannot integrate content across shots and understand how space is represented in edited video. Film literacy may come about through exposure.

Match-on-Action

Match-on-action refers to an editing technique where a subject begins an action in one shot and carries it through to completion in the next (Bordwell and Thompson 2001) The action bridge between shots distracts the viewer from noticing the cut (i.e., edit blindness; Smith and Henderson 2008; Smith and Martin-Portugues Santacreu 2017) and provides a foundation for the perception of continuity. It is also known that it enables even first-time adult viewers, who are not able to do so in the absence of continuing action through the cuts, to perceive spatiotemporal continuity between shots (Ildirar and Schwan 2014). This technique is believed to function by both cuing attentional shifts pre-cut and using motion blur post-cut (Pepperman 2004) to limit the availability of attention and perceptual discrimination ability of viewers towards the cut (Smith 2012; Smith and Martin-Portugues Santacreu 2017). Or, in a simpler explanation: "so powerful is our desire to follow the action flowing across the cut we ignore the cut itself" (Bordwell and Thompson 2001: 70). Do the infants also have such a desire to follow the actions?

Falck-Ytter et al. (2006) found that 12-month-old babies (but not 6-month-olds) do perform goal-directed, anticipatory eye movements when observing actions performed by others. In their study, an actor placed objects in a bucket, and both 12-month-old infants and adults fixated the goal of an ongoing manual action. Six-month-olds, however, tracked the moving hand rather than fixating the goal. Imagine a newborn, who cannot know where the bed ends and where the curtain begins, since it does not know what they are. Discriminating and categorizing actions are even harder than objects, as evidenced by the fact that verbs are more difficult to learn than nouns. So it cannot know where peeling the banana ends and eating the banana begins. In time, babies learn to use information about the goal or intention of the acting person to segment events into meaningful units. In one study (Baldwin et al. 2001), for example, 10- to 11-month-old infants were familiarized with one of two movies depicting a woman cleaning a kitchen. Each movie depicted a salient goal-directed action (e.g., replacing a fallen dishtowel or storing an ice cream container in the freezer). After the familiarization phase, infants were presented with excerpts with one-second pauses inserted into the movie. The pauses were placed either at the moment when the woman achieved the action's goal, or several seconds before. The infants looked longer at the excerpts when the pauses were placed before the goal completions, suggesting that they found those more disruptive.

For anticipating future actions, segmenting events into units is critical for both adults and infants. Infants could use these initial groupings to discover more abstract cues to event structure, such as the actor's intentions, which are known to play a role in adults' global event segmentation (e.g., Zacks and Tversky 2001; Zacks 2004). Visual sequence learning is a primary mechanism for event segmentation and research show that 8-month-old infants are sensitive to the sequential statistics of actions performed by a human agent (Roseberry et al. 2011). More interestingly, adults (Baldwin et al. 2008), as well as infants in their first year of life (Stahl et al. 2014), can segment a continuous action sequence based on sequential predictability alone, which suggests that before infants have top-down knowledge of intentions, they may begin to segment events based on sequential predictability. These studies do, however, use stimuli recorded or created on computers as one single shot. As has been shown by Kirkorian and Anderson (2017), these real-world perceptual skills may not automatically enable perception of similar actions when they are depicted across multiple shots, as infants are impaired in integrating content across shots and understanding how space is represented in edited video.

Eye-Line Match

Another editing technique the filmmakers found helped viewers perceive continuity between film shots is *eye-line match*, which is based on the premise that an audience will want to see what the character onscreen is seeing. A film sequence with an eye-line match begins with a character looking at something offscreen, followed by a cut of another object or person. From a developmental perspective, this refers to joint visual attention: the shared focus of two individuals on an object. This ability emerges between 6 and 12 months of age and consolidates through at least the eighteenth month of development (Butterworth and Cochran 1980; Butterworth and Jarrett 1991; Corkum and Moore 1998. It is not until 18 months, for example, that babies begin to follow others' attention to objects that are behind them (Butterworth and Cochran 1980). A recent study (McClure et al. 2017) tested 6- to 24-month-old babies to find out if they are capable of using joint visual attention (JVA) successfully in the video chat context by observing them video-chatting with their grandparents; it found that the development of screen-mediated JVA is within the timeline of general JVA development. However, it is not known if the same transfer of JVA skills will occur when the eliciting screen content is presented across a series of shots joined by cuts, as is the case in eye-line match cuts.

Ellipsis, Crosscutting, and Flashbacks

Film cuts can be between shots depicting a scene from different camera angles, or an event taking place at the same time in different places or, more challengingly, the temporal sequence of a narration can be altered by using cuts. Given the fact that before 19 months of age, they cannot even order simple actions like pouring imaginary liquid from a toy pot to a cup and (then) giving it to a doll to drink (Fenson and Ramsay 1981), it would be unfair to expect children to understand time gaps or flashbacks in the films. As a matter of fact, even for 10-year-olds flashbacks are not easy to understand. Flashbacks are not superior to jumbled editing when the children are asked to sequence the event presented (Lowe and Durkin 1999). A more recent study also found that 8-year-olds (the oldest age group in the study) have difficulties coping with narrative discontinuity (Munk et al. 2012). However, it is common in children's programs, as in the early days of cinema, to use special effects to alert the viewer that the action shown is a flashback; for example, the edges of the picture may be deliberately blurred, or unusual coloration, sepia tone, or monochrome may be used. So, once the children can learn the meaning of this cinematic symbol, then such effects might be useful.

Narration

Another strategy contemporary kid's programs borrow from the early days of cinema is using a narrator. Although originally, live narrators were used to help viewers to understand the narration in the absence of sound during the silent era of cinema (Standish 2006), today they are used as an addition to sound to help little viewers to understand the narration (for a very successful example, see *Peppa Pig*, a British animated television series for preschoolers).

Directing Infant Attention

While watching moving images, bottom-up (i.e., stimulus-driven) and top-down factors (i.e., task, preference, ongoing comprehension) influence viewers' eye movements (Henderson 2007; Tatler et al. 2011). Bottom-up influences are characterized by how well the salience of low-level stimulus features based on luminance, contrast, color, orientation, and motion accounts for eye movements, and studies show that adult viewers' eye movements when watching dynamic stimuli are influenced by bottom-up saliency (Mital et al. 2011; Borji and Itti 2013; Smith and Mital 2013). However, adult viewers' eye movements do not correlate with the most salient location in the image while watching Hollywood movies (Shepherd et al. 2010). To test the role of top-down factors on viewer's eye movements, some researchers gave the viewers some tasks and found that changing observers' tasks affects eye movements when viewing static images (Yarbus 1967), dynamic stimuli (Smith and Mital 2013), and when performing natural actions (Land et al. 1999; Hayhoe et al. 2003; Franchak and Adolph 2010). Even in the absence of an explicit task, top-down factors influence free viewing by prioritizing semantically relevant stimuli such as objects and faces. Faces attract an observer's gaze when viewing static images (Yarbus 1967; Cerf et al. 2007) or dynamic movies (Klin et al. 2002; Foulsham et al. 2010). The tendency to look at faces, which starts from the very early days of infancy, contribute to eye movement consistency among observers (Frank et al. 2009).

Whether influenced by bottom-up or top-down factors, adults' eye movements are highly consistent when freely viewing dynamic stimuli – observers tend to look at the same location at the same time (Hasson et al. 2008a; Dorr et al. 2010; Shepherd et al. 2010; Mital et al. 2011; Wang et al. 2012; Smith and Mital 2013). Hollywood movies, however, evoke greater consistency in eye movements compared to homemade, "naturalistic" movies (Hasson et al. 2008a, Hassan et al. 2008b; Dorr et al. 2010). Do the eye movements of the little viewers also remain consistent when they are watching moving images?

Studies comparing eye movements of adults and infants suggest that similarity of gaze location increases with age (Frank et al. 2009; Kirkorian et al. 2012, Franchak et al. 2016). A study shows increasing eye movement consistency across age in 3-, 6-, and 9-month-olds and adults while watching short clips from *A Charlie Brown Christmas* (Frank et al. 2009). A more recent study found the same results for 1-year-olds, 4-year-olds, and adults viewing an episode of Sesame Street mixing live action with puppetry and animation (Kirkorian et al. 2012).

Bottom-up and top-down factors influence eye movements differently in infants compared to adults. Although young infants prefer to look at faces in static image arrays over other types of stimuli (Gliga et al. 2009; Libertus and Needham 2011; Gluckman and Johnson 2013), the proportion of time spent fixating faces in static images (Amso et al. 2014) and dynamic displays (Frank et al. 2009) starts at a modest level before increasing gradually over development. Bottom-up and top-down influences are not independent and thus are difficult to disentangle.

Watch Like Mother: Accommodating Infant Cognition in Tots TV Design

Infant brains are noisier information processing systems; this means that messages intended for infants have to allow clearer differentiation between those aspects that are required for the processing message (the 'signal') and those that are not (the 'noise'). This need for simplification of the sensory environment gives rise to exaggeration and accentuation of speech by caregivers (i.e., Motherese; Ferguson 1964) and the use of primary colors and bold shapes in the design of children's toys. The same problem of cutting through the sensory noise is faced by producers of infant-directed TV (*Tots TV*), and the formal differences between Tots TV and adult-directed TV (including the increased use of animation over live-action) seem to suggest that designers have intuited the differing demands of infant cognition.

Analysis of infant gaze behavior while watching TV has indicated that the fixation locations of young infants (3–6 months) is more predicted by visual salience than by semantic features of the scene such as faces (Frank et al. 2009). However, visual salience can also be used to guide attention to the most important area of an image, typically the face of the speaking character. Franchak et al. (2016) compared eye movements between 6- and 24-month-old infants and adults during free viewing of a one-minute-long clip from *Sesame Street* and found that while adults fixated on the human actor's face more frequently than infants did, infants spent more time fixating on the highly salient Muppet faces. This potential for well-designed animated or puppet faces to attract immature gazes was also demonstrated in a developmental study from our lab. Smith et al. (2014) compared the gaze behavior of 6-month-old,

12-month-old, and adult participants viewing excerpts from baby DVDs including live-action clips of animals or of children interacting and 2D animations of cartoon shapes moving across the screen. Infants had less *attentional synchrony* (i.e., spatiotemporal clustering of gaze across participants; Smith and Mital 2013) than adults (Frank et al. 2009; Kirkorian et al. 2012) but these differences were mostly due to scenes with high feature entropy: for example, no clear peaks of high flicker, luminance, or color contrast. Such scenes tended to be live-action depictions of complex visual scenes, in which the foreground objects (e.g., cows) were hard to discern from the background (e.g., fields and bushes). During scenes with low entropy (e.g., simple animations of cartoon animals or of real objects shot against a white backdrop) or the presence of a face, infant gaze behavior was indistinguishable from adult gaze patterns. These results suggest that the designers had optimized these shots to accommodate the limited top-down control of infant gaze and to guide attention to the most informative part of the image: a face.

Further evidence that designers of Tots TV optimize the audiovisual stimulus to simplify their infant viewers' task of deciding what to attend to (i.e., the signal) over the irrelevant background features (e.g., noise) comes from a computational corpus analysis performed in our lab. Wass and Smith (2015) compared the distribution of visual features (i.e., luminance, colors, edges, flicker, and motion) in high-quality Tots and Adult TV and found that Tots TV had a better signal-to-noise ratio than Adult TV, with peaks in low-level visual features predicting the location of the speaking face (the *signal*) more often than in Adult TV. The editing rate of Tots TV was slower and the average shot size larger (i.e., more long shots), which may give the slower attentional system of young children longer to find the focal object within a frame. Camera movements were less frequent, and in combination, all of these design decisions allowed the composition to point directly to the speaking face in most shots. By comparison, Adult TV was frenetic, with rapid editing, highly mobile cameras, and a muted palette, which allocate as much saliency to peripheral features as speaking faces, making the task of finding character faces a more effortful/cognitive task. As we and others have demonstrated, this can result in greater variance in how infants distribute their gaze across the frame and a lower likelihood of finding the speaking face (Frank et al. 2009; Kirkorian et al. 2012; Smith et al. 2014; Franchak et al. 2016). Interestingly, these formal differences between Tots TV and Adult TV were not entirely due to the Tots TV being animated. The Tots TV programs we analyzed included live action (e.g., *Teletubbies, In the Night Garden*), 2D and 3D animation (*Charlie & Lola, Tree Fu Tom, Octonauts*), and mixtures (*Baby Jake, Abadas*). We also included a selection of adult-directed animation (2DTV), puppetry (*Mongrels*), and stop motion animated programs (*Rex The Runt*), and while these shared similar brightness and color profiles to Tots TV, they were shot and edited similar to the Adult TV, suggesting that their creators understood the need to tailor the flow of audiovisual information to their older audiences.

Of course, ensuring an infant attends to the part of the image you want does not guarantee they perceive the content in the intended way. Pempek and colleagues (2010) showed 6-, 12-, 18-, and 24-month-old babies both normal and distorted versions (in which shots were randomly ordered, and the dialogues it included were reversed) of the Teletubbies, a television program designed for very young children. They found that the youngest infants (6-, 12-, and to some degree 18-month-olds) looked at the normal and distorted versions for the same amount of time, suggesting they could not discern any perceptual difference in the two types of video. Only 24-month-olds distinguished between normal and distorted video by looking for longer durations towards the normal version (Pempek et al. 2010). You can lead a horse to water, but you can't make it drink!

How Babies Perceive Faces and the Emotions They Express

The studies above demonstrate the significant role faces play in structuring film and TV content and guiding viewer gaze. But what evidence is there that infants respond to the depicted faces once they attend to them? Children older than three months old show a clear face preference in either dynamic displays or static stimulus arrays (see Frank et al. 2014 for a review), which might explain why trains, cars, flowers, etc., have faces in animated films. This preference varies with individual differences in attentional control. Infants watched two different videos (the animated *Charlie Brown* and a live-action clip from *Sesame Street*), and the scholars tested not only their looking at faces but also their attentional abilities (Frank et al. 2014). Replicating previous findings, they found that looking at faces increased with age. In addition, they found that infants who showed weaker attentional abilities also looked less at faces and more at salient regions. This relation was primarily seen in the youngest infants (the 3-month-old group), and was stronger than the relation between chronological age and face looking (both in that group and in the 6- and 9-month-old groups).

There are also studies about how infants scan individual components of a face. There is evidence that one-month-olds fixate primarily on the outer contour of the face but, by two months old, focus on internal elements, mostly the eyes and mouth (Maurer and Salapatek 1976; Hainline 1978). When scanning of the internal features of static faces, young infants spend more time attending to the eyes than the mouth (Haith et al. 1977; Hunnius et al. 2011). Most faces infants see, however, are not static but dynamic and viewed within a social context. A study (Wilcox et al. 2013) exploring infants' scanning of dynamic faces, in which an adult female spoke and acted in a positive and engaging way, found that by 3–4 months of age, infants perceive both eyes and mouth as important sources of information and scan faces accordingly. In contrast, the 9-month-olds spent a significantly greater proportion of time looking at the eyes than the mouth. These scholars conclude that with time and experience infants identify that a great deal of socially relevant information can be quickly and effectively gathered from the eyes, making mouth scanning redundant and unnecessary.

When looking into another's eyes, infants prefer direct gaze: Two- to five-day-old newborns prefer to look at a direct gaze when presented alongside an averted gaze of the same person (Farroni et al. 2002), and contemporary infant-directed television programs seem to use this information as well by breaking the fourth wall (see *Teletubbies* for an example). The position of a face relative to the observer has an important role on emotion detection and recognition due to the availability of information presented in the face. A study (Goren and Wilson 2006) found that happiness is the least affected by peripheral presentation.

Which expressions can be discriminated in the first few days after birth and whether there is a particular expression that is preferred over others are the initial questions tried to be answered by the scholars working on the emotion perception in infancy. Given the results of adult cognitive neuroscience, studies found that fearful faces may maximally engage rapid and subcortical processing (Adolphs and Tranel 2003) and, as the fearful expression contains wide eyes and an open mouth, one might think that newborns must be sensitive to faces that display fear. However, newborns cannot discriminate between the neutral and fearful faces (Farroni et al. 2007, experiment 2), but they do discriminate between happy and fearful faces and prefer to look at happy faces, not fearful ones (Farroni et al. 2007, experiment 3). Studies have also demonstrated that infants display a wide range of emotional expressions at as early as three months of age, including interest, enjoyment, surprise, sadness/distress, anger, and discomfort/pain (Malatesta and Haviland 1982; Haviland and Lelwica 1987).

Many mother–infant studies using live interaction paradigms suggest that infants recognize the emotional expressions of their own caregivers and respond to them meaningfully as early as 2–3 months of age (e.g., Field 1977; Beebe and Gerstman 1980; Cohn and Ellmore 1988). At approximately 3 months of age, infants can discriminate among facial expressions of happiness, anger, fear, surprise, anger, and disgust (e.g., Barrera and Maurer 1981; Kuchuck et al. 1986; Serrano et al. 1992). Again by 3 months of age, infants have 'expectations' about their mother's behaviour during social interactions and respond to violations of those expectations with meaningful affective changes (Gusella et al. 1988; Izard et al. 1995). In contrast to interaction studies, findings from experimental investigations of infants' recognition of emotional expressions suggest that only 7-month-olds are capable of discriminating among happy, interested, angry, and sad expressions of strangers (Soken and Pick 1999). By 7 months, infants who hear a happy vocalization look longer at a 'happy face' than at a 'sad face' (e.g., Soken and Pick 1992; Kahana-Kalman and Walker-Andrews 2001). As babies gain mobility and begin to explore the world, they instinctively return to the caregiver periodically for emotional cues and respond to the emotional signal conveyed (Sigman and Capps 1997). By 12 months, infants are thought to use this early understanding of facial expressions to guide their own behavior through social referencing (e.g., Hertenstein and Campos 2004). It is now known that for testing young infants' emotion recognition, videos are better stimuli than still images since the crucial affective information is conveyed in the dynamic motion is lost in static photographs (Ekman et al. 1972). It is also known that multimodal displays are better. Experiments conducted on infants' intermodal perception of emotions demonstrate that 5- to 7-month-old infants look preferentially to a dynamic facial expression accompanied by its characteristic vocal expression even when many of the relations are distorted or eliminated (Walker-Andrews 1986; Soken and Pick 1992). For example, Walker-Andrew (1986) presented infants with two films portraying a woman with two different expressions along with a single vocal expression corresponding to one of the facial expressions. In a series of experiments, both 5- and 7-month-old infants looked more to all facial expressions (happy, sad, angry, and neutral) when they were sound specified than when they were not. Another factor effecting the difference that may contribute to the reported age difference is that in most studies the emotional expressions are portrayed by an unfamiliar actress, whereas in interaction studies they are typically portrayed by a familiar person (i.e., mothers). Indeed, Barrera and Maurer (1981) showed that 3-month-olds find it easier to discriminate among facial expressions portrayed by their own mothers than among the same expressions portrayed by a stranger. Kahana-Kalman and Walker-Andrews (2001) also found that person familiarity plays an important role on infants' early recognition of emotional expression. In contrast to an earlier study (Walker 1982), which used strangers to test the between the face and voice and found that not 5-month-olds but 7-month-olds prefer the affectively concordant display, Kahana-Kalman and Walker-Andrews (2001) found that 3.5-month-old infants detect and respond to the affective correspondences in their own mothers' facial and vocal expressions, even when synchrony relations between the face and voice are disrupted.

In the aforementioned experiments, the stimuli are typically presented in a very accessible format: at eye level, large enough so that all details can be appreciated. To be able to understand how infants actually see the faces in real life, Franchak et al. (2010) used head-mounted eye-trackers and found that 14-month-olds rarely fixated on their mother's face, even when she spoke to them directly. They looked instead at her hands or other parts of her body. The authors interpreted that this result might have been due to the mother's location, usually high above the child. Frank (2012) recorded 2–3 hours of the visual experience of a single child at ages 3, 8, and 12 months with a head-mounted camera and found systematic changes in the visibility of faces across the first year, showing postural shifts (lying, sitting, standing, crawling, or being held) as a possible reason for that.

However, in contrast to mobile mothers, screens can be placed at the eye level of babies regardless of their postures, maximizing the probability that the baby looks at the screen. But how do we ensure they find the face or perceive the expressions once their gaze lands there? As discussed previously (Wass and Smith 2014), creators of Tots TV see to have intuited the use of animation as a way to simplify this task for their immature viewers. By minimizing background features and limiting camera movements and editing, Tots TV make the faces of speaking characters more salient relative to the background, enabling viewers' gazes to find them faster. Also, we have shown that visual features are actually more clustered in the faces in Tots TV compared to Adult TV, with specific areas of high contrast around the eyes, the center of emotional expression (Wass and Smith 2014). These high-contrast eyes (think the classically enlarged and babylike 'Disney eyes') help guide immature gaze to the most emotionally rich element in each frame, potentially aiding narrative comprehension and understanding of character intentions. Empirical studies of the impact of caricature on adult face recognition have confirmed cartoonists' intuitions that by caricaturing a person, they are making recognition faster and easier than when using a realistic likeness (Rhodes et al. 1987). Ironically, simplification of the facial features in Tots TV might inadvertently lead to simplified potential for a range of emotional expressions (often this is exacerbated by limited range of movements in puppeted heads or time constraints on drawing complex facial action units). However, the remaining extremes of emotion that are possible may mirror the simplification of the narratives and characterization of Tots TV typically used. As audiences mature, so does the complexity of such features, as well as the migration towards the nuanced performances of live-action actors (or more lifelike animation; see Japanese Anime).

How Babies Perceive Emotions Portrayed by Fictitious Characters

One example of clear social learning from TV is learning an emotional response from an actor. For example, 12-month-olds avoid a novel toy after watching a televised model that showed negative reaction toward it (Mumme and Fernald 2003). In their study, Mumme and Fernald (2003) showed infants a televised scenario of an actress reacting with neutral, positive, or negative emotion to one of two interesting novel objects in front of her, then gave them an opportunity to interact with the real-world versions of the two objects to find out how the emotional reactions of the actress influenced the infant's own reactions. After witnessing the televised adult react negatively towards one object, 12-month-old infants avoided that object once it was within reach. In the positive condition, however, there was no significant change in infants' tendency to touch the target object. In contrast to the differential responding of the 12- month-old infants, the 10-month-old infants did not vary their behavior toward the objects in response to positive and negative emotional reaction. Learning appropriate emotional reactions through simulation of others is a key developmental process. Research on infants' emotional life suggests that dramatic and rapid changes occur in the first two years of life with respect to infants' abilities to perceive and respond to the emotions of the others (see Walker-Andrews 1997, for a review). Such developmental changes contribute to infants' ability to become active participants in social interactions (Malatesta et al. 1989) and may also influence how infants emotionally respond to screen-based content, although considerably more research is required on this developmental question.

Although differentiating emotions in stories is more difficult than in pictures, studies have shown that children can label the emotion conveyed by brief stories describing causes and consequences (e.g., Reichenbach and Masters 1983; Widen and Russell 2002). Even 3-year-olds can differentiate situations that elicit positive emotions from those that lead to negative emotions (Stein and Levine 1989). However, it is more difficult to establish the causes of negative emotions. Furthermore, it is not clear that young children are interpreting what they perceive in terms of discrete separate emotions. Children use different emotion labels with different frequencies even when presented with an equal number of facial expressions for each emotion; the order from highest to lowest is typically happiness, sadness, anger, fear, surprise, and disgust (Izard 1994; Gosselin and Simard 1999; Widen and Russell 2003). This pattern has been observed for children's 'correct' responses, but the same order was also found for children's 'incorrect' uses (Widen and Russell 2003), suggesting that differential use of emotion labels reflects children's developing category system.

Two-year-old children can only divide emotions into two broad categories – feeling good or feeling bad. The older they get, the more precise their ability to make a distinction becomes (Widen and Russell 2010). Widen and Russell (2010) asked to label the emotion conveyed by each of five facial expressions and, separately, by stories about the corresponding emotion's antecedent cause and behavioral consequence. They did not require children to choose from a prespecified list of labels but asked instead how the character felt. They categorized the labelling levels of children into four groups: The children at labeling level 1 (mean age 33 months) used happiness to label not only the smiling 'happy face' and the happy story, but, indeed, all faces shown to them and all stories told to them. At labeling level 2 (mean age 37.9 months), some children used happiness and sadness; others used happiness and anger. In either case, children used these labels liberally. Happiness was used more narrowly than in labeling level 1, and the negative term was used broadly for most negative faces and stories. At labeling level 3 (mean age 41.4 months), children used three labels (happiness, sadness, anger) with fewer events falling into each category, but still more events than would be seen with adults. At labeling level 4 (mean age 48.1 months), children used four labels (happiness, sadness, anger, fear) to cover the 10 emotional stimuli. For example, even though they did not use the label of disgust, they were not silent when faced with a disgust face or story. They assimilated these stimuli to their four categories. By the age of 4 or 5, all basic emotions (Ekman and Friesen 1975) are recognized (Camras and Allison 1985). By the age of 5, children can distinguish fear and sadness (Harris et al. 1989), whereas the discrimination between sadness and anger is difficult even for 6- to 7-year-olds (Levine 1995).

As a matter of fact, emotions portrayed by fictitious characters is important part of all kind if narrative media and requires inference generation and building situation models accordingly. The ability to build emotional inferences depends on several factors, such as the sufficiency of background information (Molinari et al. 2009), the reader's knowledge about emotions (Gernsbacher et al. 1992) and age (Diergarten and Nieding 2015). By constructing various kinds of inferences, we combine information given in the narration with our own world knowledge to form a sophisticated representation of the state of affairs described or just implied. Whereas most of the research on emotional inferences concentrates on written text, films are capable of generating perceptually enriched situation models given that perceptible information enhances emotional inferences in comparison with nonperceptible information. For example, Gillioz et al. (2012) found that behavioral information about emotion led to greater differences in reading times than in emotional labels (e.g., "She danced all night" vs. "Suzanne was feeling happy," p. 240). This is also supported by research on the modality effect, which shows that a dual presentation (audio and visual) is superior to a visual presentation alone (Leahy and Sweller 2011). However, every kind of medium is based on a certain set of symbol systems, and understanding these systems is essential for understanding the content. So, film-specific media literacy is also required to build the situation models and generate emotional inferences. By the age of 3 years, children are able to comprehend simple edited video stories as well as they comprehend unedited stories (presented as one continuous shot), and by the age of 4 years, they are able to substantially comprehend shot sequences conveying spatial relations, such as those implied by deleted actions, simultaneity of action, and character point of view (Smith et al. 1985). However, comprehension of video sequences during early childhood is limited. It continues to improve throughout middle childhood (Smith et al. 1985; Calvert 1988).

Potter (1998, 2013) distinguishes between rudimentary and advanced skills of media literacy. Rudimentary skills include the fundamental abilities to recognize the symbols used by media, recognize patterns composed by these symbols, and ascribe meaning to them; these abilities are developed between 3 and 5 years of age. Nieding and Ohler (2008) call this "media sign literacy" ("Mediale Zeichenkompetenz," p. 382), and together with their colleagues, they suggest that the ages between 4 and 8 years are crucial for the development of rudimentary media literacy skills. Advanced media literacy skills develop during school years and adulthood (Munk et al. 2012).

Conclusion

Babies' media exposure and developmental processes can no longer be studied in isolation from one another, due to the fact that many infants begin consistently viewing moving images at four months of age and become regular viewers when they are only two years old. In spite of the usage of the same perceptual and cognitive skills used to perceive the moving images and real visual environment, the differences between moving images and real life should not be underestimated. Films systematically deviate from the course of natural perception. For example, often the film anticipates certain events, cutting to a place immediately before something important will happen there (Bordwell 2005). As demonstrated by recent studies (Smith et al. 2014; Wass and Smith 2015), creators of kids' media seem to have intuited how to optimize the audio-visual content in order to simplify the viewing process for their audience's immature brains by relying heavily on the potential of animation, puppetry, and cartoonlike live-action scenes (think clowns and *Teletubbies*). Also, even simple dialogue scenes contain abrupt changes of viewing points, which are impossible in real-world situations. By utilizing formal features, films induce and shape predictive inferences in a manner that is different from real-world cognition (Magliano et al. 1996). Hence, while films may make use of principles of natural perception (Anderson 1996; Smith 2012), they also contain numerous deviations from real-world conditions, possibly requiring viewers to possess sufficient knowledge of cinematic conventions to be able to comprehend the films content. Even up to 11 years of age, children struggle to distinguish reliably between reality and fiction (Woolley and Ghossainy 2013; Mares and Sivakumar 2014) and need to be educated in media literacy, preferably from as early as preschool (Diergarten et al. 2017). However, our scientific understanding of how media literacy develops, and especially its origins in typical infant cognitive development, is still very poorly understood. As we have attempted to lay out in this review chapter, collaborations between developmental psychologists, media researchers, and content producers (e.g., directors, producers, animators, etc.) are sorely needed to further our understanding. Until this gap in knowledge is filled, parents, teachers, and content producers should be aware of the difficulties children face when decoding the audiovisual codes used in films. The immaturity of their viewers audiovisual perceptual systems should be respected in the design of content, and, where possible, caregivers should be encouraged to coview content with their children to help maximize learning and the socio-emotional richness of the experience.

Acknowledgment

The research for this paper has received funding from the European Union's Horizon 2020 research and innovation programme under the Marie Skłodowska-Curie grant agreement No 656779.

References

AAP Council on Communications and Media. "Media and Young Minds." *Pediatrics*, 138(5), 2016: e20162591.

Abel, Richard. "Yhcam Discoursing on Cinema: France, 1912." *Framework*, 32(33), 1986: 150–159.

Adolphs, Ralph and Daniel Tranel. "Amygdala Damage Impairs Emotion Recognition from Scenes only When They Contain Facial Expressions." *Neuropsychologia*, 41(10), 2003: 1281–1289.

Amso, Dima, Sara Haas, Elena Tenenbaum, Julie Markant, and Stephen J. Sheinkopf. "Bottom-Up Attention Orienting in Young Children with Autism." *Journal of Autism and Developmental Disorders*, 44(3), 2014: 664–673.

Anderson, Daniel R. and Katherine G. Hanson. "From Blooming, Buzzing Confusion to Media Literacy: The Early Development of Television Viewing." *Developmental Review*, 30(2), 2010: 239–255.

Anderson, Daniel R. and Tiffany A. Pempek. "Television and Very Young Children." *American Behavioral Scientist*, 48(5), 2005: 505–522.

Baldwin, Dare A., Jodie A. Baird, Megan M. Saylor, and Angela M. Clark. "Infants Parse Dynamic Action." *Child Development*, 72(3), 2001: 708–717.

Baldwin, Dare, Annika Andersson, Jenny Saffran, and Meredith Meyer. "Segmenting Dynamic Human Action via Statistical Structure." *Cognition*, 106(3), 2008: 1382–1407.

Barr, Rachel and Harlene Hayne. "Developmental Changes in Imitation from Television During Infancy." *Child Development*, 70(5), 1999: 1067–1081.

Barr, Rachel, Paul Muentener, Amaya Garcia, Melissa Fujimoto, and Verónica Chávez. "The Effect of Repetition on Imitation from Television during Infancy." *Developmental Psychobiology*, 49(2), 2007: 196–207.

Barr, Rachel. "Transfer of Learning between 2D and 3D Sources during Infancy: Informing Theory and Practice." *Developmental Review*, 30(2), 2010: 128–154.

Barrera, Maria E. and Daphne Maurer. "Recognition of Mother's Photographed Face by the Three-Month-Old Infant." *Child Development*, 1981: 714–716.

Beebe, Beatrice and Louis J. Gerstman. "The 'Packaging' of Maternal Stimulation in Relation to Infant Facial-Visual Engagement: A Case Study at Four Months." *Merrill-Palmer Quarterly of Behavior and Development*, 26(4), 1980: 321–339.

Bordwell, David and Kristin Thompson. *Film Art: An Introduction.* New York: McGraw-Hill, 2001.

Bordwell, David. *Narration in the Fiction Film.* Routledge, 2005.

Borji, Ali and Laurent Itti. "State-of-the-Art in Visual Attention Modeling." *IEEE Transactions on Pattern Analysis and Machine Intelligence*, 35(1), 2013: 185–207.

Bronson, Po and Ashley Merryman. "Baby Einstein vs. Barbie [Electronic Version]. Time. Retrieved February 21, 2008." 2006: http://content.time.com/time/nation/article/0,8599,1538507,00.html (14.11.2017).

Brown, Angela M. and Misao Yamamoto. "Visual Acuity in Newborn and Preterm Infants Measured with Grating Acuity Cards." *American Journal of Ophthalmology*, 102(2), 1986: 245–253.

Butterworth, George and Edward Cochran. "Towards a Mechanism of Joint Visual Attention in Human Infancy." *International Journal of Behavioral Development*, 3(3), 1980: 253–272.

Butterworth, George and Nicholas Jarrett. "What Minds Have in Common is Space: Spatial Mechanisms Serving Joint Visual Attention in Infancy." *British Journal of Developmental Psychology*, 9(1), 1991: 55–72.

Calvert, Sandra L. "Television Production Feature Effects on Children's Comprehension of Time." *Journal of Applied Developmental Psychology*, 9(3), 1988: 263–273.

Camras, Linda A. and Kevin Allison. "Children's Understanding of Emotional Facial Expressions and Verbal Labels." *Journal of Nonverbal Behavior*, 9(2), 1985: 84–94.

Cerf, Moran, Jonathan Harel, Wolfgang Einhäuser, and Christof Koch. "Predicting Human Gaze Using Low-Level Saliency Combined with Face Detection." *Advances in Neural Information Processing Systems*, 2008: 241–248.

Certain, Laura K. and Robert S. Kahn. "Prevalence, Correlates, and Trajectory of Television Viewing Among Infants and Toddlers." *Pediatrics*, 109(4), 2002: 634–642.

Christakis, Dimitri A. and Michelle M. Garrison. *Teacher in the Living Room? Educational Media for Babies, Toddlers, and Preschoolers.* Menlo Park, CA: Kaiser Family Foundation, 2005.

Cleveland, Allison and Tricia Striano. "Televised Social Interaction and Object Learning in 14-And 18-Month-Old Infants." *Infant Behavior and Development*, 31(2), 2008: 326–331.

Cohn, Jeffrey F. and Marquita Elmore. "Effect of Contingent Changes in Mothers' Affective Expression on the Organization of Behavior in 3-Month-Old Infants." *Infant Behavior and Development*, 11(4), 1988: 493–505.

Corkum, Valerie, and Chris Moore. "The Origins of Joint Visual Attention in Infants." *Developmental Psychology*, 34(1), 1998: 28–38.

Courage, Mary L. and Russell J. Adams. "Visual Acuity Assessment from Birth to Three Years Using the Acuity Card Procedure: Cross-Sectional and Longitudinal Samples." *Optometry & Vision Science*, 67(9), 1990: 713–718.

Csibra, Gergely. "Goal Attribution to Inanimate Agents by 6.5-Month-Old Infants." *Cognition*, 107(2), 2008: 705–717.

Cutting, James E. and Ayse Candan. "Shot Durations, Shot Classes, and the Increased Pace of Popular Movies." *Projections*, 9(2), 2015: 40–62.

de Klerk, Carina, Victoria Southgate, and Gergely Csibra. "Predictive Action Tracking without Motor Experience in 8-Month-Old Infants." *Brain and Cognition*, 109, 2016: 131–139.

DeLoache, Judy S., Cynthia Chiong, Kathleen Sherman, Nadia Islam, Mieke Vanderborght, Georgene L. Troseth, Gabrielle A. Strouse, and Katherine O'Doherty. "Do Babies Learn from Baby Media?" *Psychological Science*, 21(11), 2010: 1570–1574.

Dickerson, Kelly, Peter Gerhardstein, Elizabeth Zack, and Rachel Barr. "Age-Related Changes in Learning across Early Childhood: A New Imitation Task." *Developmental Psychobiology*, 55(7), 2013: 719–732.

Diergarten, Anna Katharina and Gerhild Nieding. "Children's and Adults' Ability to Build Online Emotional Inferences during Comprehension of Audiovisual and Auditory Texts." *Journal of Cognition and Development*, 16(2), 2015: 381–406.

Diergarten, Anna Katharina, Thomas Möckel, Gerhild Nieding, and Peter Ohler. "The Impact of Media Literacy on Children's Learning from Films and Hypermedia." *Journal of Applied Developmental Psychology*, 48, 2017: 33–41.

Dmytryk, Edward. *On Filmmaking*. Woburn, MA: Focal Press, 1986.

Donnelly, Katherine E., Nathalia L. Gjersoe, and Bruce Hood. "When Pictures Lie: Children's Misunderstanding of Photographs." *Cognition*, 129(1), 2013: 51–62.

Dorr, Michael, Thomas Martinetz, Karl R. Gegenfurtner, and Erhardt Barth. "Variability of Eye Movements When Viewing Dynamic Natural Scenes." *Journal of Vision*, 10(10), 2010: 28–28.

Ekman, Paul and Wallace V. Friesen. Unmasking the Face: A Guide to Recognizing Emotions from Facial Cues. Oxford: Prentice Hall, 1975.

Ekman, Paul, Wallace V. Friesen, and Phoebe Ellsworth. Emotion in the Human Face: Guide-lines for Research and an Integration of Findings: Guidelines for Research and an Integration of Findings. Braunschweig: Pergamon, 1972.

Falck-Ytter, Terje, Gustaf Gredebäck, and Claes von Hofsten. "Infants Predict Other People's Action Goals." *Nature Neuroscience*, 9(7), 2006: 878–879.

Farroni, Teresa, Enrica Menon, Silvia Rigato, and Mark H. Johnson. "The Perception of Facial Expressions in Newborns." *European Journal of Developmental Psychology*, 4(1), 2007: 2–13.

Farroni, Teresa, Gergely Csibra, Francesca Simion, and Mark H. Johnson. "Eye Contact Detection in Humans from Birth." *Proceedings of the National Academy of Sciences*, 99(14), 2002: 9602–9605.

Farroni, Teresa, Mark H. Johnson, Enrica Menon, Luisa Zulian, Dino Faraguna, and Gergely Csibra. "Newborns' Preference for Face-Relevant Stimuli: Effects of Contrast Polarity." *Proceedings of the National Academy of Sciences of the United States of America*, 102(47), 2005: 17245–17250.

Fenson, Larry and Douglas S. Ramsay. "Effects of Modeling Action Sequences on the Play of Twelve-, Fifteen-, and Nineteen-Month-Old Children." *Child Development*, 1981: 1028–1036.

Ferguson, Charles A. "Baby Talk in Six Languages." *American Anthropologist*, 66(2/6), 1964: 103–114.

Ferguson, Christopher J. and. Brent M Donnellan. "Is the Association between Children's Baby Video Viewing and Poor Language Development Robust? A Reanalysis of Zimmerman, Christakis, and Meltzoff (2007)." *Developmental Psychology*, 50(1), 2014: 129.

Field, Tiffany Martini. "Effects of Early Separation, Interactive Deficits, and Experimental Manipulations on Infant-Mother Face-to-Face Interaction." *Child Development*, 1977: 763–771.

Flavell, John H., Eleanor R. Flavell, Frances L. Green, and Jon E. Korfmacher. "Do Young Children Think of Television Images as Pictures or Real Objects?" *Journal of Broadcasting & Electronic Media*, 34(4), 1990: 399–419.

Forsdale, Joan Rosengren and Louis Forsdale. "Film Literacy." *Journal of the University Film Producers Association*, 18(3), 1966: 9–27.

Foulsham, Tom, Joey T. Cheng, Jessica L. Tracy, Joseph Henrich, and Alan Kingstone. "Gaze Allocation in a Dynamic Situation: Effects of Social Status and Speaking." *Cognition*, 117(3), 2010: 319–331.

Franchak, John M. and Karen E. Adolph. "Visually Guided Navigation: Head-Mounted Eye-Tracking of Natural Locomotion in Children and Adults." *Vision Research*, 50(24), 2010: 2766–2774.

Franchak, John M., David J. Heeger, Uri Hasson, and Karen E. Adolph. "Free Viewing Gaze Behavior in Infants and Adults." *Infancy*, 21(3), 2016: 262–287.

Frank, Michael C., Dima Amso, and Scott P. Johnson. "Visual Search and Attention to Faces during Early Infancy." *Journal of Experimental Child Psychology*, 118, 2014: 13–26.

Frank, Michael C., Edward Vul, and Rebecca Saxe. "Measuring the Development of Social Attention Using Free-Viewing." *Infancy*, 17(4), 2012: 355–375.

Frank, Michael C., Edward Vul, and Scott P. Johnson. "Development of Infants' Attention to Faces during the First Year." *Cognition*, 110(2), 2009: 160–170.

Gernsbacher, Morton Ann, H. Hill Goldsmith, and Rachel R.W. Robertson. "Do Readers Mentally Represent Characters' Emotional States?" *Cognition & Emotion*, 6(2), 1992: 89–111.

Gillioz, Christelle, Pascal Gygax, and Isabelle Tapiero. "Individual Differences and Emotional Inferences during Reading Comprehension." *Canadian Journal of Experimental Psychology/Revue canadienne de psychologie expérimentale*, 66(4), 2012: 239.

Gliga, Teodora, Mayada Elsabbagh, Athina Andravizou, and Mark Johnson. "Faces Attract Infants' Attention in Complex Displays." *Infancy*, 14(5), 2009: 550–562.

Gluckman, Maxie, and Scott P. Johnson. "Attentional Capture by Social Stimuli in Young Infants." *Frontiers in Psychology*, 4, 2013.

Goren, Deborah and Hugh R. Wilson. "Quantifying Facial Expression Recognition across Viewing Conditions." *Vision Research*, 46(8), 2006: 1253–1262.

Gosselin, Pierre and Janik Simard. "Children's Knowledge of Facial Expressions of Emotions: Distinguishing Fear and Surprise." *The Journal of Genetic Psychology*, 160(2), 1999: 181–193.

Granrud, Carl E. "Size Constancy in Newborn Human Infants." *Investigative Ophthalmology and Visual Science*, 28(5), 1987.

Gusella, Joanne L., Darwin Muir, and Edward Z. Tronick. "The Effect of Manipulating Maternal Behavior During an Interaction on Three-And Six-Month-Olds' Affect and Attention." *Child Development*, 1988: 1111–1124.

Hainline, Louise. "Developmental Changes in Visual Scanning of Face and Nonface Patterns by Infants." *Journal of Experimental Child Psychology*, 25(1), 1978: 90–115.

Hains, Sylvia M. J. and Darwin W. Muir. "Infant Sensitivity to Adult Eye Direction." *Child Development*, 67(5), 1996: 1940–1951.

Haith, Marshall M. Rules That Babies Look By: The Organization of Newborn Visual Activity. Hillsdale: Lawrence Erlbaum Associates, 1980.

Haith, Marshall M., Terry Bergman, and Michael J. Moore. "Eye Contact and Face Scanning in Early Infancy." *Science*, 198(4319), 1977: 853–855.

Harris, Paul L., Carl N. Johnson, Deborah Hutton, Giles Andrews, and Tim Cooke. "Young Children's Theory of Mind and Emotion." *Cognition & Emotion*, 3(4), 1989: 379–400.

Hasson, Uri, Eunice Yang, Ignacio Vallines, David J. Heeger, and Nava Rubin. "A Hierarchy of Temporal Receptive Windows in Human Cortex." *Journal of Neuroscience*, 28(10), 2008a: 2539–2550.

Hasson, Uri, Ohad Landesman, Barbara Knappmeyer, Ignacio Vallines, Nava Rubin, and David J. Heeger. "Neurocinematics: The Neuroscience of Film." *Projections*, 2(1), 2008b: 1–26.

Haviland, Jeannette M. and Mary Lelwica. "The Induced Affect Response: 10-Week-Old Infants' Responses to Three Emotion Expressions." *Developmental Psychology*, 23(1), 1987: 97.

Hayhoe, Mary M., Anurag Shrivastava, Ryan Mruczek, and Jeff B. Pelz. "Visual Memory and Motor Planning in a Natural Task." *Journal of Vision*, 3(1), 2003: 6.

Hayne, Harlene, Jane Herbert, and Gabrielle Simcock. "Imitation from Television by 24-and 30-Month-Olds." *Developmental Science*, 6(3), 2003: 254–261.

Henderson, John M. "Regarding Scenes." *Current Directions in Psychological Science*, 16(4), 2007: 219–222.

Hertenstein, Matthew J. and Joseph J. Campos. "The Retention Effects of an Adult's Emotional Displays on Infant Behavior." *Child Development*, 75(2), 2004: 595–613.

Hespos, Susan J. and Philippe Rochat. "Dynamic Mental Representation in Infancy." *Cognition*, 64(2), 1997: 153–188.

Hunnius, Sabine, Tessa C. J. de Wit, Sven Vrins, and Claes von Hofsten. "Facing Threat: Infants' and Adults' Visual Scanning of Faces with Neutral, Happy, Sad, Angry, and Fearful Emotional Expressions." *Cognition and Emotion*, 25(2), 2011: 193–205.

Ildirar, Sermin and Louise Ewing. "Revisiting the Kuleshov Effect with First Time Viewers." *Projections*, ISSN 1934–9688 (2018) 32, 1986: 150.

Ildirar, Sermin and Stephan Schwan. "First-Time Viewers' Comprehension of Films: Bridging Shot Transitions." *British Journal of Psychology*, 106(1), 2015: 133–151.

Izard, Carroll E. "Innate and Universal Facial Expressions: Evidence from Developmental and Cross-Cultural Research." *Psychological Bulletin*, 115(2), 1994: 288–99.

Izard, Carroll E., Christina A. Fantauzzo, Janine M. Castle, O. Maurice Haynes, Maria F. Rayias, and Priscilla H. Putnam. "The Ontogeny and Significance of Infants' Facial Expressions in the First 9 Months of Life." *Developmental Psychology*, 31(6), 1995: 997.

Johnson, Mark H., Suzanne Dziurawiec, Hadyn Ellis, and John Morton. "Newborns' Preferential Tracking of Face-Like Stimuli and its Subsequent Decline." *Cognition*, 40(1), 1991: 1–19.

Johnson, Scott P., Gavin J. Bremner, Alan Slater, Uschi Mason, Kirsty Foster, and Andrea Cheshire. "Infants' Perception of Object Trajectories." *Child Development*, 74(1), 2003: 94–108.

Johnson, Scott P., Leslie B. Cohen, Kathryn H. Marks, and Kerri L. Johnson. "Young Infants' Perception of Object Unity in Rotation Displays." *Infancy*, 4(2), 2003: 285–295.

Kahana-Kalman, Ronit and Arlene S. Walker-Andrews. "The Role of Person Familiarity in Young Infants' Perception of Emotional Expressions." *Child Development*, 72(2), 2001: 352–369.

Kellman, Philip J. and Elizabeth S. Spelke. "Perception of Partly Occluded Objects in Infancy." *Cognitive Psychology*, 15(4), 1983: 483–524.

Kibbe, Melissa M. and Alan M. Leslie. "What's the Object of Object Working Memory in Infancy? Unraveling 'What' and 'How Many.'" *Cognitive Psychology*, 66(4), 2013: 380–404.

Kirkorian, Heather L. and Daniel R. Anderson. "Anticipatory Eye Movements While Watching Continuous Action across Shots in Video Sequences: A Developmental Study." *Child Development*, 88(4), 2017: 1284–1301.

Kirkorian, Heather L., Daniel R. Anderson, and Rachel Keen. "Age Differences in Online Processing of Video: An Eye Movement Study." *Child Development*, 83(2), 2012: 497–507.

Kirkorian, Heather L., Heather J. Lavigne, Katherine G. Hanson, Georgene L. Troseth, Lindsay B. Demers, and Daniel R. Anderson. "Video Deficit in Toddlers' Object Retrieval: What Eye Movements Reveal About Online Cognition." *Infancy*, 21(1), 2016: 37–64.

Klin, Ami, Warren Jones, Robert Schultz, Fred Volkmar, and Donald Cohen. "Visual Fixation Patterns during Viewing of Naturalistic Social Situations as Predictors of Social Competence in Individuals with Autism." *Archives of General Psychiatry*, 59(9), 2002: 809–816.

Kochukhova, Olga and Gustaf Gredebäck. "Learning About Occlusion: Initial Assumptions and Rapid Adjustments." *Cognition*, 105(1), 2007: 26–46.

Koolstra, Cees M., Juliette van Zanten, Nicole Lucassen, and Nazreen Ishaak. "The Formal Pace of Sesame Street Over 26 Years." *Perceptual and Motor Skills*, 99(1), 2004: 354–360.

Krcmar, Marina, Bernard Grela, and Kirsten Lin. "Can Toddlers Learn Vocabulary from Television? An Experimental Approach." *Media Psychology*, 10(1), (2007): 41–63.

Kuchuk, April, Martha Vibbert, and Marc H. Bornstein. "The Perception of Smiling and its Experiential Correlates in Three-Month-Old Infants." *Child Development*, 1986: 1054–1061.

Land, Michael, Neil Mennie, and Jennifer Rusted. "The Roles of Vision and Eye Movements in the Control of Activities of Daily Living." *Perception*, 28(11), 1999: 1311–1328.

Leahy, Wayne and John Sweller. "Cognitive Load Theory, Modality of Presentation and the Transient Information Effect." *Applied Cognitive Psychology*, 25(6), 2011: 943–951.

Leat, Susan J., Naveen K. Yadav, and Elizabeth L. Irving. "Development of Visual Acuity and Contrast Sensitivity in Children." *Journal of Optometry*, 2(1), 2009: 19–26.

Leigh, John R. and David S. Zee. "The Vestibular-Optokinetic System." *The Neurology of Eye Movements*, 19, 1999: 89.

Levine, Linda J. "Young Children's Understanding of the Causes of Anger and Sadness." *Child Development*, 66(3), 1995: 697–709.

Libertus, Klaus and Amy Needham. "Reaching Experience Increases Face Preference in 3-Month-Old Infants." *Developmental Science*, 14(6), 2011: 1355–1364.

Lowe, Phillip J. and Kevin Durkin. "The Effect of Flashback on Children's Understanding of Television Crime Content." *Journal of Broadcasting & Electronic Media*, 43(1), 1999: 83–97.

Magliano, Joseph P., Katinka Dijkstra, and Rolf A. Zwaan. "Generating Predictive Inferences While Viewing a Movie." *Discourse Processes*, 22(3), 1996: 199–224.

Malatesta, Carol Z., Clayton Culver, Johanna Rich Tesman, Beth Shepard, Alan Fogel, Mark Reimers, and Gail Zivin. "The Development of Emotion Expression during the First Two Years of Life." *Monographs of the Society for Research in Child Development*, 1989: i-136.

Malatesta, Carol Zander and Jeannette M. Haviland. "Learning Display Rules: The Socialization of Emotion Expression in Infancy." *Child Development*, 1982: 991–1003.

Mares, Marie-Louise, and Gayathri Sivakumar. "'Vámonos Means Go, But That's Made Up for the Show': Reality Confusions and Learning from Educational TV." *Developmental Psychology*, 50(11), 2014: 2498.

Maurer, Daphne and Philip Salapatek. "Developmental Changes in the Scanning of Faces by Young Infants." *Child Development*, 1976: 523–527.

McCall, Robert B., Ross D. Parke, Robert D. Kavanaugh, Robert Engstrom, Judy Russell, and Elizabeth Wycoff. "Imitation of Live and Televised Models by Children One to Three Years of Age." *Monographs of the Society for Research in Child Development*, 1977: 1–94.

McClure, Elisabeth R., Yulia E. Chentsova-Dutton, Steven J. Holochwost, Gerrod W. Parrott, and Rachel Barr. "Look At That! Video Chat and Joint Visual Attention Development among Babies and Toddlers." *Child Development*, 2017.

Meltzoff, Andrew N. "Infant Imitation after a 1-Week Delay: Long-Term Memory for Novel Acts and Multiple Stimuli." *Developmental Psychology*, 24(4), 1988: 470.

Mital, Parag K., Tim J. Smith, Robin L. Hill, and John M. Henderson. "Clustering of Gaze during Dynamic Scene Viewing is Predicted by Motion." *Cognitive Computation*, 3(1), 2011: 5–24.

Moher, Mariko and Lisa Feigenson. "Factors Influencing Infants' Ability to Update Object Representations in Memory." *Cognitive Development*, 28(3), 2013: 272–289.

Möhring, Wenke and Andrea Frick. "Touching Up Mental Rotation: Effects of Manual Experience on 6-Month-Old Infants' Mental Object Rotation." *Child Development*, 84, 2013: 1554–1565.

Molinari, Carlos, Débora Burin, Gastón Saux, Juan Pablo Barreyro, Natalia Irrazabal, María Susana Bechis, Aníbal Duarte, and Verónica Ramenzoni. "Fictional Characters' Emotional State Representation: What is its Degree of Specificity?" *Psicothema*, 21(1), 2009: 9–14.

Moore, David S. and Scott P. Johnson. "Mental Rotation in Human Infants: A Sex Difference." *Psychological Science*, 19(11), 2008: 1063–1066.

Muir, Darwin W., Sylvia M. J. Hains, Y. Cao, and Barbara D'Entremont. "3-To 6-Month-Olds' Sensitivity to Adult Intentionality: The Role of Adult Contingency and Eye Direction in Dyadic Interactions." *Infant Behavior and Development*, 19, 1996: 199.

Mumme, Donna L. and Anne Fernald. "The Infant as Onlooker: Learning from Emotional Reactions Observed in a Television Scenario." *Child Development*, 74(1), 2003: 221–237.

Munk, Carmen, Günter Daniel Rey, Anna Katharina Diergarten, Gerhild Nieding, Wolfgang Schneider, and Peter Ohler. "Cognitive Processing of Film Cuts among 4-to 8-Year-Old Children." *European Psychologist*, 17(4), 2012: 257–265.

Nieding, Gerhild and Peter Ohler. "Mediennutzung und Medienwirkung bei Kindern und Jugendlichen." [Media Use and Media Effects in Children and Young People.] In: Batinic, Bernad and Markus Appel (Eds.). *Medienpsychologie*. Berlin/Heidelberg: Springer, 2008: 379–400.

Pempek, Tiffany A., Heather L. Kirkorian, John E. Richards, Daniel R. Anderson, Anne F. Lund, and Michael Stevens. "Video Comprehensibility and Attention in Very Young Children." *Developmental Psychology*, 46(5), 2010: 1283.

Pepperman, Richard. *The Eye is Quicker: Film Editing; Making a Good Film Better*. Los Angeles: Michael Wiese Productions, 2004.

Phillips, Ann T., Henry M. Wellman, and Elizabeth S. Spelke. "Infants' Ability to Connect Gaze and Emotional Expression to Intentional Action." *Cognition*, 85(1), 2002: 53–78.

Pierroutsakos, Sophia L. and Georgene L. Troseth. "Video Verite: Infants' Manual Investigation of Objects on Video." *Infant Behavior and Development*, 26(2), 2003: 183–199.

Potter, W. James. *Media Literacy*. [1st Edition]. Thousand Oaks, CA: Sage Publications, 1998.

——— *Media Literacy*. [6th Edition]. Thousand Oaks, CA: Sage Publications, 2013.

Reichenbach, Lisa and John C. Masters. "Children's Use of Expressive and Contextual Cues in Judgments of Emotion." *Child Development*, 1983: 993–1004.

Rhodes, Gillian, Susan Brennan, and Susan Carey. "Identification and Ratings of Caricatures: Implications for Mental Representations of Faces." *Cognitive Psychology*, 19(4), 1987: 473–497.

Rochat, Philippe and Susan J. Hespos. "Tracking and Anticipation of Invisible Spatial Transformations by 4-to 8-Month-Old Infants." *Cognitive Development*, 11(1), 1996: 3–17.

Roseberry, Sarah, Kathy Hirsh-Pasek, Julia Parish-Morris, and Roberta M. Golinkoff. "Live Action: Can Young Children Learn Verbs from Video?" *Child Development*, 80(5), 2009: 1360–1375.

Roseberry, Sarah, Russell Richie, Kathy Hirsh-Pasek, Roberta Michnick Go-linkoff, and Thomas F. Shipley. "Babies Catch a Break: 7-To 9-Month-Olds Track Statistical Probabilities on Continuous Dynamic Events." *Psychological Science*, 22(11), 2011: 1422–1424.

Schwarzer, Gudrun, Claudia Freitag, and Nina Schum. "How Crawling and Manual Object Exploration are Related to the Mental Rotation Abilities of 9-Month-Old Infants." *Frontiers in Psychology*, 4, 2013.

Serrano, Juan M., Jaime Iglesias, and Angela Loeches. "Visual Discrimination and Recognition of Facial Expressions of Anger, Fear, and Surprise in 4-to 6-Month-Old Infants." *Developmental Psychobiology*, 25(6), 1992: 411–425.

Shepherd, Stephen V., Shawn A. Steckenfinger, Uri Hasson, and Asif A. Ghazanfar. "Human-Monkey Gaze Correlations Reveal Convergent and Divergent Patterns of Movie Viewing." *Current Biology*, 20(7), 2010: 649–656.

Sigman, Marian and Lisa Capps. *Children with Autism: A Developmental Perspective*. Vol. 34. Cambridge, MA: Harvard University Press, 1997.

Slater, Alan, Anne Mattock, and Elizabeth Brown. "Size Constancy at Birth: Newborn Infants' Responses to Retinal and Real Size." *Journal of Experimental Child Psychology*, 49(2), 1990: 314–322.

Slater, Alan, Scott P. Johnson, Elizabeth Brown, and Marion Badenoch. "Newborn Infant's Perception of Partly Occluded Objects." *Infant Behavior and Development*, 19(1), 1996: 145–148.

Slater, Alan, Scott P. Johnson, Philip J. Kellman, and Elizabeth S. Spelke. "The Role of Three-Dimensional Depth Cues in Infants' Perception of Partly Occluded Objects." *Infant and Child Development*, 3(3), 1994: 187–191.

Slater, Alan, Victoria Morison, Marcia Somers, Anne Mattock, Elizabeth Brown, and David Taylor. "Newborn and Older Infants' Perception of Partly Occluded Objects." *Infant Behavior and Development*, 13(1), 1990: 33–49.

Smith, Robin, Daniel R. Anderson, and Catherine Fischer. "Young Children's Comprehension of Montage." *Child Development*, 1985: 962–971.

Smith, Tim J. "An Attentional Theory of Continuity Editing." Doctoral thesis, University of Edinburgh, 2006: doi:10.3167/proj.2012.060102.

——— "The Attentional Theory of Cinematic Continuity." *Projections*, 6(1), 2012: 1–27.

Smith, Tim J. and Irati R. Saez de Urabain. "Eye Tracking. " In: Hopkins, Brian, Elena Geangu, and Sally Linkenauger (Eds.). *Cambridge Encyclopedia of Child Development*. Cambridge: Cambridge University Press, 2017: 97–101. doi:10.1017/9781316216491.

Smith, Tim J. and Janet Yvonne Martin-Portugues Santacreu. "Match-Action: The Role of Motion and Audio in Creating Global Change Blindness in Film." *Media Psychology*, 20(2), 2017: 317–348.

Smith, Tim J. and John M. Henderson. "Edit Blindness: The Relationship between Attention and Global Change Blindness in Dynamic Scenes." *Journal of Eye Movement Research*, 2(2), 2008: 1–17.

Smith, Tim J. and Parag K. Mital. "Attentional Synchrony and the Influence of Viewing Task on Gaze Behavior in Static and Dynamic Scenes." *Journal of Vision*, 13(8), 2013: 16–16.

Smith, Tim J., Sam Wass, Tessa Dekker, Parag K. Mital, Irati Rodriguez, Annette Karmiloff-Smith. "Optimising Signal-to-Noise Ratios in Tots TV

Can Create Adult-Like Viewing Behaviour In Infants." 2014 International Conference on Infant Studies, Berlin, Germany, July 3–5, 2014.

Soken, Nelson H. and Anne D. Pick. "Intermodal Perception of Happy and Angry Expressive Behaviors by Seven-Month-Old Infants." *Child Development*, 63(4), 1992: 787–795.

——— "Infants' Perception of Dynamic Affective Expressions: Do Infants Distinguish Specific Expressions?" *Child Development*, 70(6), 1999: 1275–1282.

Stahl, Aimee E., Alexa R. Romberg, Sarah Roseberry, Roberta Michnick Golinkoff, and Kathryn Hirsh-Pasek. "Infants Segment Continuous Events Using Transitional Probabilities." *Child Development*, 85(5), 2014: 1821–1826.

Standish, Isolde. A New History of Japanese Cinema. Bloomsbury Publishing, 2006.

Stein, Nancy L. and Linda J. Levine. "The Causal Organisation of Emotional Knowledge: A Developmental Study." *Cognition & Emotion*, 3(4), 1989: 343–378.

Strouse, Gabrielle A. and Georgene L. Troseth. "'Don't Try This at Home': Toddlers' Imitation of New Skills from People on Video." *Journal of Experimental Child Psychology*, 101(4), 2008: 262–280.

Tatler, Benjamin W., Mary M. Hayhoe, Michael F. Land, and Dana H. Ballard. "Eye Guidance in Natural Vision: Reinterpreting Salience." *Journal of Vision*, 11(5), 2011: 5.

Tincoff, Ruth and Peter W. Jusczyk. "Some Beginnings of Word Comprehension in 6-Month-Olds." *Psychological Science*, 10(2), 1999: 172–175.

Troseth, Georgene L. "Is it Life or is it Memorex? Video as a Representation of Reality." *Developmental Review*, 30(2), 2010: 155–175.

Troseth, Georgette L. and Judy S. DeLoache. "The Medium Can Obscure the Message: Young Children's Understanding of Video." *Child Development*, 69(4), 1998: 950–965.

Walker, Arlene S. "Intermodal Perception of Expressive Behaviors by Human Infants." *Journal of Experimental Child Psychology*, 33(3), 1982: 514–535.

Walker-Andrews, Arlene S. "Infants' Perception of Expressive Behaviors: Differentiation of Multimodal Information." *Psychological Bulletin*, 121(3), 1997: 437.

——— "Intermodal Perception of Expressive Behaviors: Relation of Eye and Voice?" *Developmental Psychology*, 22(3), 1986: 373.

Wang, Helena X., Jeremy Freeman, Elisha P. Merriam, Uri Hasson, and David J. Heeger. "Temporal Eye Movement Strategies during Naturalistic Viewing." *Journal of Vision*, 12(1), 2012: 16.

Wass, Sam V. and Tim J. Smith. "Visual Motherese? Signal to Noise Ratios in Toddler Directed Television." *Developmental Science*, 18(1), 2015: 24–37.

Widen, Sherri C. and James A. Russell. "Gender and Preschoolers' Perception of Emotion." *Merrill-Palmer Quarterly*, 48(3), 2002: 248–262.

——— "A Closer Look at Preschoolers' Freely Produced Labels for Facial Expressions." *Developmental Psychology*, 39(1), 2003: 114.

——— "Differentiation in Preschooler's Categories of Emotion." *Emotion*, 10(5), 2010: 651.

Wilcox, Teresa, Jessica A. Stubbs, Lesley Wheeler, and Gerianne M. Alexander. "Infants' Scanning of Dynamic Faces during the First Year." *Infant Behavior and Development*, 36(4), 2013: 513–516.

Woolley, Jacqueline D. and Maliki E. Ghossainy. "Revisiting the Fantasy-Reality Distinction: Children as Naïve Skeptics." *Child Development*, 84(5), 2013: 1496–1510.

Yarbus, Alfred L. "Eye Movements during Perception of Complex Objects." In: Yarbus, Alfred L. *Eye Movements and Vision*. Springer US, 1967: 171–211.

Zacks, Jeffrey M. "Using Movement and Intentions to Understand Simple Events." *Cognitive Science*, 28(6), 2004: 979–1008.

Zacks, Jeffrey M. and Barbara Tversky. "Event Structure in Perception and Conception." *Psychological Bulletin*, 127(1), 2001: 3.

Zimmerman, Frederick J., Dimitri A. Christakis, and Andrew N. Meltzoff. "Television and DVD/Video Viewing in Children Younger than 2 Years." *Archives of Pediatrics & Adolescent Medicine*, 161(5), 2007: 473–479.

Films & TV series

A Charlie Brown Christmas. Directed by Bill Melendez. 1965; USA: Lee Mendelson Films.

Baby Jake: UK 2011–2012, CBeebies, created by Darrall Macqueen Ltd.

Charlie & Lola: UK 2005–2008, CBeebies, created by Lauren Child.

In the Night Garden: UK 2006–2009, BBC, created by Andrew Davenport.

Le Voyage Dans la Lune [A Trip to the Moon.] Directed by Georges Méliès. 1902; France: Star Film Company.

Looney Tunes: USA 1930–1969 (original; 1987–present (revival)), Cartoon Network, Nickelodeon, ABC, created by Warner Brothers.

Mongrels: UK 2010–2011, BBC Three, created by Adam Miller.

Octonauts: UK 2010–present, CBeebies, created by Vicki Wong and Michael C. Murphy.

Peppa Pig: UK 2004–present, Channel 5 and Nick Jr., created by Andrew Davenport.

Rex The Runt: UK 1998–2001, BBC Two, created by Richard Goleszowski.

Sesame Street: USA 1969-present, NET, PBS, HBO, created by Joan Ganz Cooney and Lloyd Morrisett.

Teletubbies: UK 1997–2001, BBC, created by Anne Wood and Andrew Davenport.

Tree Fu Tom: UK 2012–2016, CBeebies, created by Daniel Bays and Dan Hodgkins.

Part VI

Excurse

11 "Portraying emotions is fundamental to animated film"

An Interview with Felix Gönnert

Meike Uhrig

Felix Gönnert (born in 1975 in Lüneburg, Germany) is working as Professor of Computer Animation in the Animation Department at the Film University Babelsberg KONRAD WOLF. He was the lead character animator for the CGI-animated feature *Lissi und der Wilde Kaiser* (Lissi and the Wild Emperor, 2007). His films have been shown at more than 300 film festivals across the world and have won him more than 30 awards and prizes.

The Meaning of Emotions and How to Display/Elicit Them

Noel Carroll described film emotions as "glue that holds the audience's" attention to the screen." Animated films especially seem to be linked to emotions and are, for example, often recalled when people are asked for the saddest movies they have ever seen.

—Animated films are usually based on a clear communication of thoughts and feelings in order to stage the acting emotionally and cognitively comprehensible for the viewer. Most of the principles that are used in the classically animated films draw on the insights that Disney's animators have worked out in the last century. Even though computer animation has expanded the range of possibilities, these principles are still the basis of this clear communication. For me, the most important principle is staging, which is also the most complex, because it is interwoven with the visual syntax of the medium in which a story is told.

The scene in *Dumbo*, for example, in which Dumbo creeps up to his mother's cage at night, and they can only touch by using their two trunks, still affects me deeply. Otherwise, animated films are exciting for me because they work like visualized dreams. Even though we, as viewers, know that everything we see is artificially or even grotesquely stylized, we empathize with the characters. Of course, this is not just about a successful performance in character animation, but also about the overall staging with all its components, which makes it possible for us to sympathize.

What role do emotions play when making a computer-animated film?

—Basically, emotions and their unfolding in space and time in all animation techniques determine the expression of the figure. Here it is important that the emotion precedes a thought process or that one has, as a viewer, the impression that the figure thinks and then, according to its character and its respective situation, emotionally reacts. This is the foundation of the *Illusion of Life*, after which the well-known book by the two Disney veterans, Frank Thomas and Ollie Johnston, is named. When we talk about computer-animated films, we usually mean those films that are shown in cinema and that are supposed to appeal to the widest possible audience. Most studios use the potential computer animation as a means of expressing emotions from very subtle to 'cartoony'. Facial expressions are like a universal code that can turn thoughts and emotions into a credible performance in conjunction with gesture and dialogue, allowing us to successfully follow animated characters for 90 minutes or longer. In a way, facial expressions allow the viewer to attribute character and soul to these characters. In my opinion, the option to use this level of imagination has established computer animation as the dominant animation technique, usually in conjunction with successful voice acting. The uniqueness of the representation of emotions in computer-animated films is, thus, that one has the opportunity to introduce extremely subtle movements in the actions of the figure, because computer animation allows this precision.

Would you say that animated films and emotions have a specifically close relationship?

—Yes and no. I believe that portraying emotions is fundamental to animated film. But I do not think that distinguishes it from feature films, documentaries, or other visual media. Emotions show us the basic themes of our life, which evolution has anchored deep within us. The cinematic narrative usually unfolds through the characters. It is they who stimulate our emotions and make us feel how close we are to the very core of the story. In production of an animated film, many things have to come together, and many people have to understand their craft well – I do not really see any significant difference to other narrative forms. However, animation is special, as it is, first of all, a technique. The different animation techniques can represent certain things well, but in some cases, they are limited. In a way, a technique of animation abstracts life and shows it to us in a different way. Sometimes this can be very poetic, sometimes very flat or funny. We viewers recognize that and, if necessary, let ourselves be part of this synthesis. The British stop motion animator Barry Purves once said: "Animation is the device."

Style and Levels of Engagement

Emotions can be displayed and elicited on various levels, including a film's narration, its world and characters, as well as elements such as color and sound. In popular real-life movies, you often find a 'subordination of style to story' and all elements support the emotional content rather invisibly. This quite strict hierarchic approach makes them interesting, especially for empirical studies. Does this hierarchy also appear in popular animated films?

— Basically, the story should determine everything in a production of an animation project: character design, colors, character animation, production design, voices, music, sound design, and so forth. Just as with live-action film, the animated film is also subdivided into genres and styles that may vary depending on the animation studio or country. The French are, for example, quite daring with 2D animated long movies, like *Tante Hilda!* (https://fr.wikipedia.org/wiki/Tante_Hilda_!), whose style reminds one of the '70s animation. Pixar and Disney are very classic in the area of 3D computer animation, where 'classic' combines many attributes that are probably only of interest to animators. It seems like the studios pick a style and then create a story for it. In a way, that may be true because the established studios have all come a long way developing and establishing their stylistic traits, stories, and characters as corporate identities. Within these stylistics, however, there is nevertheless a set of rules in which all the means and steps of design are subordinated to the story. It's hard to create real emotions and not just stage well-known formulas. In the context of character animation, I find the concept of truthfulness, which Stanilslawski actually coined for acting in the theater, equally valid. The development and production conditions of animated films, however, apparently only allow very few studios to bring great potential into their characters. A key point is the immense effort that must be made for an animated film. A whole world has to be created! After all, the style of an animated film does not just come from the story, but it is largely determined by the resources available for its production.

Furthermore, in addition to their choices being determined by narration and resources, and as we can see especially in your short films, computer-animated films are diverse concerning the filmic levels they use: There are close-ups and muted colors to support the narration of *Loup,* but also effects caused by self-references in *Bsss* by embodied metaphors, by surreal and avant-gardist elements in *Lucia,* and by fantastic happenings in *Apollo.* This diversity is a characteristic especially of computer animation and film art in general. However, would you agree that animated films are met with a greater flexibility on the part of the viewers concerning freedom of style, messaging, etc.?

— Animated films often invite you to a kind of fantastic journey in which you are introduced to worlds that you can only portray with animation. As far as the characters and their conflicts are concerned, I believe we as spectators must be able to identify with them. As fantastic as the world may be, we must be emotionally attached to the characters in the first place. This usually implies a rather classical dramaturgy. But as long as the story works, and you're well-established in the fantasy world, animated films are a great way to do this. Many, probably the largest number of blockbusters in the cinema, are augmented with animation and VFX to increase visual possibilities and create imaginary worlds. These hybrid films are widely established so I would say that we are ready to accept strong abstractions as long as they are linked to a story and characters that relate to our real existence. An example of this would be *Father and Daughter* by Michael Dudok de Wit. The film has a graphic representation without us having to see the facial expressions of the characters but still allows us a great emotional involvement.

The mood of a film might be determined by a film's style already. In animated films – more than in any other film form – there are numerous possibilities to choose from. In terms of film style, the Uncanny Valley Effect and the strive for Believability are often mentioned. According to theories by Barbara Flückiger, Patrick Powers, or Nichola Dobson (see Chapter 7) it is not so much the realism of a film, but rather the way it balances the amount of realism on its various levels. How do you decide how stylized the world is that you animate, how fantastic the narration, and how fictive the characters – and then how to balance it all?

— In most of my films (animaflix.com), the main characters appear to me in my sketchbooks as a small maquette or through other authors such as Walter Moers before I develop a story and a world around them. In that sense, the style may also reflect my taste, and the abstraction is a mix of what fits that style and what I was able to do with the resources I have at my disposal. My films are characterized by certain types of characters, but I can also imagine completely different types, styles, and stories. I just have not yet had the opportunity to make them. The balancing of stylization and realism is essential in the design process. For me it is not about realism but about an authentic expression that can then be interpreted. This plays the central role especially in character animation. The character animation in turn is influenced by the design.

Animated Worlds and Character Design

One major elicitor of emotions is via engaging characters, here, animated films are able to create characters according to personality or change their appearance according to their current mood. Is there a formula for creating emotionally believable characters?

— Exciting characters have a good story, an adequate design, and are so staged and animated that we viewers believe they have a life of their own. But beyond that, I believe that one senses whether an animator has really put himself emotionally into the figure when he animated it. I believe that, as with actors, this is an essential foundation that distinguishes a solidly crafted representation from an artistically outstanding performance.

Characters in your films are often reoccurring – Lucia, for example, appears in *Lucia, Loup,* and *Apollo* – and are almost always children. Why?

— I first developed the girl's figure for *Lucia.* Then came the boy, for *Apollo.* Since both were similar in design, I thought it would be appropriate for them to meet. That they are children may have something to do with the stories being based on their imagination and curiosity. It's all about escaping the world, discovering something, and finally returning. I was probably able to imagine that better with children than with adolescents or adults where other topics would have had priority (Figure 11.1).

It seems a common feature that (computer-)animated characters appear with dominant features such as extremely big eyes. These seem to be due to better emotional display, for reasons of beauty/cuteness, and/or simply being the state of the art. Would you say there are features that are specific to computer-animated films, and if so, what's the reason?

— The big eyes are not computer-animation specific. But they help, for example, to show clear acting and are usually part of the design language of the cartoony design, which is dominant in commercial animated film as a whole. Small or naturalistic eyes usually fall quickly into the area of the Uncanny Valley and are therefore deliberately avoided. Basically, I would say that character design and rigging require more or less consideration of anatomical and physical basics. Due to the precise

Figure 11.1 Apollo. Directed by Felix Gönnert.

spatial representation, deformations must be credible (not necessarily realistic). This is a general requirement for computer animation, even more than drawn animation and stop motion. Hair and clothing and possibly muscle and adipose tissue also need to be credibly animated or simulated to give the design adequate complexity in movement.

Animation and Science

Your experiments with Maya were a starting point for *Bsss*, which is a hybrid of computer animation and real-life background; *Loup* is partly drawn; *Adolf* is based on ideas by Walter Moers, and *Lucia* is based on your own artistic idea. In general, computer animations may be defined by a characteristic combination of art and technology. Is that what causes your emotional bonding with computer animation? What's your fascination?

— I was electrified when I first saw images of 3D renderings in the early 1980s. They were simulated buildings and a figure following a light in the dark. I have been working freelance with this technique since the mid-nineties, but I still enjoy drawing with a pencil. For some reason, I'm still interested in working and experimenting with it. Sometimes I wonder if it would not be better to use a technique that produces less iconic images and leaves more room for the viewer to imagine. Maybe it's because I'm interested in the presence of animated characters in computer animation. That's something I want to tie in with.

You conducted studies in context of emotions using computer animation. Why?

— For me, a solid understanding of emotions, of facial expressions, and gestures is elemental. Every emotion, every movement has a reason – every animator should have that internalized. Darwin, Stanislawski, Bammes, Ekman and many others are important pillars of knowledge.

In terms of emotion elicitation, computer animations prove to be highly valuable – their capacity to manipulate images on all levels and their calculatory nature is a major advantage especially for empirical studies. What else makes them interesting as a research object – maybe even more than other film forms?

— For me, computer animation was and is primarily interesting because it allows you to create photo-surreal characters and worlds. The convergence between the analog world and the digital will increase more and more, and so the real world will become increasingly synthesized with the tools of computer animation and therefore able to be analyzed. For me, that has little to do with art, so I prefer to be inspired by the real world and try to translate that in my own way into the digital world.

How could animation filmmakers and animation researchers be of mutual benefit to each other? The results of which study would be most interesting for you?

— I think that animation tools such as performance capturing offer interesting possibilities for data analysis of emotions. In this area, there is also rapid progress with the current image recognition methods. I think that the study of such data can be very complex. The animator can interpret it in an artistic way. If it should be done in a scientific way, in my opinion, different areas would be in demand, like neuroscience, psychology, computer science, etc. For convincing animation of realistic characters, for example, the detailed analysis of facial expressions may be helpful if it results in certain laws that go beyond the already known. But even here it will be animators who make the final decisions to bring the character to life. Artificial intelligence could change that, but there is still some way to go.

Part VII
Annex

Authors

Katalin E. Bálint
Assistant Professor at the Tilburg Center for Cognition and Communi-cation at Tilburg University, The Netherlands

Katalin E. Bálint researches viewers' psychological responses to audio-visual media. She conducts empirical studies into how formal features, such as shot scale, cut rate, or gaze behavior of characters, influence empathy, theory of mind, and narrative engagement in viewers. Katalin E. Bálint is currently an Assistant Professor at Tilburg University at the New Media Design MSc program and a research associate at Radboud University Nijmegen, where she investigates the potentials of narra-tive health communication. She was a postdoc at Utrecht University (2012–2014) and University of Augsburg (2014–2016). Her background is in Psychology (BA, MA, PhD) and Film Studies (BA, MA). She has published in peer-reviewed journals (*Scientific Study of Literature*, Projections, *Journal of Media Psychology*) and edited books (*Making Sense of Cinema*. Bloomsbury Publishing 2016; *Handbook of Narrative Absorption*. John Benjamins Publishing).

Nichola Dobson
Teaching Fellow at Edinburgh College of Art at the University of Edinburgh, Scotland

Nichola Dobson is a theorist and historian in animation studies with a broader interest in moving image culture and production. As part of the Design & Screen Cultures team, she teaches across disciplines within the Design School with a focus on Animation, Visual Narratives, and Screen Cultures. She began teaching at Edinburgh College of Art in 2010, prior to which she lectured at Glasgow Caledonian University and Queen Margaret University, where she received her PhD.

   Nichola Dobson is the founding editor of *Animation Studies* from 2006 until 2011 and the academic blog *Animation Studies 2.0* (2012–present). She has published on both animation studies and television, most recently *Norman McLaren, Between the Frames* (Bloomsbury 2018); *The A to Z of Animation and Cartoons* (Rowman & Littlefield 2010), and *Historical*

Dictionary of Animation and Cartoons (Rowman & Littlefield 2009) for Scarecrow Press. She has published in anthologies on fan fiction, *Crime Scene Investigation* and *Life on Mars* as well as shorter works for the on-line journal *FLOW*. She is currently working on a book on TV animation with Paul Ward for Edinburgh University Press. She began a new role as President of the Society for Animation Studies in winter 2014.

Kathrin Fahlenbrach
Professor at the Department for Media and Communication at the University of Hamburg, Germany

Kathrin Fahlenbrach's main research focus lies on cognitive film and media theory, embodiment, and moving images as well as on cognitive metaphors in audiovisual media; another area of her work is on images and media in protest performances.

Kathrin Fahlenbrach is author of several articles on metaphors in moving images. In her book on audiovisual metaphors (Schueren 2010), she introduces a theoretical framework on embodied and emotion metaphors in audiovisual mass media, including film and television. Most recently, she has edited a volume on *Embodied Metaphors in Film, Television, and Video Games: Cognitive Approaches* (Routledge 2016).

Torben Grodal
Professor of Film and Media Studies at the University of Copenhagen, Denmark

Torben Grodal is an author and Professor Emeritus of Film and Media studies at the University of Copenhagen in Denmark. In addition to having written books and articles on literature Torben Grodal has authored *Moving Pictures: A New Theory of Genre, Feelings, and Emotions* (Oxford University Press 1997), *Embodied Visions: Evolution, Emotion, Culture and Film* (Oxford University Press 2009); and an advanced introduction to film theory in Danish, *Filmoplevelse* (Tusculanum 2005). He has further published a series of articles on film, emotions, narrative theory, art films, video games, and evolutionary film theory. His most recent article is "How Film Genres Are a Product of Biology, Evolution, and Culture – an Embodied Approach." *Palgrave* Communications, 3, Article number: 17079, 2017: doi:10.1057/palcomms.2017.79.

Over the course of several articles, Torben Grodal has developed a model for how humans process film called the PECMA flow – short for "Perception, Emotion, Cognition and Motor Action." In his more expansive book on the topic *Embodied Vision: Evolution, Emotion, Culture and Film* (Oxford University Press 2009), Grodal elaborates on the PECMA flow model and how evolutionary approaches to film analysis are flexible enough to take into account cultural variations in perceptions of film.

Patrick Colm Hogan

Board of Trustees Distinguished Professor in the Department of English at the University of Connecticut, USA

Patrick Colm Hogan is a Board of Trustees Distinguished Professor at the University of Connecticut, where he is a member of the Department of English, the Program in India Studies, the Program in Comparative Literature and Cultural Studies, and the Program in Cognitive Science. He is the author of twenty books, including political work, such as *The Culture of Conformism: Understanding Social Consent* (Duke University Press 2001), and work on cognitive studies, such as *What Literature Teaches Us About Emotion* (Cambridge University Press 2011). Hogan's best-known book is *The Mind and Its Stories: Narrative Universals and Human Emotion* (Cambridge University Press 2003). Hailed as "a landmark in modern intellectual life" by Steven Pinker of Harvard University, this book examines cross-cultural patterns in narrative genre. One important structure discussed in this book is the sacrificial plot. In the Christian world, this plot is epitomized by the story of Jesus, but it is found in a range of other traditions, including in South Asian stories concerning the death of the Goddess.

Prior to his book *The Death of the Goddess* (2Leaf Press 2014), Patrick Colm Hogan published fiction in *The Journal of Irish Literature* and poetry in *Minnesota Review, Kunapipi, The Journal of Commonwealth and Postcolonial Studies*, and elsewhere. He has also published and exhibited photography *(New Letters),* collaborated with director Ken Kwapis on two short films, and worked with composer Paul Goldstein on several musical pieces.

Sermin Ildirar Kirbas

Postdoctoral Research Fellow at Centre for Brain and Cognitive Development, Birkbeck, at the University of London, UK

Sermin Ildirar is a Marie S. Curie postdoctoral research fellow at the Centre for Brain and Cognitive Development, Birkbeck, University of London. She studied Film and Media studies at Istanbul University and University of Vienna and works on perceptual and cognitive processes during viewing by adults and infants. She is also director of several short movies and co-scriptwriter of a feature movie and a computer game.

Her publications include *Watching Film for the First Time: How Adult Viewers Interpret Perceptual Discontinuities* (Film. Psychological Science 2010), *First-time viewers' comprehension of films: Bridging shot transitions* (British Journal of Psychology 2015), and *Indexing the Events of an Art Film by Audiences with Different Viewing Backgrounds. Making Sense of Cinema: Empirical Studies Into Film Spectators and Spectatorship* (Bloomsbury 2016).

Chris Landreth (Foreword)
Animator, Filmmaker, and Teacher, Canada

Chris Landreth worked as a mechanical engineer, until he started working with animations in 1990. He's created several CG-animated short films, including *The End* (1995), Bingo (1998), *Ryan* (2004), and *The Spine* (2009). He has received the Academy Award in 2005 for Best Animated Short Film and 60 other international awards. Chris Landreth's films explore storytelling based on human psychology as much as photorealistic character animation, an approach he calls 'psychorealism.' His latest short film to continue this exploration, *Subconscious Password*, received the 2013 Annecy Cristal for Best Short film.

In addition to filmmaking, Chris Landreth has created a course called *Making Faces*, an intensive masterclass on Facial Animation, which he teaches at schools, universities, and animation studios worldwide.

Maike Sarah Reinerth
PhD Candidate in Media Studies at the Film University Babelsberg KONRAD WOLF, Germany

Maike Sarah Reinerth is currently finishing her dissertation on representations of subjectivity in cinema at the Film University Babelsberg KONRAD WOLF, partly funded by a grant from the Brandenburgisches Zentrum für Medienwissenschaften (ZeM) in Potsdam, Germany.

Maike Sarah Reinerth has worked as a researcher at the Johannes Gutenberg University Mainz, the University of Hamburg, and the Hamburg University of Applied Sciences. She is co-editor of several books and has published numerous academic essays and film reviews. Her most recent publications include texts on the transmediality of animated films (Springer VS 2016) and on representations of subjectivity in early cinema (Routledge 2016) as well as two edited volumes, *Subjectivity across Media. Interdisciplinary and Transmedial Perspective* (Routledge 2017), and *In Bewegung setzen ... Beiträge zur deutschsprachigen Animationsforschung [Setting in Motion ... Contributions to German-language Animation Studies]* (Springer VS 2017).

Maike Sarah Reinerth is the co-coordinator of AG Animation, a German-language working group that advocates the academic and scientific recognition of animation, a speaker of the initiative for good working conditions in academic media studies, and, since 2015, the mother of a son.

Brendan Rooney
Assistant Professor at the School of Psychology at University College Dublin, Ireland

Brendan Rooney is an assistant professor at University College Dublin, Ireland. He is currently chair of the Psychological Society of Ireland's Special Interest Group for Media, Art, and Cyberpsychology. Brendan

Rooney's research interests include the interaction between cognition and emotion in the context of film and other entertainment. He is particularly interested in processes associated with appraisals of realism in film and their relationship to emotional regulation.

He has published original papers in journals such as *Media Psychology, Frontiers in Perception Science, Virtual Reality*, and *Poetics*. He has also published chapters in edited books for Psychology Press, Oxford University Press, and Routledge.

Tim J. *Smith*
Reader in Cognitive Psychology at the Department of Psychological Sciences, Birkbeck, at the University of London, UK

Tim J. Smith is a Reader in Cognitive Psychology in the Department of Psychological Sciences, Birkbeck, University of London. His research covers all aspects of Visual Cognition with a special focus on the active perception of naturalistic scenes via eye movements. His personal and professional passion for film has led to his applying his empirical methods to the issue of how we perceive film. How do we attend to, perceive, and remember static, dynamic and real-world scenes? How do visual features of a scene command our attention, and how do higher-order cognitive factors compete with these factors? How do we program eye movements around a complex visual scene and process information at fixation and in the periphery? How does our understanding of naturalistic Visual Cognition allow us to understand how we perceive visual media such as Film, TV, and Digital Media? He investigates these issues using a combination of behavioral experiments, eye tracking, cognitive modeling and electrophysiology.

He is a board member of the Society for Cognitive Studies of the Moving Image and an editor of Projections: The Journal of Movies and Mind. His publications include numerous articles in international encyclopedias, prominent anthologies, and renowned periodicals in the areas of Cognitive Psychology and Film theory.

Kirsten Moana Thompson
Professor and Director of Film Studies at Department of English at Seattle University, USA

Kirsten Moana Thompson is Professor of Film and Director of the Film Programme at Seattle University. Previously, she was Professor of Film Studies and Director of the Film Programme at Victoria University, in Wellington, New Zealand, and (previously) Associate Professor and Director of the Film Program at Wayne State University in Detroit. She teaches and writes on animation and color studies as well as classical Hollywood cinema, German, and New Zealand and Pacific studies. She is the author of *Apocalyptic Dread: American Cinema at the Turn of the*

Millennium (SUNY Press 2007), *Crime Films: Investigating the Scene* (Wallflower 2007), and co-editor with Terri Ginsberg of *Perspectives on German Cinema* (GK Hall: NY 1996). She is currently working on a new book on *Colour, Visual Culture and American Cel Animation*.

Meike Uhrig
Research Associate at the Department of Media Studies at the University of Tuebingen, Germany

Meike Uhrig is a Research Associate at the Department of Media Studies at the University of Tuebingen and coordinator at the Tuebingen Centre for Animation Studies. She spent a research year as Visiting Researcher at the Department of Psychology at Stanford University, USA. In her dissertation project, she studied the representation, reception, and effects of emotions in film.

Meike Uhrig has been awarded several times for her interdisciplinary projects that span across psychology, film, media, and communication studies. She is author and editor of several books and numerous articles on emotion and animated films. Her publications include *Darstellung, Rezeption und Wirkung von Emotionen im Film [Representation, Reception and Effects of Emotions in Film]* (Springer VS 2014), *Visual Communication Effects: Moving Images* (Wiley-Blackwell 2016), *Emotion Elicitation. A Comparison of Images and Films* (Frontiers 2015), and *In the Face of... Animated Fantasy Characters* (Routledge 2018).

Paul Ward
Professor and Course Leader for MA Animation Production, Arts University Bournemouth, UK

Paul Ward is Professor of Animation Studies in the Faculty of Media and Performance at the Arts University Bournemouth. His main research interests are in the fields of animation and documentary film and television, animation pedagogy, production cultures, communities of practice, and film and media historiography.

Published work includes articles for the journals *animation: an interdisciplinary journal*, *Animation Journal*, and the *Historical Journal for Film, Radio and Television*, as well as numerous anthology essays. He serves on the Editorial Boards of *animation: an interdisciplinary journal* and *Animation Studies* and was a member of the UK Arts and Humanities Research Council Peer Review College with special interest in animation and documentary research proposals. He was also the President of the Society for Animation Studies from 2010 to 2015 and the inaugural Fellow of the Holland Animated Film Festival (HAFF) in 2012. He was a Visiting Professor in the Design School at the Politecnico di Milano in November 2013. His work has been translated into German, Czech, Korean, Farsi, and Japanese.

Paul Ward is Series Co-Editor (with Caroline Ruddell) for the book series Palgrave Animation.

Paul Wells

Professor and Drama Director of the Animation Academy at the School of the Arts, English and Drama at Loughborough University, UK

Paul Wells is Director of the Animation Academy, a research group dedicated to cutting-edge engagement with animation and related moving image practices. Paul is an internationally established scholar, screenwriter, and director, having published widely in Animation and Film Studies and written and directed numerous projects for theatre, radio, television, and film.

His books include *Understanding Animation* (Routledge 1998), *Animation and America* (Rutgers University Press 2002), *The Fundamentals of Animation* (AVA 2006), and *The Animated Bestiary: Animals, Cartoons and Culture* (Rutgers University Press 2009), now all standard texts in the study, practice and research of animation as a field. His work also embraces collaborative texts, including *Drawing for Animation* (AVA 2009) with master animator Joanna Quinn and *Re-Imagining Animation* (AVA 2008) with Johnny Hardstaff, leading graphic designer and filmmaker with Ridley Scott Associates.

Paul Wells' text *Scriptwriting* (AVA 2007), forms the basis of workshops and consultancies he has conducted worldwide. His continuing professional engagements include working with writers from *The Simpsons* and *SpongeBob SquarePants* and developing animated shorts, children's series, documentaries, and features in Norway, Sweden, Belgium, The Netherlands, and the United States.

Spinechillers, Paul Wells' radio history of the horror film, won a Sony Award, while *Britannia – The Film* was chosen as an Open University set text. His recent TV documentaries on John Coates, Geoff Dunbar, and John Halas – the latter based on his book *Halas & Batchelor Cartoons – An Animated History* (Southbank Publishing 2006, with Vivien Halas) – have been presented at festivals globally. He was also a consultant for the BBC's *Animation Nation*.

Paul Wells is Chair of the Association of British Animation Collections (ABAC), a collaborative initiative with the BFI, BAFTA, and the National Media Museum.

Index

For Product Safety Concerns and Information please contact our EU
representative GPSR@taylorandfrancis.com
Taylor & Francis Verlag GmbH, Kaufingerstraße 24, 80331 München, Germany

www.ingramcontent.com/pod-product-compliance
Ingram Content Group UK Ltd.
Pitfield, Milton Keynes, MK11 3LW, UK
UKHW021430080625
459435UK00011B/216